# DEVOTIONS FOR DAILY LIVING

# $\mathcal{D}$EVOTIONS
# FOR DAILY LIVING

HAL M. HELMS

PARACLETE PRESS
BREWSTER, MASSACHUSETTS

Library of Congress Cataloging-in-Publication Data

Helms, Hal McElwaine.
     Devotions for daily living / by Hal M. Helms.
        p.   cm.
     ISBN 1-55725-207-6
     1. Devotional calendars.  I. Title.
BV4811.H385  1998
242'.2—dc21                    97-52658
                                  CIP

10 9 8 7 6 5 4 3 2 1

Published by Paraclete Press
Brewster, Massachusetts
www.paraclete-press.com

Printed in the United States of America.

# Table of Contents

# PRESSING ON

SECTION ONE

# LIGHT TO A NEEDY WORLD

*Let your Light
so shine
before men,
that they
may see
your good
works and
give glory
to your Father
who is
in heaven.*

*Matthew 5:16*

## DAY 1 • YOU ARE THE LIGHT OF THE WORLD

Daily Reading: Matthew 5:1-16

*You are the light of the world. A city set on a hill cannot be hid. Nor do men light a lamp and put it under a bushel, but on a stand, and it gives light to all in the house. (vv. 14, 15)*

What a breath-taking dignity the Lord bestows on his followers—calling us "the light of the world"!

When we think about our own imperfections and failures, this seems too high a title for us. Yet there it is, and it is not so much compliment as fact.

Think about it this way: in the dark world in which we live, where can people look for light, if not to those who know and follow Jesus Christ? What other "light sources" are there? To be sure, there is the Bible, the "lamp of purest gold," as the hymn calls it. But what is the light there, if it is not the result of God's Spirit in the lives of those who knew and loved him? In other words, even the Word of God was given to us through those whom Jesus called "the light of the world." It was his will that they have this part in the plan of salvation.

What does this mean in practical terms? To me it says that everything I am, and everything I do either brings his light into my world or obscures it under some "bushel." That "bushel" was a measuring container which was used to measure wheat or other grains. When it was put over a light, the light was totally blotted out from view. That's what happens if we allow the "bushel" of self-indulgence, self-pity, anger, etc. to blot out the light in us.

So let your light shine!

1. In what ways can you let the Beatitudes apply in your life?

2. How can you specifically let your light shine today?

## Day 2 • I Am the Light of the World

Daily Reading: John 8:1-20

*Again Jesus spoke to them saying, "I am the light of the world; he who follows me will not walk in darkness but will have the light of life." (v. 12)*

Lest we begin to think that we are the light, this is an important corrective. We are light-bearers, but the Light is always he, never we.

Walking in darkness is a very frightening experience. Not only can you not see what you're bumping into, but the mind suggests frightening possibilities that are even more alarming—"things that go bump in the night."

Jesus knows this, and makes a spiritual point of it. When we "walk in darkness"—we are not safe. Many dangers, toils and snares are about our path.

In *Pilgrim's Progress* Christian finds himself in a very narrow pathway. "When he sought, in the dark, to avoid the ditch on one hand, he was ready to tip over into the mire on the other; and when he sought to escape the mire, without great care he was ready to fall into the ditch." But after he had gotten through he looked back as the sun was rising and saw where he had been. Then he said, "His candle shines on my head, and by his light I go through darkness" (Job 29:3).

1. How have you let Jesus be your "light" today and followed him?

## Day 3 • Discerning Thoughts and Intentions

Daily Reading: Hebrews 4:1-16

*For the word of God is living and active, sharper than any two-edged sword, piercing the divisions of soul and spirit, of joints and marrow, and discerning the thoughts and intentions of the heart. (v. 12)*

If we are to exchange our old lamps for new ones, we must come more and more to a healthy distrust of our own thoughts and intentions. We must be willing to have the innocent mask which our heart presents to us (and to others) taken off, and the real thing exposed. That is what the writer here says is the power of the Word of God. Its piercing, lively effect is to unmask what is hidden in us. The searchlight of God's truth pierces like a shaft into the darkness exposing what was not seen or understood before.

This has been the experience of countless Christians who have allowed the Holy Spirit to convict them of sin beyond their initial conversion experience. The history of Christianity is filled with the testimonies of people who began to find their relationship with Jesus growing stronger, their ability to cope with their own life situation radically improved—when they allowed the Word of God to pierce to the separation even of soul and spirit, to expose sinful attitudes, buried hurts, stubborn opinions, etc.

All that is religious is not truly of the Spirit of God. We can be very religious, very "spiritual," and still be operating out of unrecognized motivations, "thoughts and intentions" of our hearts which we ourselves do not understand. When a counselor has been given permission to be honest with you, it may be devastating. We would expect "piercing" to have some pain (Hebrews 4:12). It will be healing, however, and freeing beyond our imagination, if we will go on through the experience and seek the Holy Spirit's light in and through it. He will not let us down! And his Word is faithful!

1. Where have you ever experienced the Word of God confronting you about something in your life? What have you done with the conviction?

2. Ask the Holy Spirit to reveal your hidden motives. What are some of them?

## DAY 4 • IN HIM IS NO DARKNESS

Daily Reading: 1 John 1:1-10

*This is the message we have heard from him and proclaim to you, that God is light and in him is no darkness at all. (v. 5)*

Jesus is the brightness of the Father's glory. In him there is no darkness of ignorance, error, untruthfulness, sin or death.*

Think for a moment what it would mean if we were in a world of darkness. We see pictures of space, where the darkness seems illuminated only in spots, with stars, suns and heavenly bodies. But the Bible calls the Lord the Sun of Righteousness, risen with healing in his wings.

Life depends upon light. It cannot exist in total darkness. And God is light, from whom all life comes—physical and spiritual. His nature has the quality of light about it—life-giving, revealing, outgoing. Darkness is the absence of light.

Whenever we give in to doubts, to despair, to hopelessness—to guilt, anger, depression—to any darkness whatsoever, we are shutting out the light which God seeks constantly to pour into us by his Spirit. We *choose* darkness rather than light in such cases.

Light can be fearsome, threatening. This is especially so if we want to cling to some secret sin within. But "in him is no darkness at all," and we as Christians have committed ourselves to walk in light rather than in darkness.

> Great Father of glory, pure Father of light,
> Thine angels adore thee, all veiling their sight.
> All praise we would render, O help us to see
> 'Tis only the splendor of light hideth thee!
> *(Walter Chalmers Smith, 1867)*

\* A.R. Fausset.

1. What are the results of walking in the light, according to this Scripture?

## DAY 5 • WALK AS CHILDREN OF LIGHT

Daily Reading: Ephesians 5:1-20

*Once you were darkness but now you are light in the Lord; walk as children of light. (v. 8)*

This week we are thinking about "New Lamps for Old," as we go on in our upward climb. We are seeking to trade the old light of self-understanding and self-direction for the new light of yieldedness and obedience to the Holy Spirit.

Our Scripture today takes into account the reality of who we are—by nature, children of disobedience (v. 6). Whether or not we have carried out all the things alluded to in verses 3 and 4, we can by this time know enough about ourselves to know that "there is not a choice between us"— we are all made out of the same clay!

Paul says, "Once you were darkness." Not just *in* darkness, but darkness. That is the truth about our old Adamic nature, inherited from our human past. All the darkness that we see and abhor in others is potentially lurking in our old nature, given the right circumstances. "There, but for the grace of God, go I," said a famous Christian seeing a drunkard wallowing in the gutter. He knew what the apostle was talking about when he says, "Once you were darkness." Only the Pharisee continues to believe that he is good within himself.

But now, says Paul, "you are light in the Lord." Not just that you are in the light, but that your new nature "in the Lord" partakes of that very light itself. He has put his Spirit (his light) within you, and there is no darkness at all in that Spirit.

The only thing we have to do is "walk as children of light." This sounds simple, but it takes a lot of dying to the old darkness and choosing the new light on our part every day, including this one!

1. What is the result of living in the Light?

## DAY 6 • THE LIGHT SHINES IN THE DARKNESS

Daily Reading: John 1:1-18

*The light shines in the darkness and the darkness has not overcome it. (v. 5)*

As Christians, we need to remember that the Light is victorious! In spite of everything—sin, death and hell—Jesus Christ *is* victor.

The very nature of light is that when it comes, darkness cannot stand before it. Whether it is a candle or an incandescent lamp, light dispels darkness. Darkness cannot overcome light!

What a cheering and encouraging word this can be to us who struggle with the dark vestiges of our old nature—our untrained appetites, our longings for things we know we should not have, our unsatisfied desire for others to love and understand us. All these things belong to the darkness of our human condition.

But Jesus Christ is alive, and he is stronger than all of these appetites. He is able to strengthen and help us in the hour of temptation. He is able to bring us through. "Because he himself has suffered and been tempted, he is able to help those who are tempted" (Hebrews 2:18).

> "Can God?" the subtle Tempter breathes within,
> When all seems lost, excepting sure defeat.
> "Can God roll back the raging seas of sin!"
> "Can God?" the fainting heart doth quick repeat.
> "God can!" His Saints of old did ever give
> Their fullest confirmation o'er and o'er.
> And He who made the long-dead bones to live,
> E'en now can bring the dead to life once more!
> *(Anonymous)*

8

"The light shines on in the dark, and the darkness has never quenched it." *(NEB)* Hallelujah!

1. Where have you experienced the power of light over darkness in your life?

## Day 7 • How Were Your Eyes Opened?

Daily Reading: John 9:1-41

*They said to him, "Then how were your eyes opened?" (v. 10)*

We are thinking this week about trading old lamps for new, old eyes for new, an old life for a new one. Even those who have long been in the way of Jesus find this is a daily choice we have to make. Thank God, however, that as we go, seeing more and more reality about ourselves and our need for Jesus, our faith grows stronger, and we know that there is no other way!

This man in the story today was "born blind." His condition was as natural to him as breathing. He had known no other. Like him, we may have lived a long time in the darkness of our own thinking until Jesus came into our lives. Whether that happened to you in a sudden, dramatic way, or as a gradual dawning of light does not matter. What does matter is that the blind now see.

The skeptical and unfriendly neighbors and others who had seen him before as a beggar, asked the newly sighted man, "How were your eyes opened?" His reply, "The man called Jesus. . . ." He had met Jesus, Jesus had touched him, then had given him a discipline to follow ("Go, wash in the pool of Siloam") and, as the man testified, "I went and washed and received my sight."

Can we see the parallel to our own situation? The Lord touches us with his loving hand. Our hearts quicken in response. He gives us a discipline which will result in greater sight and greater freedom. And we have the choice. Like this man, we too can go . . . obey, and receive our sight!

1. What specific action is God calling you to do that will lead you into the light?

2. Do you understand that you will influence others when you choose to walk in the light? When have you seen this happen?

# LEARNING TO LIVE WITH ME

*He destined us*
*in love to*
*be his sons*
*through Jesus*
*Christ, according*
*to the purpose*
*of his will.*

*Ephesians 1:5*

## DAY 1 • BELOVED AND CHOSEN

Daily Reading: 2 Thessalonians 2:1-16

*But we are bound to give thanks to God always for you, brethren, beloved of the Lord, because God chose you from the beginning to be saved through sanctification by the Spirit and belief in the truth. (v. 13)*

Here we have a beautiful description of our inheritance as God's children. We are "beloved by the Lord," chosen "from the beginning to be saved. . . ." What a glory has been bestowed on us!

There is never a cause for despair or discouragement in this life if we keep our eyes on the Lord and remember how much he loves us.

Our greatest problem, of course, is ourselves. We see in the holy and perfect light of Jesus Christ how far we are from our goal of being like him. But wait! He loves you! He has chosen to save you through sanctification and through your belief in the truth. The more you believe that truth, live in it, allow the Lord to mold and form you in your new nature, the more cause there is for rejoicing.

He is not through with you and me yet. The work is still going on. There is every reason to believe that he will not give up on us, so there is no good reason for giving up on ourselves.

Don't let discouragement overtake you! Counter it with the truth: I am a blood-bought child of Jesus Christ. I am chosen and precious in his sight "So then, stand firm!" (v. 15)

1. How is God changing you?

2. In what truth or truths about yourself are you standing fast?

## DAY 2 • ARE YOU NOT OF MORE VALUE?

Daily Reading: Matthew 6:1-34

*Look at the birds of the air: they neither sow nor reap, nor gather into barns, and yet your heavenly Father feeds them. Are you not of more value than they? (v. 26)*

Learning to live with ourselves means learning to see how our lives are rooted in the love of God. It is not because we are great, worthy, successful, beautiful, intelligent, rich or poor, young or old that he loves us. He loves us because he loves us. We are precious to him.

Is not the same true of any real love in the world? A parent does not love a child because the child is great, but because the child is his or her own. There is no "logical" explanation, and the child does not *earn* the love of a good parent. Love *is*.

Learning to live with myself means putting aside life-long demands that I be reassured over and over again of my worth, my intelligence, my abilities, my beauty. It means relaxing and living in God's love. He loves you because you are you and he is God. He made you, and he has a perfect image in his heart which you are meant to be. Only as that image comes into reality is the real you going to be seen. What you and I have done with ourselves—in self-hate and self-love—is to distort and twist that image badly. Restoration has begun. That is what your life in Christ is about: being restored in the image which God had in mind when he made you and set his love on you.

> The soul that on Jesus hath leaned for repose,
> I will not, I will not desert to its foes.
> That soul, though all hell should endeavor to shake,
> I'll never, no never, no never forsake!
> *(Anonymous)*

1. In what present situation do you need to trust God to care for you?

2. What keeps you from accepting and resting in his care and love?

## DAY 3 • ONCE LOST, NOW FOUND!

Daily Reading: Luke 15:11-32

*It was fitting to make merry and be glad, for this your brother was dead and is alive, he was lost, and is found. (v. 32)*

One thing is very clear in this story of Jesus'. The father never stopped loving either of his sons. When the younger son demanded his share of the inheritance before his time, the father did not stop loving him. When he wasted his substance in loose living, the father did not stop loving him. When he returned home, while he was yet a great way off the father ran to meet him and welcomed him back. He always loved him.

Nor did the elder brother suffer. "All that is mine is yours," the father told him, pleading with him to come in and join the celebration that the lost had been found, the wandering one had returned home.

Whether you see yourself as the younger or the elder son, the run-away or the stay-at-home, the message is the same—the Father has never stopped loving you! One step toward him, and he meets us with rejoicing, and all heaven rejoices with him.

You don't have to prove anything to God. He loves you and longs to see you come into complete "sonship," that for which he created you.

> I sought the Lord, and afterward I knew
> He moved my soul to seek him, seeking me.
> It was not I that found, O Saviour true;
> No, I was found of thee.

1. Where do you see yourself trying to prove yourself to God?

2. Where will you not accept what God says about you?


## DAY 4 • NO LONGER STRANGERS

Daily Reading: Ephesians 2:1-22

*So then you are no longer strangers and sojourners but you are fellow citizens with the saints and members of the household of God. (v. 19)*

It could not be said much plainer than that: we are members of God's household, God's family!

Someone has said that one of the most beautiful words in the English language is the word "home." In it is contained much of what we long for, even subconsciously—a sense of belonging and acceptance by people near and dear to us. We find our true humanity not only in being loved, but in being enabled to love others. The family is the place where this is meant to take place at its deepest level, but it is not to stop there. There must be more.

Thomas Kelly in his *Testament of Devotion* has a chapter on "The Blessed Community." In it he speaks of the small group which can become an outbreaking of that larger, divine Community which manifests the Kingdom of God in our midst.

Two people, three people, ten people may be in living touch with one another through him who underlies their separate lives. This is an astounding experience, which I can only describe but cannot explain in the language of science. But in vivid experience of divine Fellowship it is there. We know that these souls are with us, liking their lives and ours continuously to God and opening themselves, with us, in steady and humble obedience to him. It is as if the boundaries of our self were enlarged, as if we were within them and as if they were within us.

Acceptance of ourselves, with all our limitations and shortcomings, is greatly helped as we allow the group of people God has given us to take such a place as Kelly describes. It *can* be happening with you—if you let it.

1. Notice all that God has done for you as written in this chapter. List five things you know God has done for you personally.

2. How are you learning to become more a part of God's family?

## DAY 5 • THE SPIRIT OF SONSHIP

Daily Reading: Romans 8:1-17

*For you did not receive the spirit of slavery to fall back into fear, but you received the spirit of sonship. When we cry, "Abba! Father!" it is the Spirit himself bearing witness with our spirit that we are children of God. (vv. 15, 16)*

*Children of God.* The thought is almost more than we can take in! As God's children, we have access to him, just as we have enjoyed access to our earthly fathers. We did not (as little children) think them too great, too busy or too unapproachable to be concerned with our little hurts and needs. Neither should we ever think that our little hurts and needs are too unimportant for the Father's care. He loves us, and that is enough.

Part of our learning to live with ourselves is seeing our true inheritance as children of God. The world seeks to make us its children. Forces all about us, temptations and pressures of many kinds, seek to mold us after the world's image. But think of how the world really sees people—sellers see us as potential customers to be exploited; politicians often see us as potential votes to be manipulated; the entertainment media sees us as gullible and ready to swallow the next wave of filth and junk that comes in the name of culture. On and on we could go. That is the way the world sees us.

But God sees us through Christ. He looks at us in the reality in which we were created to live, and patiently works with us in becoming what he sees as our true selves. "For your life is hid with Christ in God. When

Christ who is our life appears, then you also will appear with him in glory" (Colossians 3:3b,4).

1. How has God been a father to you?

2. How have you been like a child to God?


## DAY 6 • IF GOD IS FOR US

Daily Reading: Romans 8:18-39
*If God is for us, who is against us? (v. 31)*

Paul is talking about suffering in this passage. He knows what he is talking about because of his own experience. Some physical ailment ("a thorn in the flesh") plagued him throughout much of his ministry. Some have suggested severe eye trouble; others have suggested other ailments. Whatever it was, it caused him suffering, though he refers to it only once, and then to explain that it was given him to keep him from being "exalted beyond measure" because of all the spiritual revelations and gifts which God had entrusted to him. No self-pity there! Then he had the suffering of being rejected and persecuted by his own people, those who were closest to him. We can only imagine the cost of that suffering to someone who had been as ardent and zealous an upholder of the traditions of the fathers as Paul had been before he met Jesus. But added to that, Paul suffered opposition and misunderstanding within the Church itself. Certain men took it upon themselves to do everything possible to discredit his ministry. They spread false rumors about him, they twisted what he said to make it sound as though he was teaching false doctrine. Through it all, Paul went steadily on with his purpose.

Look at whatever you are called to suffer—misunderstanding, rejection, physical difficulty—and see how small it is in comparison with what God is giving continually from his love. If God is for us, who is against us? Who can put us down, raise us up—but God himself?

Away with any feeling of despondency or self-pity! It is enough to know that you are God's child, and he is *for* you. Everything that he allows to come into your life is meant to your good and not your hurt. You can absolutely believe that!

1. How does God help you when you are in difficulty?

2. How does God's promise of no separation from him help you live as his child?


## DAY 7 • BEHOLD, A NEW CREATION!

Daily Reading: 2 Corinthians 5:1-21

*Therefore if anyone is in Christ he is a new creation; the old has passed away, behold the new has come. (v. 17)*

Here again, Paul is talking about our new life in Christ, and the wonder of it. Truly it is past understanding, and we are "lost in wonder, love and praise," when we let it sweep over us like a great wave of God's love.

The choices we face day by day are important, and they need to be talked about and considered. "Catch us the foxes, the little foxes that spoil the vineyards" (Song of Solomon 2:15). These "little foxes" can spoil a day, or a long period of fruitful growth, if they are not seen and caught!

*But* (and this is important) we must not forget the larger view, the overriding reality. Looking unto Jesus we see where we are going and how we are going to get there! Looking to Jesus we can get our eyes out of the mud and into the stars from time to time.

If anyone is in Christ—if anyone has relied on him, made the heart commitment which he must have, stopped trusting in self and begun the process of trusting him for life and life to come—that person is a new work of God, created by the presence and power of the Holy Spirit. And that is you and that is everyone who belongs to him. Don't lose sight of that glorious truth!

> Since my eyes were fixed on Jesus
> I've lost sight of all beside—
> So enchained my spirit's vision
> Looking on the Crucified.
> *(Mary D. James)*

1. Where can you begin to see some changes in your life—the old things passing away and the new emerging?

# LEARNING TO LIVE WITH OTHERS

*Bear one*
*another's burdens,*
*and so fulfill*
*the law*
*of Christ.*

*Galatians 6:2*

## DAY 1 • BEAR ONE ANOTHER'S BURDENS

Daily Reading: Galatians 6:1–18

*Bear one another's burdens, and so fulfill the law of Christ. (v. 2)*

Last week we thought about learning to live with ourselves. This week we are thinking about learning to live with others. Don't you ever think life would be very simple, and very happy, if it were not for the people you have to live or work with? That is an easy thought to entertain if we do not want to look at what makes us difficult for other people to live with!

"Bear one another's burdens," says the apostle. What does that mean? Just before this he says that if anyone is "taken in any trespass, you who are spiritual should restore him in a spirit of gentleness." Bearing one another's burdens means, at least in part, learning the costly business of forgiveness. The burden of someone else's wrong can be heavy indeed, especially if you are the one who has been hurt or wronged in the process.

Our relationship with others cannot be what it should be unless there is a constant willingness to forgive. When sinners live or work together, they inevitably hurt one another. To cover over the hurt, ignore it, pretend it isn't there does nothing but cause a festering within. We must acknowledge that the wrong exists and then "restore" the wrong one in a spirit of gentleness. In this way, the wonderful, supernatural unity of spirit can be maintained within the fellowship. Even our relationships with nonbelievers will respond to this readiness to forgive. Pray for a forgiving spirit! It is necessary if we are to fulfill the law of Christ.

> Help me the slow of heart to move
> By some clear, winning word of love;
> Teach me the wayward feet to stay
> And guide them in the homeward way.
> *(W. Gladden)*

1. Whom do you need to forgive?

## DAY 2 • LOVE NEVER ENDS

Daily Reading: 1 Corinthians 13
*Love bears all things, believes all things, hopes all things, endures all things. Love never ends. (vv. 7,8a)*

This is Paul's great hymn of love. But it is more than a praise and exaltation of the greatest of all virtues. It is a description and a definition which we cannot afford to ignore.

How easy it is to tell ourselves that we love others, that we are at heart loving people, ignoring the evidence that our feelings and actions do not correspond to this description of love.

It is important, too, to remember that the Greek word which the Bible uses here is the word *agape*. Two other words were available—*phileo* (friendship), and *eros* (sexual or romantic love). Paul uses this word, *agape*, referring to the spiritual and divine quality of the love which binds the Body of Christ together. In our relationships we experience the other types of loves but only of this one, *agape*, can it be said, "Love never ends."

In your relationship with others, are you looking for a love that will fulfill and satisfy you? Pray that the Lord will show you the difference between that kind of love and the kind Paul is talking about here. Read Bonhoeffer's chapter again on "Community," to see the difference he sees between spiritual and human (read *spiritual* and *soulish*) love. Learning to live with others means seeking the kind of love that doesn't give up!

1. Where do you need to redefine love in your life?

2. How are you putting the "agape" love to work in your life?

## DAY 3 • THOUGH MANY, ONE BODY

Daily Reading: 1 Corinthians 12:1-31

*For just as the body is one and has many members, and all the members of the body, though many, are one body, so it is with Christ. (v. 12)*

Members of God's family. Bearing one another's burdens. And now, members of the same body. In this chapter the apostle uses the metaphor of the body to show how intimately and organically we Christians are related to one another.

21

Learning to live with others involves learning to accept the fact that others have gifts differing from our own and that they have functions differing from ours. Until we make peace with that truth and learn to be grateful for what the Lord has given to us—talent, ability, position or whatever—we will be plagued with a low-rumbling jealousy somewhere deep within us that will play us false in our relationship with others.

A body cannot function except as a whole. Any part that is cut off from the rest will quickly die, and the whole body suffers. So with Christ—we must seek to maintain the unity of the spirit in the bond of peace. This is not done by hiding our feelings or denying them but by being willing to deal honestly with them, that love might replace resentment, hurt, anger or even hate.

> We are not divided, all one body we,
> One in hope and doctrine, one in charity!
> *(S. Baring-Gould, 1864)*

1. What keeps you separated from the body of Christ, i.e., your family, your church group, etc.? Is it hurt? Fear? Jealousy? What else? Be specific.

2. How are you learning to replace resentment, hurt, anger, jealousy, with love?

## DAY 4 • LET ALL BE DONE IN LOVE

Daily Reading: 1 Corinthians 16:1-24

*Be watchful, stand firm in your faith, be courageous, be strong. Let all that you do be done in love. (v. 13, 14)*

It is interesting that Paul puts all these instructions together. The infant church at Corinth was experiencing many difficulties. There was jealousy, contention, even getting drunk at Communion (1 Cor. 11:21)! It was important, then, for those who were serious about their walk with Jesus to "be watchful," "to stand firm," to be courageous and strong. Otherwise the sin within the church would bring humiliation and shame to the entire Body of Christ among outsiders.

But notice the injunction which immediately follows: "Let all that you do be done in love." How important it is when we start to defend the truth, to uphold a point of honor or principle, that we remember, "Let all that you do be done in love." We may be ever so right, but still bring nothing but the savor of death, if our hearts are hard, self-righteous, legalistic. "He who abides in love abides in God and God abides in him" (1 John 4:16). Our righteousness does not amount to anything if we do not learn truly to love others, and we can only do that as we allow God's love to flow through us, burning out all that is self-directed in our idolatrous and selfish "loves."

As we relate to family, husband, wife, in-laws, church groups, friends—we should seek constantly to let this be our guide: "Let all that you do be done in love." It will not always mean being "soft," nor will it mean being a doormat for others. Real love is often "tough love." But God will show us whether we are operating out of love or out of some other motive.

1. Can you recall something you've said to another person which though possibly right was not done in love?

2. How can you be watchful and firm today?

## DAY 5 • LOOK TO THE INTEREST OF OTHERS

Daily Reading: Philippians 2:1-18

*Let each of you look not only to his own interests but also to the interests of others.* (v. 4)

Being genuinely interested in and concerned for others can be costly. It can mean putting their interests ahead of your own, even if you are tired, if you want time to read the paper, or to watch a favorite TV program, take a nap or work at your hobby. Getting involved with people is a little frightening for some people.

An octogenarian had lived all her life in a careful, guarded way. Never married, she had maintained her independence, and at 82 had never shared a bedroom with anyone else! Her first 3D experience was a challenge. Not so much the diet, but that requirement to contact a member of the group every week. Everything in her resisted it. But she was determined that she would be obedient to the discipline. To her surprise and joy, the weekly telephone calls made more difference in her life than the diet!

One of the main aspects of the 3D program is to challenge us to get out of the rut of self-concern and to open our lives and hearts to others. We all need practice in the art of living with others. The key is to seek to be a blessing, to be actively looking to the interests of others, instead of being wrapped up and smothered in your own.

Having come this far along the path you should be affirming the truth of this, and seeking further ways to bring the light of Jesus' love into others' lives—without trying to convert them! The Holy Spirit will take genuine acts of love and use them in his own way to draw souls to Jesus.

1. What specifically keeps you from caring about others?

2. List three things you will do today to care for others.

## DAY 6 • FIRST, TAKE OUT THE LOG

Daily Reading: Matthew 7:1-12

*Why do you notice the speck that is in your brother's eyes but do not notice the log that is in your own eye? Or how can you say to your brother, "Let me take the speck out of your eye," when there is a log in your own eye? You hypocrite, first take the log out of your own eye, and then you will see clearly to take the speck out of your brother's eye. (vv. 3-5)*

Here is a basic principle for us all: being the greater sinner in our own eyes. Until and unless that happens, we are going to do exactly what the Lord describes here—we are going to concentrate on our brother's sin (read: husband's sin, wife's sin, parent's sin, etc.) and overlook our own. It will seem as though the log is in the other person's eye, and the speck, the insignificant small flaw, is in our own.

But Jesus knows who we are, and calls us "hypocrites" as long as that is our approach. It is dangerous to speak to others about their wrong until and unless we have looked at our own, and have taken responsibility before a holy God for it.

Perhaps the reason many Church members have become so reluctant to live together in any kind of real openness is a fear of appearing self-righteous and judgmental. So instead, many have chosen to live with a surface politeness and acceptance which masks a lot of unreality underneath and keeps people from experiencing genuine fellowship. We avoid conflicts because we have not learned how to handle them in Christ.

This Scripture points the way: we are to deal first with the log in our own eye. We are to recognize with St. Paul, that we are "chief of sinners" (1 Timothy 1:15). This is the only cure for self-righteousness, and when the truth penetrates our hearts, we can then show mercy on others as we help them remove the speck out of their eyes!

1. What is the "beam in your eye"? How can you get rid of it?

2. Can you recall where you have judged someone else and thereby excused yourself? Where?

## DAY 7 • AGREE IN THE LORD

Daily Reading: Philippians 4:1-23

*I entreat Euodias and I entreat Synteche to agree in the Lord. And I ask thou also, true yokefellow, help these women, for they have labored side by side with me in the gospel together with Clement and the rest of my fellow workers, whose names are in the book of life. (vv. 2,3)*

Christians disagree. Sometimes it is the fault of one, sometimes of the other, sometimes of both. Paul here repeats the word, "I entreat," as if to make no judgment as to which one is at fault and it may even suggest that he holds them both at fault for not being reconciled. He then asks someone whom he refers to as "true yokefellow" to "help these two women." They would need help in settling their disagreement and coming into reconciliation.

This is a labor of love which has to take place in the Christian fellowship from time to time. In spite of the fact that we love the Lord, love one another and may have worked hard in the cause of Christ, we still get hurt by one another, and opinions sometimes clash. What should we do in such a case? It is often very wise to go to someone whom you trust and ask that person to go with you to speak to the one with whom the disagreement has occurred. Go in the spirit of lowliness and openness. If you have been hurt, be ready to admit it, and to recognize that it is probably pride or the desire to be loved which is hurting in you. Then you can seek a genuine reconciliation that will enable you to go on together in Christ.

One wonders how Euodias and Synteche settled their difference. But there can be little doubt that, with Paul's urging, they quickly did it!

1. Is there someone you need to go to, to get things straightened out? Who?

2. What keeps you from being in harmony with that person? Pride? Rightness?

# LEARNING TO LIVE OPENLY

*Therefore*
*putting away*
*falsehood, let*
*every one speak*
*truth with his*
*neighbor, for*
*we are members*
*one of another.*

*Ephesians 4:25*

## DAY 1 • IF WE SAY WE HAVE NOT SINNED

Daily Reading: 1 John 1:1-10

*If we say we have not sinned, we make him a liar, and his word is not in us. (v. 10)*

One commentator in writing on this verse says that the Greek construction used in the original makes it very clear that the apostle is talking here about "actual sins" committed even after our regeneration—"not merely before but after conversion."*

Jesus, in one of his parables, told of two men who went to the temple to pray. One of them, the Pharisee, congratulated God on the splendid job he had done in creating him, the Pharisee. "I thank thee that I am not as this sinner," he said. But the other, a tax-gatherer, knew how wrong he was, and simply smote his breast crying, "God be merciful to me a sinner." "Which man," asks the Lord, "do you think went away justified?"

It is one of the strange paradoxes of life that we Christians find it so hard not to be like the Pharisee, even though we call Jesus our "Savior." How easy it is to go about seeking to establish our own *rightness* and how hard it is to face being wrong in any situation! So much for the degree of spiritual pride which we grasp. It is one of the greatest struggles most of us have to face to be willing to see our wrongness in any given situation without going into anger, accusation of others, self-pity and despair. How that pride does cling so closely to us!

Here is a simple remedy for us. "He who humbles himself" . . . "confess your faults one to another" . . . "if we say we have not sinned." That's the pivotal point on which our spiritual lives turn—either in pride and self-righteousness or in humility and thanksgiving for Jesus.

*Jamison, Fausett and Brown, *Commentary*, p. 630

1. What do you accuse God of being when you don't admit your own sin?

2. What are you hiding about yourself, to yourself? Why?

## Day 2 • Speaking the Truth In Love

Daily Reading: Ephesians 4:1-16

*Rather, speaking the truth in love, we are to grow up into him who is the head, into Christ. (v. 15)*

It is a common malady of Christians to mistake "love" for a soft, permissive attitude towards others. We have been thinking about the necessity of going before God first with our own sin before we dare say anything to anyone else about the "speck" that is in his or her eye. But, as we see here, we are responsible for "speaking the truth."

An old movie about an angel come to earth played some very funny scenes as the angel innocently upset a formal social affair simply by telling the truth. As the plot went on, the angel was told that telling the truth was bound to make trouble, and that people could not bear to hear it. We may think more like those people than we realize, and use that excuse to judge our brother or sister silently rather than chance offending him or her by telling the truth.

Of course we need wisdom in following the apostle's instruction. We are told to speak the truth "in love," which will involve having the self-control not to blurt out everything we think, no matter what! Love is patient and kind. Therefore, whatever truth we are given to say to someone else will be measured by the wisdom and mercy of God, who knows much more than we do about when we should speak and how much.

Nonetheless, the instruction to "speak the truth in love" does bind us to the obligation to care enough to say what love calls us to say, realizing that silence can be as cruel as words. "A word fitly spoken is like apples of gold in a setting of silver" (Proverbs 25:11). "A word in season, how good it is!" (Proverbs 15:23).

1. How do you see that being honest is really showing love?

2. When is honesty not loving?

29

## DAY 3 • PUTTING AWAY FALSEHOOD

Daily Reading: Ephesians 4:17-32

*Therefore, putting away falsehood, let every one speak the truth with his neighbor, for we are members one of another. (v. 25)*

Jesus calls himself "the truth." The Holy Spirit is referred to as "the Spirit of truth." On the other hand, Satan is called "a liar and the father of lies." It is very clear then that the introduction of falsehood into our relationships opens those relationships to the influence of the devil and clouds our life "in the Spirit."

To put away falsehood is to put away deceit in its manifold forms. Yet most of us, even unconsciously, practice deceits of various kinds. We have made them so habitual that we are often not even aware of them. But the Spirit of truth will show them to us if we are truly desirous, and will press on through our inner barriers. Even when we pray we must be like the widow in the story Jesus told, and persevere with God. In this case, it is not because he is unwilling to hear and answer, but because there are so many conflicting things within us that we have to pray earnestly and sometimes persistently over a period of time before we are ready to hear and receive the answer the Lord is giving us. Praying in such a case is simply giving God permission to show us his answer to our need. When our eye of faith becomes single, clear and undivided, then we can see with God's light.

Putting away falsehood also involves giving up the false things we have believed about ourselves. Our friends in Christ can help us, if we give them permission to speak honestly to us. This may be painful, but it will lead to joy and a fellowship deeper than we have known before.

1. Why is speaking or thinking falsely so serious?

2. What are two places where the Holy Spirit convicts you that you have lived dishonestly?

## Day 4 • Pleasing Men or Serving Christ

Daily Reading: Galatians 1:1-24

*Am I now seeking the favor of men or of God? Or am I trying to please men? If I were still pleasing men, I should not be a servant of Christ. (v. 10)*

Paul wrote this letter when he was under attack by a group of Christians who were trying to discredit him and his ministry. In another place he says that he had become all things to all men in order that he might by any means win some (1 Cor. 9:22). So we know that he was not a rigid, opinionated stick-in-the-mud. But his very freedom had opened him up to the criticism of power-seeking and people-pleasing! So he opens the letter to his spiritual children at Galatia, who are in danger of being lured away by some new teaching, with a double curse on anyone who is preaching a false gospel. Such is his intensity of feeling that you can almost feel it even now, almost 2,000 years later. The converts for whom he had given all to win, for whom he had risked his life, were ready to turn to others and reject the truth he had given them at such great cost.

How is it with you? Do you live to please other people or to please God? Sometimes those two things go happily together, and what we do to please God also pleases others. At other times, we face a clear choice between doing what we know is right, saying what we believe we ought to say and displeasing others, and doing something else or being quiet in order to please them.

Learning to live openly involves this costly choice. If we do not choose rightly we are locked in shades of deception and falsehood. But with the right choice, we bring God's benediction, which works for everyone's good.

1. Whom do you try to please? Why?

2. Does attempting to please someone else keep you from Christ? How?

## DAY 5 • IN WEAKNESS, FEAR AND TREMBLING

Daily Reading: 1 Corinthians 2:1-16

*And I was with you in weakness and in much fear and trembling, and my speech and my message were not in plausible words of wisdom, but in demonstration of the Spirit and power. (vv. 3,4)*

This is an interesting insight into Paul's vulnerability before the people he sought to reach. He had not tried to hide the fact that he was weak and afraid. We do not know the exact circumstances when he first went to Corinth, nor what caused his weakness. But he took that weakness as a positive thing—so that, as he says in verse 5, "your faith might not rest in the wisdom of men but in the power of God."

If we are to experience the depth and blessing of Christian fellowship God intends us to have, we must choose to let our weakness be known by those we are close to. Hiding it only means trying to protect the inner pride which wants to "have it all together." Think, however, how you feel towards others who are experiencing difficulty. Do you despise them? Rather, do you not care more deeply for them as they reveal that they are not supermen or superwomen?

Paul was so grounded in Jesus Christ that he no longer had to protect himself, trying to look good. He could be himself, knowing that the treasure he held was in an earthen vessel, and that it was safe to be Paul. He did not need to put on airs, trying to appear "spiritual," or even good. He only needed to walk in obedience to the Lord and trust that God would use him, in spite of who he was, to God's glory and to the good and salvation of others.

The same heritage waits for you and me for the taking.

1. Where are you weak and yet afraid to admit it?

2. To whom do you need to admit your weakness?

## DAY 6 • NOT THE RIGHTEOUS, BUT SINNERS

Daily Reading: Mark 2:1-17

*And when Jesus heard it, he said to them, "Those who are well have no need of a physician, but those who are sick; I came not to call the righteous, but sinners." (v. 17)*

The righteous truly had no use for Jesus when he lived on earth. They saw no need of him, and the things he said threatened that for which they had worked and striven.

What use do the righteous have for him today? Since he came to call sinners, and gave his life for the salvation of those who had no righteousness of their own—the righteous are excluded. Paul said of the Jews, his own people, "Being ignorant of the righteousness that comes from God, and seeking to establish their own, they did not submit to God's righteousness" (Romans 10:3).

Jesus is not condemning right living! He speaks strongly against sin, and says, "Blessed are those who hunger and thirst for righteousness." What then does he mean when he says, "I came not to call the righteous, but sinners?" He refers, I believe, to those who are righteous in their own eyes. They have used good behavior to dull their eyes to their need for a righteousness greater than the scribes' and Pharisees'—God's righteousness.

What has this to do with living openly? Unless we are willing to abandon our pretense at being right, and join the fellowship of sinners who are forgiven and are continuing to be forgiven, we cannot live in openness and honesty with our fellow Christians. Self-righteousness is a solitary prison cell.

1. How has your pretense of "having it all together" kept you from growing in Jesus?

2. Why do you need to be right, or appear to be "on top"?

## DAY 7 • BUT WHEN YOU HAVE TURNED AGAIN

Daily Reading: Luke 22:24-46

*Simon, Simon, behold, Satan demanded to have you, that he might sift you like wheat, but I have prayed for you that your faith may not fail; and when you have turned again, strengthen your brethren. (vv. 31, 32)*

The scene is the Last Supper. Bewildered, and hardly daring to ask questions, the disciples have gathered with the Lord to celebrate Passover. The foreboding must have been intense. Yet in spite of it all, an argument arose among them as to who would be first in the kingdom (v. 24)! Jesus' answer should forever put a stop to the kind of striving which is so natural to us all. "The kings of the Gentiles exercise lordship over them, and those in authority over them are called benefactors. But not so with you! Rather let the greatest among you become as the youngest, and the leader as one who serves. . . . I am among you as one who serves."

The Lord then looks at Peter, calling him by his old name, "Simon," rather than the name he had given him, "Peter: the Rock." He knows that just ahead lies a great temptation, and great suffering for Peter. But the Lord himself has prayed that Peter's faith will not fail him. And after he has gone through this suffering, Peter will be able to strengthen others.

Don't waste your suffering! Don't let it turn you into a bitter, complaining soul. Let it break you of your demand to have your own way. Let it press you to that wounded side of him who bled and died for your sins, and make you able to strengthen others. In your circle there are those who may need your prayerful and loving support and concern. Let your own suffering prepare you to help. None can comfort quite so well as those who themselves have received God's comfort in time of great need.

1. Does it help you to know that Christ prays for you in your time of testing? Why?

2. How have your defeats or failures helped you to grow as a Christian?

# DEALING WITH HURTS

*I will turn*
*their mourning*
*into joy;*
*I will comfort*
*them, and*
*give them*
*gladness for*
*sorrow.*

*Jeremiah 31:13b*

## DAY 1 • FILLED WITH BITTERNESS

Daily Reading: Lamentations 3:1-39

*He has filled me with bitterness and sated me with wormwood. (v. 15)*

This week we are thinking about the whole problem of hurt and how to handle it. There is no loving without the possibility of being hurt. There is no living person who is not susceptible to hurt. So we must learn to deal with hurt constructively or we will remain as the prophet felt when he wrote, "He has filled me with bitterness . . . my soul continually thinks of it and is bowed down within me" (v. 20).

Do you carry bitterness in your heart as a result of some hurt inflicted on you in the past? Bitterness has a way of turning into hardness, and the person who carries it is the one most hurt by it.

The prophet here moves from the bitterness of soul to make some very strong affirmations about the Lord. Even though the situation Jeremiah faced was brought about by human agencies, he considered his affliction as being from God. That is how directly he felt God was in charge of his life. Anything in his life was there by God's allowance.

But even though he was broken-hearted and bitter in soul about what had happened, he knew that God's love never ceases and his mercies are endless. "He does not willingly afflict or grieve the sons of men" (v. 33). His way out of bitterness was to let it press him even closer to God. This is what all our hurts should do: drive us to Jesus.

> Child of My love, lean hard,
> And let me feel the pressure of thy care;
> I know thy burden, child. I shaped it;
> Poised it in Mine own hand; made no proportion
> In its weight to thine unaided strength.
> For even as I laid it on, I said,
> "I shall be near, and while she leans on Me
> This burden shall be Mine, not hers;
> So shall I keep My child within the circling arms
> Of Mine own love." Here lay it down, nor fear
> To impose it on a shoulder which upholds
> The government of worlds. Yet closer come;
> Thou art not near enough. I would embrace thy care;
> So I might feel My child reposing on My breast,
> Thou lovedst me! I knew it. Doubt not then;
> But loving Me, lean hard.
> *(Anonymous)*

1. Can you identify some hurt, or hurts, you are carrying? What are they?


## DAY 2 • WHAT ARE YOU DOING HERE?

Daily Reading: 1 Kings 19:1-18

*And there he came to a cave, and lodged there; and behold, the word of the Lord came to him, and said to him, "What are you doing here, Elijah?" (v. 9)*

This is one of the most exciting stories in the Bible, and one in which we can all see ourselves portrayed. Elijah was a brave and stalwart hero of faith, standing before the king and queen and all the prophets of Baal in that great contest on Mount Carmel. But then Jezebel threatened his life, and Elijah fled far into the wilderness to escape her clutches.

He had stood strongly for God, and now here he was, hiding in a cave! Self-pity flooded him there in the desert, and he wanted to die.

Most of us are well-acquainted with self-pity, which can come over us like a flood, accusing everyone, even God, of not understanding. When asked what he was doing there, Elijah pictured the black scene of circumstances and declared that he alone was led to serve the Lord, and now men were seeking his life, too.

Then comes that famous scene, where he stands at the door of the cave, "and the Lord passed by." A great wind, an earthquake and a fire—but the Lord was not in them. Then "a still, small voice" came to Elijah, again asking, "What are you doing here?"

The same question can be asked of us when we get locked in self-pity of any kind. What are you doing hiding away, trying to comfort yourself? Look at how the story ends, and see what a waste of time Elijah's self-pity was. God is still God, and self-pity clouds the reality of it. Be done with it!

1. Where do you feel sorry for yourself? Identify the hurt behind the self-pity.

2. How can God help you get rid of your self-pity?

## Day 3 • Hurt but Forgiving

Daily Reading: 2 Timothy 4:1-22

*At my first defense no one took my part; all deserted me. May it not be charged against them! (v. 16)*

Paul knew what it was to be hurt. If we think we have cause to nurse old grievances against those who have hurt us, how much more he did! But he knew that carrying such a grievance around in his heart would do no good. In another place he writes this beautiful word: "And be kind to one another, tenderhearted, forgiving one another, as God in Christ forgave you" (Ephesians 4:32). The love of Jesus demanded that he forgive others, and makes the same demand on us. "Even as God in Christ forgave you," is the touchstone against which we must measure every grudge or hurt we have against someone else.

Do you know how much it cost God to forgive you? Do you know that your sin against God brought Jesus to the cross? If so, how can you withhold forgiveness from those who have hurt you much less, and still call yourself a follower of Jesus?

Dealing with hurts constructively and positively involves forgiving those who have wronged us. It does not mean to excuse them or to deny that a wrong has been done. Rather, looking the wrong straight in the face, we can say, "Whatever wrong was done to me—I choose in the name of Jesus to forgive it. Lord, may it not be charged against them!" You may find then, as many of us have, that you must confess the sin of holding back forgiveness for too long a time! Then you can go on rejoicing!

1. Recount the way in which holding onto the place where you've been hurt has really hurt you instead.

2. Recall where you have hurt others, and see how destructive that was. Ask God to forgive you.

## Day 4 • A Little Foolishness

Daily Reading: 2 Corinthians 11:1-33
*I wish you would bear with me in a little foolishness. Do bear with me! (v. 1)*

I'm glad that Paul wrote this particular section for two reasons: first we get a glimpse of his life as "apostle to the Gentiles" that we have nowhere else. And what a life it was: labors, imprisonments, countless beatings almost to death. Five times he had been beaten with rods, once he was stoned, three times he was shipwrecked, and so on. We can only begin to imagine what life was like for Paul after he met Jesus on the road to Damascus. If we are ever tempted to think that we have it hard, it would not be a bad idea to turn to this chapter and read again what this one soldier of Christ endured for his sake and for the sake of spreading the gospel.

And there is a second reason why I am glad that he wrote this. Paul was hurt and upset with the way the Corinthians were treating him and his message. He had hoped for better from them! And so, in working through his reaction to this ill-treatment, he asks them to bear with him in "a little foolishness." Many times that is exactly what is needed to deal with our hurts. We need to express, even at the risk of being totally wrong and looking foolish, the way we feel, the hurt we have experienced. Then, having expressed those feelings, we can say with Paul, "I have been a fool!" (2 Corinthians 12:11). Then we can be open to reconciliation with the one by whom we have felt hurt and from whom we have felt estranged. Getting our differences out "in the light" really is important.

1. What keeps you from expressing your hurt to others?

2. Have you ever experienced the relief of sharing your hurt with others? When?

## Day 5 • What Can Flesh Do to Me?

Daily Reading: Psalm 56:1-13
*In God I trust without a fear. What can flesh do to me? (v. 4)*

The Psalmist knew that he had enemies aplenty. But he had chosen to live in faith, with his life directed toward God, rather than in fear or in reaction to what man had done or could do to him.

In our own situation, we probably do not have human enemies who have the same malicious intent which David knew. But we do have enemies! They are spiritual foes which seek to do us harm at every turn. What then, does this psalm say to us about the challenge of today?

First, that fleeing to God in genuine trust frees us from the fears that plague us. One of our worst fears, one which controls our lives more than we realize, is the fear of being rejected by others. The hurts which we have experienced as children often remain as traumas or scars on our souls, motivating us to act irrationally in the present. True faith in God is a healing thing. It brings the Balm of Gilead to the hurts, scars, memories—even of terrible wrongs that may have happened to us. It is not unusual for adults to have deep, painful memories of wrongful things done to them when they were children. Only God by his Holy Spirit can reach down and heal those hurts. But he can and will, as we allow his gentle Spirit to probe the depths of our hidden hurts.

The second thing the Psalm says is that real *harm* comes from our reactions to what others do. The pain we feel cannot harm us if we let God do his perfect work in us. Let every hurtful thing press you to Jesus. He is the Healer of the broken heart!

1. What is the remedy available to us when we get hurt?

2. Has God used pain and hurt to help you? When?

## DAY 6 • A TIMELY WARNING

Daily Reading: Proverbs 28:1-28

*If one turns away his ear from hearing the law, even his prayer is an abomination. . . . He who conceals his transgressions will not prosper, but he who confesses and forsakes them will obtain mercy. (vv. 9 and 13)*

Who has not been hurt by what someone else said to them or about them? The writer of these proverbs knows how easy it is to turn away the ear from hearing what one does not want to hear.

If there is someone in your life who is honest enough to speak the truth to you about yourself, about how you come across to others, about whatever it is that makes life difficult for others, then you are blessed indeed. If your desire is to live and walk in the truth, then you will need to give someone permission to be honest with you, even when it hurts to hear the truth. "He who trusts in his own mind is a fool; but he who walks in wisdom will be delivered" (v. 26). By this time we should know that our own minds tell us what we want them to tell us, and that we need the words of others if we are to live in reality. Much of what we call "hurt" is the reaction of sinful pride to the honest words of someone close to us— be it husband, wife, friend or whoever.

This warning is for the wise. The foolish will choose to go on believing whatever they choose about themselves.

1. Do you want someone to be honest with you even if it hurts? Why?

2. What is the reason for your hurt when someone else says something to you that is true?

## DAY 7 • GODLY GRIEF

Daily Reading: 2 Corinthians 7:1-16

*For godly grief produces a repentance that leads to salvation and brings no regret, but worldly grief produces death. (v. 10)*

We have an expression familiar to us all: "Good grief!" But do we think grief is ever good? This week we have been thinking about hurts and how to deal with them—the pain we all experience from some wrong inflicted on us, rejections, insults, misunderstandings, disappointments and so on. We have been reminded of the absolute necessity of forgiveness if we are to go on in Christ and enjoy the benefits of his peace and presence. We are not allowed the luxury of unforgiveness!

The question we face today is this: is hurt good for us? Paul says, "Yes." He has written this little fledgling church a strong, rebuking letter. They were stung by it to the very quick. Perhaps they shed tears, and spent some sleepless nights wondering what to do and how to correct the situation which had so upset him, their father in the faith. Now he writes again having heard that they were moved to action by his strong words. The pain he inflicted has been for their good and not their harm. "Even if I made you sorry with my letter, I do not regret it," he says, "for I see that the letter grieved you, though only for a while. . . . You felt a godly grief, so that you suffered no loss through us." The difference for the

Corinthians was that they let their pain move them to repentance. When we allow any criticism, correction, or rebuke to *work for us* the pain of it will go away. You can absolutely depend on it! The pain lasts only as long as it is needed to do its work!

1. How does self-pity harm you?

2. How can hurt or pain help you?

# FORGIVING ONE ANOTHER

*If one has a
complaint against
another, forgiving
each other;
as the Lord
has forgiven you,
so you also
must forgive.*

Colossians 3:13

## Day 1 • You Must Forgive

Daily Reading: Colossians 3:1-17

*Forbearing one another and, if one has a complaint against another, forgiving each other; as the Lord has forgiven you, so you also must forgive. (v. 13)*

Last week, in thinking about hurts we talked about the importance of forgiving. This week we are again focusing our attention on this all-important aspect of Christian life. There can be no Christian fellowship in the true sense of the term without it. It is not possible for Christians to live together, work together, or associate together in a meaningful way without the necessity of forgiveness arising. If we think that we can cover up and ignore the little hurts, breaches and wounds of everyday associations, we do not know ourselves or others very well.

What to do when such a thing happens? Here is the testimony of one person I ran across recently.

> I found myself one midnight wholly sleepless as the surges of a cruel injustice swept over me, and the love which covers seemed to have crept out of my heart. Then I cried to God in an agony for the power to obey his injunction, "Love covereth."
>
> Immediately the Spirit began to work in me the power that brought about the forgetfulness.
>
> Mentally I dug a grave. Deliberately I threw up the earth until the excavation was deep.
>
> Sorrowfully I lowered into it the thing which wounded me. Quickly I shoveled in the clods.
>
> Over the mound I carefully laid the green sod. Then I covered it with white roses and forget-me-nots, and quickly walked away.
>
> Sweet sleep came, the wound which had been so nearly deadly was healed without a scar, and I know not today what caused my grief.

This person had found the secret of forgiveness—letting go of the account held against another, not charging that person's sin against him. But make no mistake about it—there is a difference between forgiveness and repressing the memory. One involves the struggle of giving up the desire to be vindicated. The other seeks mere relief from the pain. Choose forgiveness!

1. Where are you failing to forgive others today?

2. What prevents you from forgiving that person or persons?

## DAY 2 • IF YOU DO NOT FORGIVE

Daily Reading: Matthew 6:1-15

*For if you forgive men their trespasses your heavenly Father will also forgive you; but if you do not forgive men their trespasses neither will your Father forgive your trespasses. (vv. 14, 15)*

In the 18th chapter of this same Gospel, Jesus tells a parable about a king who wanted to settle his accounts with his servants, and called them in. One of them was found to owe the incredible sum of ten thousand talents. The estimated (pre-inflation) value of a talent was about a thousand dollars, so you can see what an astronomical sum this was that the servant owed. Falling down on his knees he begged, "Lord, have patience with me, and I will pay you everything." Out of pity for him, his master "released him and forgave him the debt."

No sooner did the man go out, however, but whom should he meet, but a fellow servant who owed him a hundred denarii. A denarius, we are told, was worth about 20 cents. The servant who had been forgiven the debt of $10,000,000 seized his fellow servant by the throat and demanded payment of his $20. The servant fell down on his knees and begged, "Have patience with me, and I will pay you." But the other refused, and had him put in prison till the $20 was paid.

Jesus told the story to illustrate the vast, inconceivable difference between the things we need to forgive and those for which we need forgiveness from God. How can we, in the light of this, dare refuse forgiveness to anyone? But before you answer too glibly, check out in prayer whether you are holding on to unforgiveness! Unforgiveness is a sin that loves to pretend not to be there at all!

1. List five times when God has forgiven you in the past week.

2. Why do we find forgiving others so hard?

## DAY 3 • REFUSING TO GO IN

Daily Reading: Luke 15:11-32

We often read this parable of Jesus with the emphasis on the prodigal son who left and returned. This has been called the most beautiful short story ever written. However, Jesus' real point was the older brother who stayed home. Of course he was portraying the forgiving, merciful Father. (The well-known German preacher, Helmut Thielicke, titles his sermon on this passage, "The Parable of the Waiting Father.")

But look at where the story ends. The older brother has been the good son. As his younger, "spoiled" brother goes through all the stages of rebellion, flaunting of his father's standards, presuming on his love, total self-absorption—the older "good" son stays home, tends the farm, does his work and plods along dutifully. No doubt he judges his younger brother, and probably is jealous of what the lad seems to be getting away with!

A Bible study conducted in a Pennsylvania resort hotel was attended by a number of elderly residents. As they came to this passage, one little old lady said indignantly, "That's not fair! The younger son went out and had all the fun and then got forgiven!" "Madame," said the teacher, "is that what you think of as fun!" Silence reigned! The "good" person often secretly entertains jealous feelings toward the "bad" one who seems to be getting away with his sin!

The upshot was that the elder son would not forgive his brother and go in to the welcome-home banquet. He stayed outside, hurt, jealous and unforgiving, feeling very unhappy and right.

1. Can you identify jealousy behind your unforgiving attitude? Where?

2. Can you see where "being right" keeps you from forgiving others? How?

## DAY 4 • GO AND TELL HIM HIS FAULT

Daily Reading: Matthew 18:1-20

*If your brother sins against you, go and tell him his fault between you and him alone. If he listens to you, you have gained your brother. (v. 15)*

Recently I had the experience of being hurt by a friend. It was a trivial thing but it did hurt, and I found myself wanting to avoid that friend for two or three days. Then in some inadvertent remark, I let someone else know that I was carrying that hurt around with me.

"You must go to her and tell her that you got your feelings hurt," said the other person.

"But I don't really want to," I protested. "It's too picky and unimportant!" (Secretly, I think I was enjoying my hurt and I was not yet ready to give it up!)

"No. That won't do," said the other. "You must get this thing cleared up."

Reluctantly I contacted my friend and asked her to come and talk. (We work in the same building.) This she readily did, and I expressed my feelings about what she had said to me. I told her that I had been hurt by her attitude towards me, and to my surprise, she readily asked my forgiveness, and said that she knew she had been wrong.

Was this not what Jesus is talking about? When someone "sins against you," and you are hurt, you have a responsibility to talk with your brother or sister, and if the problem is still not cleared up, to get someone else to talk with the two of you. The object is not to be right, but to "gain your brother."

Incidentally, in that whole transaction, I, too, saw that my attitude had been wrong! The relationship between us seems stronger than before.

1. Why do we hesitate to go to others when we think they are wrong?

2. Are there times when you don't want to give up the hurt? Why?

## DAY 5 • BLESSED ARE THE MERCIFUL

Daily Reading: Matthew 5:1-16

*Blessed are the merciful, for they shall obtain mercy. (v. 7)*

> The quality of mercy is not strain'd
> It droppeth as the gentle rain from heaven
> Upon the place beneath; it is twice bless'd;
> It blesseth him that gives and him that takes.
> 'Tis mightiest in the mightiest; it becomes
> The thronèd monarch better than his crown.
> His scepter shows the force of temporal power,
> The attribute of awe and majesty,
> Wherein doth sit the dread and fear of kings;
> But mercy is above this scepter'd sway,
> It is enthroned in the hearts of kings,
> It is an attribute of God Himself

And earthly power doth then show likest God's
When mercy seasons justice.
(Shakespeare, *The Merchant of Venice*)

To be unmerciful and unforgiving is very natural to our fallen state. As I said yesterday, I was enjoying holding on to my unforgiveness of my friend, because something in me wanted go get even. But although withholding forgiveness is very natural, we Christians are called to learn "a more excellent way."

But it needs to be pointed out that this mercy neither involves excusing another person's sin nor simply saying with one's words, "I forgive you." It involves knowing how greatly we are dependent on God's mercy, and choosing to let that mercy operate in our own hearts. It truly means letting go of the demands you hold against another person. Otherwise, mercy is not truly at work.

Mercy is an attitude of heart, which goes beyond personal rights, justice or any other claims. It takes into account that only God can judge safely, and we are not safe judges of anyone.

1. What does it mean for you to be merciful?

2. Where has another person shown you mercy? How does receiving mercy help you to be merciful?

## DAY 6 • I ALSO FORGIVE

Daily Reading: 2 Corinthians 2:1-17

*So I beg you to reaffirm your love for him. Anyone whom you forgive, I also forgive. What I have forgiven, if I have forgiven anything, has been for your sake in the presence of Christ, to keep Satan from gaining the advantage over us; for we are not ignorant of his designs. (vv. 8, 10-11)*

Paul had written a strong letter of rebuke and correction concerning a scandalous sin among the members of the Corinthian church. He had upbraided them for their laxness in condoning open immorality in their midst, and urged them no longer to treat the offending member as a brother. Time had passed and, it would seem, the offending member had shown signs of change. But had he truly changed? Who could know? The members of the church were not certain.

Then came this letter from the beloved Paul, champion of the gospel. What did it say? "Reaffirm your love for him!" Why? Because the design of Satan was now to take their righteous indignation and turn it into hardened unforgiveness, to bring about a permanent separation in the body of Christ.

How does this apply to your life and mine? Where have we righteously taken a stand, but have forgotten to temper right with mercy, to "reaffirm" our love for the person? Parents need to remember Paul's injunction when they are dealing with children, and we need to remember it when dealing with those who have been "in the wrong." They need the witness of truth; they also must have the witness of forgiving love!

1. Are you aware of times when you have been "right" and yet had no mercy? When?

2. Why is it dangerous to be unmerciful and unforgiving? Who gains from your unforgiving spirit?

## DAY 7 • CHARGE THAT TO MY ACCOUNT

Daily Reading: The Book of Philemon
*If he has wronged you at all, or owes you anything, charge that to my account. (v. 18)*

Onesimus was a slave. The name means *useful*, but Onesimus had ideas of his own, and had run away from his owner, Philemon. He had become *useless* rather than *useful*. In his wild escapade (for a runaway slave was in jeopardy of his very life) Onesimus had come to know Paul, and had accepted Jesus Christ as his Savior. "I appeal to you for my child, Onesimus, whose father I have become in my imprisonment," wrote the aged apostle from his prison cell in Rome.

Another interesting twist to the story is that Philemon, "our beloved fellow worker," was apparently also a spiritual son, and owed "his very self" to Paul's labor and effort (v. 19). An estrangement existed between Onesimus and Philemon, and Paul was making an effort to bring about reconciliation. Among other things, he did not hesitate to confront the offended one with his debt to him, Paul, in order to put pressure on him to do what Christ would have him do.

Christians are called to be *peacemakers*. We are called to be ambassadors for Christ, and we have a message of reconciliation. This means that we must not hesitate to use our influence to bring about reconciliation where others are at odds. Paul sets the example and speaks frankly to his friend, counting on the love between them to become a bridge of understanding and reconciliation between Philemon and his runaway slave Onesimus.

Do not hesitate to speak the truth frankly for the sake of bringing together others who may have pulled away from each other in hurt. Prayerfully ask for the Spirit's help and guidance, and move as he leads you. Forgiveness is so essential to all our lives that it is worth paying a high price to obtain it. Be willing to pay the price!

1. Do you need to bring about reconciliation in some situation? What is it?

2. Do you see the connection between practicing forgiveness and being a peacemaker? What is it?

# PERSEVERANCE

*Therefore lift*
*your drooping*
*hands and*
*strengthen your*
*weak knees,*
*and make straight*
*paths for your feet,*
*so that what is*
*lame may not*
*be put out of joint*
*but rather be*
*healed.*

*Hebrews 12:12, 13*

## DAY 1 • SEE THAT YOU DO NOT REFUSE HIM

Daily Reading: Hebrews 12:12-29

*Therefore lift your drooping hands and strengthen your weak knees, and make straight paths for your feet, so that what is lame may not be put out of joint but rather be healed. (vv. 12, 13)*

"Perseverance: Steadfastness. Persisting in a state, enterprise or undertaking in spite of counter influences, opposition or discouragement." This is the dictionary definition of this week's theme.

What does that say to you in light of our week's theme Scripture? You may have undertaken a discipline of regular Scripture reading. No doubt you have found from time to time your enthusiasm lagging, discouragement creeping in. This happens to everyone, no matter what kind of endeavor we undertake!

But personal discipline is not just another endeavor. What you are doing is worthy of your best. It is worthy of your beginning again, if you failed in your resolve. For your goal is to become more like Jesus and to be fashioned into the person he created and redeemed you to be. That's worth a struggle.

1. What things seem to cause you the greatest temptation to "give up"?

2. Since God could save us from all difficulty if he chose to do so, why do you think he allows unfavorable circumstances to develop in our lives?

## DAY 2 • HE THAT ENDURES

Daily Reading: Matthew 10
*But he who endures to the end will be saved. (v. 22)*

This is not a popular passage of Scripture. Most of us want to read over it hastily and move on to the more positive passages. For the Lord here talks about the cost of discipleship, the price of serving him, and what it will mean if we take his call seriously.

There is no way to escape the suffering implicit in turning from the world to God. There is no easy path. "For the gate is narrow and the way is hard, that leads to life, and those who find it are few" (Matthew 7:14).

Is it worthwhile to persevere? After all, who wants to be subject to the kind of conditions described here? To answer that question one has to look realistically at the cost of following Jesus—and the cost of not following him. The cost of following him is high. It takes everything you are and have if you are truly going to be his. But what will it take to go with the world—that seemingly easy way? Will that not also take everything?

Only do not be double-minded. Remember the seed which fell on rocky ground and withered away because it had no root. The joy of the harvest cannot come without the labor of sowing and cultivating. Right now the harvest may seem a long way off. Do not despair! Endure! Keep on in the way you have been led. Follow the light you have seen! There is a life worth seeking, a purpose worth the sacrifice, and a goal worth the burden of the race. Jesus showed the way and he is the way for us.

1. When we become double-minded, joy goes out of our life. How can we get back on track when this happens?

2. Sometimes we become disappointed in ourselves and feel like giving up. Why do you think this happens?

## DAY 3 • SUFFERING PRODUCES ENDURANCE

Daily Reading: Romans 5:1-21

*More than that, we rejoice in our sufferings, knowing that suffering produces endurance, and endurance produces character, and character produces hope, and hope does not disappoint us. (vv. 3-5a)*

Yesterday we thought about enduring. "Enduring" carries a feeling of getting through, no matter what—perhaps with the head bent pressing against the wind.

But look at today's Scripture. Persevering takes on a much more positive connotation, as the apostle looks at the fruit of the suffering we are called to endure.

That suffering may be physical. Sometimes it is, but that is not the most common nor is it necessarily the hardest kind of suffering. There is the call to suffer by standing against what we want to do—to fight that in us that wants its own way. Anyone who has tried to stand against his nature knows that it entails suffering of an intense degree. Then there is the suffering of misunderstandings, rejections, disappointments, as God allows our lives to take turns which cross out the desires of our hearts and the dream-wishes of our lives. All of this, Paul is saying, "produces endurance, and, as we endure, character comes forth, and with the character, there is hope." In this process, hope is the fruit which brightens and sweetens all that has been bitter and difficult. We no longer feel that life has betrayed us and God has deserted us. We have stood in the storm and through it we have come to have hope!

Friends, wherever you are, and whatever the condition of your life, look for the loving Hand of mercy outstretched over you, to help you through your suffering.

> Be still, my soul; the Lord is on thy side;
> Bear patiently the cross of grief or pain;
> Leave to thy God to order and provide;
> In every change He faithful will remain.
> Be still my soul, thy best, thy heavenly friend,
> Through thorny ways leads to a joyful end.
> *(Katrine von Schlegel, 18th century; tr. Jane Borthwick)*

1. Give an example of growth in character and hope from an experience of suffering in your life.

2 Why is perseverance such a valuable trait?

## Day 4 • I Press On

Daily Reading: Philippians 3:12-21

*But one thing I do, forgetting what lies behind and straining forward to what lies ahead, I press on toward the goal for the prize of the upward call of God in Christ Jesus. (vv. 13b, 14)*

Pressing on toward the prize! What a picture of the Christian life. In actual reality, for Paul, that meant accepting his share of sufferings, giving himself daily for the cause of Jesus and for the sake of fellow believers. It meant doing things God's way instead of his own. That's what is summed up in the phrase, "I press on toward the goal."

There is an old story, familiar to us all from childhood, of the hare and the tortoise. They were pitted together in about as ludicrous a race as human imagination can invent. The hare with his swift hind legs and his lithe muscles was so confident of victory that he was able to indulge himself in many diversions and a rest stop or two, knowing that the race was "in the bag." The tortoise, however, had the heavy burden of his house (which he always carried on his back) and the terrible disadvantage of short legs and a slow gait. He did have one thing in his favor, however. He had perseverance. He had stick-to-it-iveness. Just because the odds were strongly against him was no excuse for not trying. So he pressed on! You know the end of the story, of course. And it should be an encouragement to you in your Christian walk. It should be a constant inspiration to become a more faithful disciple of Jesus. What does it matter if you have failed? What does it matter if you feel discouraged at times? Those are the times to *PRESS*. Pressing means going beyond the comfortable limits, the easy victories, into the uncharted path known to but few. The saints have been there. They know what it is to struggle. Jesus has been there. He cheers you on, and strengthens you as you go. Don't let down!

> "Well I know thy trouble, O my servant true:
> Thou art very weary. I was weary, too.
> But that toil shall make thee
> Some day all mine own,
> And the end of sorrow
> Shall be near my throne."
>                    *(St. Andrew of Crete, 660-732; tr. John Mason Neal)*

1. When you feel discouraged, what are the best things to do?

2. Jesus has been there, too. He has experienced discouraging times. What do you think Jesus did when these times came upon him?

## DAY 5 • NOT THOSE WHO SHRINK BACK

Daily Reading: Hebrews 10:26-39

*But we are not of those who shrink back and are destroyed, but of those who have faith and keep their souls. (v. 39)*

The author draws a frightening picture of what it means to desert once we have "signed on" with Jesus. There is nothing but waste and "a fearful prospect of judgment" if we reject and desert the "only name given under heaven by which we must be saved." There is no safe place but Calvary ground!

Yet we all know what it means to be tempted to shrink back when the way seems hard, and when we long for an easier path. We see others taking that easier path, and jealousy rises within us. "I was envious of the arrogant when I saw the prosperity of the wicked," said the psalmist (Psalm 73:3).

Bunyan, in his great classic, *Pilgrim's Progress*, tells of Christian's meeting with two fellows on the road, whose names were Timorous and Mistrust. Christian said to them, "Sirs, what's the matter? You run the wrong way." Timorous then spoke, saying that they had meant to go to the City of Zion, but that they had arrived at that difficult place. "But," said he, "the farther we go, the more danger we meet with, wherefore we turned and are going back again."

"Yes," said Mistrust, "for just before us lie a couple of lions in the way, whether sleeping or waking we do not know; and we could not help thinking that if we came within their reach, they would soon pull us to pieces."

Their words made Christian afraid, and he was in great distress not knowing what to do. Finally, however, he decided it was safer to go on than to go back, for, after all, he believed that which had started him on his journey in the first place.

Ours is a walk of faith, and if we would see its fulfillment we must be those "who have faith and keep their souls."

> The countless hosts lead on before
> I must not fear nor stray;
> With them, the pilgrims of the faith
> I walk the King's highway.
> *(Evelyn Atwater Cummins, 1922)*

1. There is a good definition of *faith* in Hebrews 11:1. Look it up and write it out in as many different translations (King James Version, Living Bible, etc.,) as possible.

2. Where have Timorous and Mistrust been influencing you lately? Like Christian in *Pilgrim's Progress*, what should you do about those negative thoughts?

## DAY 6 • THINGS HOPED FOR

Daily Reading: Hebrews 11:1-16.

*Now faith is the assurance of things hoped for, the evidence of things not seen. (v. 1)*

Yes, we are called to walk by faith and not by sight. Often we think it would be easier if we knew what lies ahead as actual knowledge, but that is not so. God knows best, and he has so planned it that we are called to walk like Abraham, "called to go out to a place which he was to receive as an inheritance . . . not knowing where he was to go" (v. 8).

In this age of instant gratification, it is easy to lose sight of the long view. We want instant weight loss, instant peace of mind, instant relief from our headaches, etc. After all, we believe, we should have what we want when we want it.

Into this kind of thinking comes the call to discipleship, to a journey of faith which does not see the end clearly, and to experiences which are new and not always easy. And this is the very making of us, if we will allow it. The plant which grows with no struggle or effort tends to be weak and easily overturned by a storm. But the plant which grows in unfavorable surroundings, with wind and cold, heat and drought to struggle with, is a plant that is resilient and tough, and able to weather the storms. We should desire to be such, so that no matter what may lie in our path, we will not be deterred from our goal to go on with Jesus.

He is our pioneer. He showed us the way, and does not ask us to go anywhere without him. Walking with us, abiding in us by his Spirit, he is the enabler even as he is the goal and the prize.

Even our faith which holds us on a steady course is his gift to us, and we have the blessed privilege of choosing, moment by moment, to keep looking to him, knowing from the past that whatever the future holds, he will not fail us.

1. How can we learn to trust God for what's ahead of us?

2. Recall something in your life that you had to work long and hard for. Do you remember the satisfaction you felt when you attained it? Write down the details.

## DAY 7 • THE GOD OF STEADFASTNESS

Daily Reading: Romans 15:1-13

*May the God of steadfastness and encouragement grant you to live in such harmony with one another, in accord with Christ Jesus, that together you may with one voice glorify the God and Father of our Lord Jesus Christ. (vv. 5, 6)*

All this week we have been thinking about steadfastness—perseverance—going on when the going is tough. When do we need such encouragement most?

One time we need it is when someone has said to us a word of "truth" which sounds like anything but truth. It may have been a husband, a wife or a Christian friend—or someone who makes no claim to be a Christian. The word may have seemed sharp, unloving and unnecessary. We were sure the person did not understand us correctly, or the word would never have been said. Friendships have been broken off in such cases, and fellowship in Christian groups broken because of something of this kind. If we are the recipient of such a word, the way to handle it is (1) assume that God is allowing it to be said for our good and (2) pray for grace to see the truth in what is being said, even if the facts are wrong. If we persevere, the Holy Spirit will turn the occasion into blessing.

Another time we need perseverance is when we have a word to speak to someone *for whom we are responsible.* I underline those words because we have no right to go around "speaking truth" to everyone. But we are responsible to speak to those who have given us permission and those for whom life commitments make us responsible—husband, wife, etc. Not to persevere because doing so might cause temporary pain is self-love. Laying down your life for your brother involves the willingness to be hated (at least temporarily!) so that the word of truth might turn the person to Jesus and to life. Silence can be the mark of betrayal rather than of life-giving love in such a case.

When you get discouraged about who you are, and the many times you fall flat on your face, look to the God of steadfastness and encouragement! He is still with you, and he will help you up and get you on the way again!

1. When you get discouraged about who you are, and the many times you fall flat on your face, what can you do about it?

# DIVIDEDNESS

*I have set*
*before you*
*life and death,*
*blessing and*
*curse; therefore*
*choose life.*

*Deuteronomy 30:19*

## Day 1 • Halting Between Opinions

Daily Reading: 1 Kings 18:1-40

*"How long will you go limping with two different opinions? If the Lord is God, follow him; but if Baal then follow him." And the people did not answer him a word. (v. 21)*

Elijah's logic is irrefutable. First, decide who God is, and then serve him. There is no half-heartedness here. Given the depth of commitment of his own heart, he cannot understand the vacillating unsteadiness of the people. How could they waver so? Did they not know that God had delivered them out of Egyptian slavery and brought them with a mighty hand across the Red Sea and through forty years of wandering in the desert? Had their parents forgotten to tell them what God had done? Did they not remember the Jordan parting, the walls of Jericho falling down, and the many other signs by which God established them in the land? How could they have forgotten that?

But before we go too far along that line, let us remember how easy it is to forget or ignore all God has done in our lives when we want willfully to go on our own way. Then we forget the inescapable logic of Elijah's words—"If the Lord is God, follow him." Instead we begin to forget what that means, and to concentrate on the immediate thing we want. This wavering is often due to nothing more profound than this: we want our own way.

There is not one who is not tempted to have a divided heart. We all feel the pull and temptation of "the world, the flesh and the devil." But we do not have to live in the limping, halting way Israel was choosing when Elijah confronted them on Mt. Carmel. The Lord *is* God. Jesus Christ *is* Lord. Since that is so, and since we believe and know it is true, "then follow him!"

> Not for weight of glory, not for crown and palm,
> Enter we the army, raise the warrior psalm;
> But for love that claimeth lives for whom He died;
> He whom Jesus nameth must be on His side.
> By thy love constraining, by thy grace divine,
> We are on the Lord's side, Saviour, we are thine.
> *(Frances R. Havergal, 1836-1879)*

1. We are constantly pulled by the world, by fleshly desires and by the devil. How do you deal with these attractions and allurements in your life?

2. To be stuck in the middle is to be in "no-man's land." There, we are exposed to attack from both sides. At times like this, we must do something. What is the best thing to do?

## DAY 2 • BRIDAL LOVE

Daily Reading: Jeremiah 2:1-13

*Thus says the Lord, I remember the devotion of your youth, your love as a bride, how you followed me in the wilderness, in a land not sown. (v. 2)*

The prophet Jeremiah is calling Judah back to her first love. The Bible uses this image over and over again to warn against the temptation to fall away, little by little, from one's initial zeal and devotion to the Lord.

This week we are thinking about having "divided hearts." This is what happened to Israel, when she went after other gods and was carried away captive by the Assyrians. Little Judah, the Southern Kingdom, was left, buffeted about by the mighty powers, and was herself often looking for help to other nations and to men rather than to the Lord. She tended to forget that she had never been strong and great in the eyes of the world. That was one of the paradoxes that marked her whole history. She was small and despised by the nations around her, and little in her own eyes in the beginning. Even Solomon, whose reign represented the "golden age" of Israel's past, was but a little child in his own eyes when he came to the throne; as a result, God was able to shower an abundance of wisdom and long life on him. Later, he became wise in his own conceits, and sowed the seed for the division between Israel and Judah, a division which was never healed. But now Jeremiah calls Judah back to her bridal days. That image of unreserved and unreasoning love was meant to rebuke her later coldness and half-obedience.

What of your early days with Christ? Have they faded into dimness? Do you recall a time when it was easier for you to see your wrongness before God, when you were more sensitive to what you believed God wanted you to do? It is dangerous to allow the heart to become divided between God and mammon, between what we know to be his will and what we ourselves want. Flee back to those bridal hours. The poet and hymn-writer William Cowper asks, "Where is the blessedness I knew when first I saw the Lord? Where is the soul-refreshing view of Jesus and his word? Return, O holy Dove, return, sweet Messenger of rest. I hate the sins that made thee mourn, and drove thee from my breast" *(O for a Closer Walk with God).*

1. Was there a time in your life when it was easier to see your wrongness before God? Take time to recall to mind that blessed time.


## DAY 3 • MY PEOPLE HAVE FORGOTTEN

Daily Reading: Jeremiah 2:14-37

*Can a maiden forget her ornaments or a bride her attire? Yet my people have forgotten me days without number. (v. 32)*

The theme is a continuation of yesterday's. How easy it is to forget even things that were important to us, which we thought would remain as bright and vivid as the day they happened. Yet time proves that this cannot be. It is surely for this reason that we are urged not to forsake the assembling of ourselves together as some were doing even in the early days of Christianity (see Hebrews 10:25). This is one of the great blessings of the Lord's Supper or Holy Communion—the recalling, the retelling in sacramental sign and symbol of the realities of Christ's suffering, representing them to our minds and hearts even as we partake of the Bread and the Cup.

Forgetting who we are and where we have been is an easy way to get off the track. If we begin to think too highly of ourselves, how easy it is for our hearts to go after other gods. If we forget where God found us in our need, our fear, our lostness, and how he set us on the Rock, Christ Jesus, giving hope for our despair, faith for our doubts, and peace of mind for our fears—we may be lured to think that the glitter and tinsel of the world are worth living and working for.

The heart cry of God to his people is contained in this chapter. God loves us, and longs for the completeness of our loyalty and faithfulness.

> See from his head, his hands, his feet
> Sorrow and love flow mingled down.
> Did e'er such love and sorrow meet,
> Or thorns compose so rich a crown!
>
> Were the whole realm of nature mine
> That were an offering far too small.
> Love so amazing, so divine
> Demands my soul, my life, my all.
> *(Isaac Watts, 1707)*

1. Are you one who is led hither and thither by your emotions? Why is this dangerous?

2. Once you have made a decision, what is the best way to stick to it?

## DAY 4 • THE DOUBLE-MINDED MAN

Daily Reading: James 1:1-27

*A double-minded man is unstable in all his ways. (v. 8, KJV) Cleanse your hands, ye sinners; and purify your hearts, ye double-minded. (James 4:8, KJV)*

Jesus told us that no one can serve two masters. "Either he will hate the one and love the other," he said, "or else he will hold to the one and despise the other" (Luke 16:13).

Double-mindedness is instability. Some of us live too much by our feelings, and find that from day to day, from circumstance to circumstance, feelings have a way of changing. So such a person is tossed to and fro on the waves of circumstance and feelings—sometimes intensely drawn to the world and all that it seems to offer. If this is your case, then the question is, "What can I do about it?"

First, don't deny it if it is there! Face that your heart is divided, and that you have difficulty sticking with a commitment. It may be that your will is so strongly bent to have your own way that you cannot (or think you cannot) bear to have it crossed. Or it may be that your feelings carry you in such a way you do not know how to stop them. Face it if that is the case. That is the first step toward healing. Talk with others, and let them know that you need help. Alcoholics help one another through organizations like AA, but the first step for them is recognition of the problem. We are all in need of the same kind of recognition of our particular ailment or sin-pattern.

Second, try obedience in little things. If you are given to double-mindedness, you can train yourself toward single-heartedness through obedience. You may even ask someone to check up on you to help you follow through on whatever step of obedience you feel the Lord is asking of you. It does help strengthen the flabby spiritual muscles of the double-minded person to become obedient (and faithful) in small things. Then we can go on to harder ones, to greater ones, as Jesus reminds us in his parable: "Well done, good and faithful servant. You have been faithful in a very little, you shall have authority over ten cities!" (Luke 19:17). That is the promise of progress as we seek to be faithful in little things.

1. How would you describe double-mindedness?

2. In this day's reading you are told how to deal with double-mindedness. What steps does James give to help you out of this state?

## DAY 5 • THE FADING GLORY

Daily Reading: Revelation 2:1-11

*But I have this against you, that you have abandoned the love you had at first. (v. 4)*

It is the common experience of those who follow Jesus in the way of discipleship, that we can easily lose sight of that first love we felt when we gave our hearts to him.

> Where is the blessedness I knew When first I saw the Lord?
> Where is the soul-refreshing view of Jesus and His word?
> *(William Cowper, 1772)*

Jesus talked about the seed that fell among thorns and lost its fruitfulness because it was choked out by cares of this world. What began in faith and zeal can easily turn into half-heartedness. In such a case we can be in great spiritual danger without even knowing it. This is the situation which faced the church at Ephesus. There were many good things that could be said about those people: their works, their toil, their patient endurance, and even their zeal for truth against false teachers All of this was to their credit, and the aged John writing from Patmos did not fail to recognize them and credit them for it. But the Lord was not wholly pleased with them. There was a flaw eating away at the heart, which sooner or later would cause terrible trouble. "Remember then from what you have fallen, repent and do the works that you did at the first. If not I will come to you and remove your lampstand from its place, unless you repent" (v. 5). Notice the repetition of the word *repent*. This was the key to restoration of "the love you had at first."

This is a key for us, if we would keep fresh the love which first we knew when we became followers and disciples of Jesus. We can allow the daily cleansing of repentance to wash the windows of our souls clear, so that we can see with his light and grow in the sunlight of his love. That first love should be a treasure never to be lost.

1. We can easily lose sight of that first love we felt when we gave our hearts to Jesus. How does this happen?

2. The key to restoration of "the love you had at first" is repentance. What does it mean to repent?

## DAY 6 • THE FLICKERING LAMP

Daily Reading: Revelation 3:1-13

*Awake, strengthen what remains and is on the point of death, for I have not found your works perfect in the sight of my God. (v. 2)*

The spiritual condition at Sardis was even more serious and advanced than that at Ephesus. Here they still had the name of being alive—they were still having certain forms and rituals which people would think marked them as being sincere—but the inside was "at the point of death," and much was dead already (v. 1).

It is good for us to look at this, as a warning of what can happen to any of us if we neglect our souls. The light first fades, and then flickers, and then it goes out. How many Christians have we known to whom this has happened? It should warn us against over-confidence in ourselves and against complacency!

"Awake," is the word the Lord sends to this sleeping church. We often must be wakened to something in our lives we have come to take for granted, and for which we make allowances. As the Lord sees it, we need to be wakened, even sharply! The sleeping guard is no guard at all!

The world and the flesh and the devil conspire to convince us that there is nothing to be alarmed at, nothing worth getting excited about. "After all, look at all the people who are getting along just fine without all this concern for religious things!"

But unless we continue to strengthen and nourish "the things that remain," the desires and intentions which God has put in our hearts to serve him, we will gradually become cold and lifeless, having no feeling or affection for the things of the Spirit.

Let grace our selfishness expel, Our earthliness refine;
And kindness in our bosoms dwell As free and true as thine.

Kept peaceful in the midst of strife, Forgiving and forgiven,
O may we lead the pilgrim's life And follow thee to heaven!
*(John Hampden Gurney, 1838)*

1. Has your faith ever been "on the point of death"? On looking back, what caused this bad time? Pay particular attention to any responsibility you had in it.

2. Even in our "down periods" Jesus is strengthening us with "those things that remain." List some of "those things that remain" that would be helpful for you to remember.

## Day 7 • Choose Life!

Daily Reading: Deuteronomy 30:1-20

*I call heaven and earth to witness against you this day that I have set before you life and death, blessing and curse. Therefore choose life, that you and your descendants may live, loving the Lord your God, obeying his voice, and cleaving to him. (vv. 19, 20a)*

All this week we have been thinking about the problem of the "fork in the road," the division in our hearts between serving God and mammon, between our loyalty to Jesus and our love of self.

In a very real sense, every day finds us in the situation described in this chapter. We are confronted with choices—today. Those choices lead in either of two directions—towards life or towards death, towards greater growth in Jesus and in the things of the Spirit of God, or towards a diminishing and weakening of those things within us. We are not always aware that these are the options. They may come dressed in such costumes that we think we are making "neutral" or harmless choices—not good perhaps but not bad either. That is one of the lies we often believe and live by. But Moses here is confronting the people of Israel with the life and death issues before them. They would be going into this good land of promise which God was giving them, and they would have to make daily choices—to conform to the world, or to be transformed by God. Little choices would make the difference.

That is so with us. It is not in the great issues that we are most likely to fail and fall, but in the small ones, in which we prefer self over God, put away the nudges the Holy Spirit is giving us, not heeding his warnings about things—these are the little decisions that make a lot of difference.

Today, if you hear his voice, cleave to him and obey him—in the little things! They are more important than you think!

1. Have you experienced blessing as described in verses 19 and 20? Relate them if you have.

2. Do you believe that God still promises "life and length of days" as a fruit of our obedience? Conversely, do you believe that we bring suffering on ourselves in disobeying his laws? Why?

# CHANGING HABIT PATTERNS

*Let us test
and examine
our ways,
and return to
the Lord.*

*Lamentations 3:40*

## DAY 1 • JESUS' CUSTOM

Daily Reading: Luke 4:14-30

*And he came to Nazareth, where he had been brought up; and he went to the synagogue, as his custom was on the Sabbath day. (v. 16)*

This week we are thinking about habits and habit patterns. Do a thing twice or three times, and soon it becomes an established pattern in one's life. The thing may be good, or it may be bad. Practice, said someone, does not make perfect. It makes *permanent*. And there is a lot of truth in that.

Mary and Joseph were pious and devout people. They looked for the coming of God's promise to his people. They were among that small group of people we meet in the early chapters of Luke who were "a small remnant" waiting for the coming of the Promised One. Then Jesus was born. The glory and unusual circumstances of his birth are recorded for us in only two Gospels—Matthew and Luke, his childhood is mentioned only in Luke, and only here do we have a reference to Jesus' custom of attending synagogue on the Sabbath. It was a habit developed no doubt from childhood training.

There are many times when habit can carry us through rough places. By doing a thing consistently, we may continue to do it when we are undergoing inner stress and turmoil, and the habit can be like a strong rudder carrying us through the storm. Worship, regularly and faithfully done, can be such a custom. It seems clear that Jesus felt the need for it in his own life.

Another custom which prevailed in times of stress for Jesus was prayer. We read in Mark 6, after the feeding of the five thousand, "And after he had taken leave of them he went into the hills to pray" (v. 46). In Luke 6, we are told "all night he continued in prayer to God" (v. 12) before calling the twelve apostles. If Jesus made a custom of prayer, how much more need we to practice his custom!

1. What habits do you feel you should cultivate as a child of God?

## DAY 2 • THE HABIT OF NEGLECT

Daily Reading: Hebrews 10:1-39

*Not forsaking the assembling of ourselves together, as the manner of some is, but exhorting one another; and so much the more, as ye see the day approaching.* (v. 25, KJV)

Even in that early time, there were already Christians who were forsaking the assembling or gathering together with other Christians. Of course they had no church buildings, but they assembled in one another's homes, especially in the homes that were large enough to accommodate a small congregation.

But some stayed away. Why do you suppose that was? Was it because they had grown weary in well-doing?

Was it because something had been said they didn't like, and their feelings had been hurt?

Had they been rebuked by a leader, and would not see that they were wrong?

Had their love simply grown cold gradually, until it was not strong enough to motivate them to go out?

They had none of the modern distractions which plague and fascinate us—television, movies, automobiles, etc. They had none of the substitutes for gathering, such as the telephone.

We do not have the danger of persecution hanging over our heads, yet the neglect some among us show at times is even greater than theirs.

What habit of neglect is alive and well in your life?

Ask for grace to give it up, and to get on with the upward call of God in Christ Jesus. Is it in your prayer life? Pray more! Is it in doing loving things for others? Do more! Whatever it is that has been so easy to neglect, start systematically to change your pattern of life. That is the only way change ever takes place.

> O Master, let me walk with Thee
> In lowly paths of service free;
> Tell me thy secret; help me bear
> The strain of toil, the fret of care.
> *(Washington Gladden)*

1. Christians need other Christians. What makes it dangerous for us to think we can "go it alone" in this life?

2. What strengths do we derive from being together with other Christians in fellowship and worship?

## Day 3 • Change Your Ways!

Daily Reading: Jeremiah 7:1-34

*Thus says the Lord of hosts, the God of Israel, Amend your ways and your doings, and I will let you dwell in this place. (v. 3)*

This chapter gives us a sad picture of the Chosen People just before the fall of Judah and Jerusalem. It was heartbreaking for Jeremiah to have to deliver the strong and seemingly hopeless message the Lord had burned within his heart. In one place he speaks of the word of the Lord as a burden, and in another, as fire in his bones. Such was the urgency and inescapable nature of the message God chose to give the people through him.

Yet even though they were very close to the brink, so that the prophet was told not even to pray for them (v. 16), there was still hope, if they would change. And so our key verse is important, as we are thinking of changing habit patterns in our own lives: "Amend your ways and your doings. . . ."

The Christian life is to be a life of change. We have here no continuing city, and we should look for no stopping place short of the Heavenly City. It is important to resist the alluring thought that repetition means stability. Ours is a journey, a pilgrimage, and the change that we should be seeking is not an outward change of scenery, but a change that reflects continual growth in Christ.

"We are 'called to be saints,'" says Spurgeon, "by that same voice which constrained (the ancient saints) to their high vocation. It is a Christian's duty to force his way into the inner circle of saintship; and if these saints were superior to us in their attainments, as they certainly were, let us follow them; let us emulate their ardor and holiness. We have the same light that they had; the same grace is accessible to us, and why should we rest satisfied until we have equalled them in heavenly character!"

1. The Christian life is a life of continual change. What causes us to get "stuck" in our old patterns?

2. In what areas do you see you have been "stuck" and need to change?

## DAY 4 • THE FRUIT OF THEIR WAY

Daily Reading: Proverbs 1:20-33

*Because they hated knowledge and did not choose the fear of the Lord, and would have none of my counsel and despised all my reproof, therefore they shall eat the fruit of their way and be sated with their own devices. (vv. 29-32)*

We learn from verse 20 that it is "Wisdom" which speaks here. This Book of Proverbs has much to say about Wisdom, even personifying it with the feminine pronoun—"In the markets she raises her voice," and so forth.

In another place we are told that the fear of the Lord is the beginning of wisdom. It is wise for us to consider where the end will be of the way we choose. Because most of us do not spend much time thinking about such things, short-range goals are more appealing. The student must learn to put the long-range goal of satisfactory grades, successful completion of courses and graduation ahead of short-range goals of watching TV, spending endless hours talking with friends, playing sports, and the like. If the long-range goal is not at least operative to some extent, he will be sure to fail.

So in life. The long-range goal requires "knowledge . . . the fear of the Lord . . . counsel . . . and reproof." Without these we go astray. If we despise them, we are given the opportunity to be "sated with our own devices." I looked up the word "sated" and the dictionary says it means "1. to cloy with overabundance: glut. 2. to appease (as a thirst or a violent emotion) by indulging in the full." Did you ever find yourself "fed up" with yourself and with your own devices? This may have to happen for us to see how bitter indeed is the fruit of our own will and willfulness.

Wisdom, then, bids us take another course. As Christians, we know that the wise choice is to seek God's will before our own. His way is best, even though it may seem hard for the moment. The easy way often turns hard in the end, and its fruit can be bitter indeed.

1. How have any of the 3D disciplines helped you choose long-range goals over short-term satisfactions?

2. What long-range goals do you need to have in order to be directed more into God's will for your life?

## DAY 5 • GOD GAVE THEM UP

Daily Reading: Romans 1:16-32

*And since they did not see fit to acknowledge God, God gave them up to a base mind and to improper conduct. (v. 28)*

"A dark picture of pagan immorality," this section of Romans has been called. In it, the apostle Paul spells out in no uncertain terms what happens when we insist on our way too strongly and too long. Three times in this passage we read, "God gave them up." And that is all that has to happen to have the worst elements in human nature bloom like some rank and stinking blossom; if God removes his grace and gives us up, we are led to become what we are without him. This chapter gives a sad picture of human nature left to itself, and we can read in it a fairly apt description of the time in which we live!

When we are struggling with all that is unlovely and ungodly within us, and the need and desire to change the habit patterns in our lives, let us keep in mind that we are not simply doing something optional, if we feel like it, when we feel like it. We are in a spiritual battle against those thought patterns, feeling patterns, and behavior patterns which wreak destruction in our own lives and in the lives of those we love. It is vital that we be open to changing.

Yet the power of old habits is very strong and resists any attempt on our part to change. Just as we tend to wake up at a regular time every morning, and get hungry at regular times during the day, habits are deeply ingrained. Remember what Dr. Jay Adams says in his little book, *Godliness Through Discipline*, and re-read it from time to time: "There is only one way," he says, "to become a godly person, to orient one's life toward godliness, and that means pattern by pattern. The old, sinful ways, as they are discovered, must be replaced by new patterns from God's Word."

God will work with us and in us, as long as we acknowledge him and in our hearts desire to change. He is faithful and loving and cannot fail us! Be of good cheer!

1. The desire to change is very important. Without it no permanent change can take place in our lives. How is the Lord increasing your desire to change?

## DAY 6 • LET US TEST AND EXAMINE

Daily Reading: Lamentations 3:31-66

*Let us test and examine our ways and return to the Lord! (v. 40)*

Yesterday we thought about what Dr. Jay Adams said about the necessity of changing our habits, pattern by pattern. Let's think again about what he says in this matter: "Discipline first requires self-examination, then it means crucifixion of the old sinful ways (saying 'no' daily), and lastly, practice in following Jesus Christ in new ways by the guidance and strength that the Holy Spirit provides through his Word. The biblical way to godliness is not easy or simple, but it is the solid way."

Jeremiah in today's Bible reading faces the ruin and sorrow of Jerusalem and the entire nation. All its glory is gone, and the people are being carried off into forced labor. It would have seemed hopeless to most eyes. But even in the midst of his lamentations and expressions of grief, he calls on the people to "test and examine our ways and return to the Lord." He knew that God's purpose and will towards his people was good, and that if they met the conditions God had to require in order to restore them, miracles could and would happen.

Look at your own life in the light of this passage, and "test and examine" the patterns which seem so natural and right. Perhaps the Lord is waiting to show you where you can begin to change by crucifying the old sinful ways and by using his promised strength to build new patterns of obedience!

1. Discipline first requires self-examination—then saying "no" daily to what is not God's will. What about your judgments? Are you a habitual "judge" of others? If so, what do you think you can do to change your habit of judging?

## Day 7 • Turn Back, Turn Back

Daily Reading: Ezekiel 33:1-20

*Say to them, As I live, says the Lord God, I have no pleasure in the death of the wicked, but that the wicked turn from his way and live; turn back, turn back from your evil ways; for why will you die, O house of Israel? (v. 71)*

What a word of encouragement to you and me! What an enticement from God to "get on" with the business of changing our habit patterns. This is the voice of the Father of love, mercy and goodness, pleading with us not to go on headstrong in the ways of the world. "Evil ways" correspond to "his ways" earlier in the verse. In other words, *our* way is the evil way in God's sight when we are opposed to him and his will. Our ways do not have to be grossly immoral, they do not have to be criminal or illegal. They have only to be our way in opposition to God to be evil!

Here we see in this chapter the juxtaposition of God's justice and his mercy. His holiness requires that wickedness be punished. Not to react in revulsion against wickedness and wrong would compromise God's own righteousness and holiness. But there is another dimension or attribute which God reveals here: his great mercy and compassion on the sinner.

"Lest the sternness of God's threats against the disobedient should drive to despair those who are conscious of their transgressions and sins which deserve the wrath of God, Ezekiel assures us that God has no pleasure in the death of the wicked but that what gives our loving God pleasure is, 'that the wicked should turn from his way and live.' . . . Oh what infinite compassion, tenderness, and love! Who can harden himself against such an appeal?" (Fausett)

Such is the appeal of God to us—the appeal from his heart to ours: to allow him to do a mighty work of changing within us, patiently, step by step, habit by habit, until our lives are turned to his praise and glory.

"Turn back, turn back. . . for why will you die?"

1. How do you know God loves you? Give as many reasons for your answer as you can.

# THE PEACE OF GOD

*What you
have learned
and received
and heard
and seen in me,
do; and the God
of peace will be
with you.*

*Philippians 4:9*

## DAY 1 • THE GOD OF PEACE

Daily Reading: I Thessalonians 5:1-28

*May the God of peace himself sanctify you wholly; and may your spirit and soul and body be kept sound and blameless at the coming of our Lord Jesus Christ. (v. 23)*

This is a beautiful title for our Heavenly Father: the God of peace. Turmoil and confusion are not marks of his presence. Yet turmoil and confusion often characterize our experience here. Why? Because we do not stay in harmony with the God of peace.

Let us think about this title, and what it means. The word "peace" carries a wealth of meaning. In the Hebrew language, which would be so familiar to Paul, it is the word *shalom*. So much more than simply an absence of hostility, it is filled with a sense of well-being or salvation.

The God of peace carries peace within himself. He is our peace, and his presence in our lives is our surety of peace. When peace is missing, it is a signal that some barrier has come between us and our Heavenly Father, the Source of peace.

The God of peace brings peace to those who are at war with him. "God was in Christ, reconciling the world to himself, not counting their trespasses against them . . ." (2 Corinthians 5:19).

When the angels sang to the shepherds that first Noel, it was to announce "Peace, good will towards men." Out of his generosity and love, the God of peace brings peace to the earth, taking on himself the burden and result of our sin through Jesus Christ on the cross. Suffering in our stead, Jesus becomes the peacemaker between God and man, and forever the door of access to the Father is open to all who come this way.

May the God of peace himself sanctify you wholly; and may your spirit and soul and body be kept sound and blameless at the coming of our Lord Jesus Christ.

> At the heart of the cyclone tearing the sky
> And flinging the clouds and the towers by,
> Is a place of central calm;
> So here in the roar of mortal things,
> I have a place where my spirit sings,
> In the hollow of God's palm.
> *(Edwin Markham, 1852-1940)*

1. How have you let your Heavenly Father be the God of peace in your life?

## Day 2 • The Peace of God

Daily Reading: Philippians 4:1-23

*And the peace of God, which passes all understanding, will keep your hearts and your minds in Christ Jesus. (v. 7)*

Yesterday we thought about the God of peace. Now we can turn our attention to the peace of God. God's peace is not a passive state of suspended animation! Yet that is what we often think of when we use the term "peace."

We were reminded that in Hebrew the word *shalom* had many more connotations than we can put into our English word "peace." It is in this sense that St. Paul uses the word frequently in opening his epistles: "Grace, mercy and peace."

In addition to the normal sense of rest and a feeling of peace, the word conveys "a state of reconciliation with God." Did you ever find yourself engaged in a sharp difference with someone in your life—having strong feelings and perhaps a lot of anger and hostility in the midst of the quarrel? Then have you had the experience of talking it out, and being reconciled, truly reconciled in mutual forgiveness and repentance? If so, you know from experience something of what Paul is talking about when he uses the word in the sense of reconciliation with God. Where there was estrangement, fear, and anxiety, now there is a free and joyful state of fellowship. How does this come about? Through Jesus Christ and his cross. Our peace rests right there—in who he is and what he has done for us. The moment we try to base our relationship with God on anything else, peace goes! Striving and ego come in.

The peace of God is Jesus. He is one with the Father, and when we live in him, we enjoy that oneness, too. It is beyond understanding. Flee to the Father, and ask the Lord Jesus to become that peace. Give up anything that is blocking the fulfillment of that prayer, and believe.

> Peace, perfect peace In this dark world of sin?
> The blood of Jesus Whispers peace within.
> *(Edward Bickersteth, 1875)*

1. In what relationship recently have you had differences and have experienced reconciliation?

2. What did you have to give up to come to peace with one from whom you were estranged?

## DAY 3 • NO PEACE FOR THE WICKED

Daily Reading: Isaiah 57:1-21

*Peace, peace to the far and to the near, says the Lord; and I will heal him. (v. 19)*
*There is no peace, says my God, for the wicked. (v. 21)*

One might think of this as the Lord's greeting to all who draw near to him: "Shalom, shalom, to the far and to the near! And I will heal him!" What a vision of the way the Father greets us as we turn, wearied of our ways, and seek heart-rest in him. All the striving, the seeking, the unfulfilled longings of our hearts are set at rest as we hear these blessed words.

> Far, far away, like bells at evening pealing,
> The voice of Jesus sounds o'er land and sea,
> And laden souls, by thousands meekly stealing,
> King Shepherd, turn their weary steps to thee.

Yet there is a condition of peace. Although the heart and love of God reach out to the uttermost there must be a desire on the part of those who would find peace to be healed and forgiven, restored and renewed in spirit. It would not do for God to ignore the real nature of rebellion against him, the wickedness and evil which so readily find lodging in human hearts. For that would be a false peace, a mere temporary truce, instead of the peace of God.

The wicked deny themselves that peace. All of us do, when we refuse God's loving condition of peace. "The impenitent are self-doomed to continuing turbulence." *(Interpreter's Bible)*

It is no false peace we seek as we go through the times of discipline seeking to progress in our life in Jesus. It is the joyful fellowship we know is there, when we are low enough, humble enough, and contrite enough (v. 15) to be able to experience it.

> Take from our souls the strain and stress,
> And let our ordered lives confess
> The beauty of thy peace.

1. Where have you tired of "your ways" and turned to Jesus to find heart-rest in him?

2. How can you tell "your ways" from "God's ways"?

## DAY 4 • THE WAY OF PEACE

Daily Reading: Isaiah 59:1-21

*The way of peace they know not, and there is no justice in their paths; they have made their road crooked, no one who goes in them knows peace. (v. 8)*

What a sad thing that the prophet had to say about his people. They did not know the way of peace. It was not that the Lord's hand was shortened, nor his ears dull; there was every willingness on his part to be found and known. But the paths they had chosen were paths of separation from God. "Your iniquities have made a separation between you and God" (v. 2). It is the sad truth in every generation of God's people that they lose their peace and fellowship with God when they forsake his paths. We make our roads crooked (seeking to hide) and we lose the peace which he longs to share with us from his own nature.

The way of peace is the way of the straight path. The straight path represents directness, steady aim, consistency of speech and purpose. The crooked way is the way of the half-truth, the backbiter, the gossiper, the devious and the manipulator—and all of us have been all of these things at one time or many in our lives. In order to find and walk the way of peace, we must let the Holy Spirit draw us back into his light, his truth, his way—so that there is an inner integrity and singleness of heart. "Blessed are the pure in heart, for they shall see God," said Jesus. The pure heart is the single-minded heart, and when we allow the Lord to sweep away the confusion of our own thoughts, excuses, demands, and accusations, we begin to see more clearly the way of peace. The God of peace desires all his children to share in the blessing of his fellowship. He is peace, and his way is peace.

> With eager heart and will on fire,
> I strove to win my great desire.
> "Peace shall be mine," I said; but life
> Grew bitter in the barren strife.
>
> My soul was weary, and my pride
> Was wounded deep; to Heaven I cried,
> "God grant me peace or I must die;"
> The dumb stars glittered no reply.

> Broken at last, I bowed my head,
> Forgetting all myself, and said,
> "Whatever comes, His will be done;"
> And in that moment peace was won.
> *(Henry Van Dyke, 1852-1933)*

1. We learn that the way of peace is a straight path and represents directness, steady air, consistency of speech and purpose. Where have you put it into practice?

2. How have you been able to let the Lord sweep away confusion from your life and to live in greater peace?

## DAY 5 • NOT AS THE WORLD GIVES

Daily Reading: John 14:1-31

*Peace I leave with you; my peace I give to you: not as the world gives do I give to you. Let not your heart be troubled, neither let it be afraid. (v. 27)*

This is Jesus' last talk with his disciples. You might call it his "Farewell Address." It was meant to hold them steady during the difficult hours and days that he knew would follow, when their faith would be tested to the utmost, and when the true mettle of their commitment to him and the truth he had taught them would be tried.

He wants them to know that, in spite of all the pain and difficulty which lay ahead, both for himself and for them, his peace would prevail. "Not as the world gives do I give to you." What the world gives, the world can take away. If we live by the surface feeling of peace when things are going well, we will lose it and be thrown into turmoil and confusion the moment the outward circumstances change. And change they do, for all of us. The peace that Jesus gives is a deeper, more lasting peace, even amid surface turmoil. Like the deep ocean which remains steady in spite of the storm raging on the surface of the water, this peace abides. But it is not a cheap peace which avoids all pain and difficulty. That we must understand, or else we will keep pursuing that ephemeral, worldly peace which can never last. This peace, this strange peace, this lasting peace, this peace that passes understanding—a pearl of great price—is the gift of Jesus to all who will walk the way of the cross with him.

They cast their nets in Galilee,
Just off the hills of brown;
Such happy, simple fisherfolk,
Before the Lord came down.

Contented, peaceful fishermen
Before they ever knew
The peace of God that filled their hearts
Brimful, and broke them too.

Young John who trimmed the flapping sail,
Homeless in Patmos died.
Peter, who hauled the teeming net,
Head-down was crucified.

The peace of God, it is no peace,
But strife closed in the sod.
Yet, brothers, pray for but one thing:
The marvelous peace of God.
    *(William Alexander Percy, 1924;*
    *Copyright, Church Pension fund)*

1. Where do you know you have sought surface peace to avoid pain and difficulty rather than seeking for God's perfect will?

2. How can you cooperate with God in your own life and receive the peace that passes understanding?

## DAY 6 • IN PERFECT PEACE

Daily Reading: Isaiah 26:1-21

*Thou dost keep him in perfect peace, whose mind is stayed on thee, because he trusts in thee. (v. 3)*

"There are multitudes who can bear witness that their first discovery of peace of mind came to them, when, weary with struggle and baffled in their quest, they cast their burden on God and were sustained" *(Interpreter's Bible)*.

The prophet here gives us a clear indication as to how peace can be found and sustained: by keeping our mind stayed on God. The mind is a fretful, impulsive thing, and will quickly wander to many things, like a child straying from the family to investigate something by itself. The mind often has to be treated like a child, with a firm "no" when it seeks to go wandering in forbidden paths. The paths may be gross and sensual, or they may be very respectable and refined. But if they are the wrong paths, they will lead to a loss of peace and fellowship with God.

One of the things we all have to watch is "getting into self." We may be doing a good thing, well-intent on doing it for a good purpose, but subtly slip into pride and ego, and in so doing, our minds are not stayed on God. We have begun to trust ourselves rather than God.

This perfect peace of which Isaiah sings is the natural result of being in right relationship with God. The key is trust, the giving up of our striving and burden-carrying, in order that we might know this blessed peace of heart.

1. How do you keep your mind stayed on God?

2. How can you watch "getting into self" without becoming introspective and self-centered?

## DAY 7 • ON EARTH PEACE

Daily Reading: Luke 2:1-20

*Glory to God in the highest, and on earth peace among men with whom he is pleased! (v. 14)*

The angels who announced the birth of Jesus did so with a song of praise and promise. It was not enough simply to get word to the shepherds that a great and wonderful thing was happening at the nearby town of Bethlehem. Such an event was so full of promise that the only way to speak of it was in song! The echoes of that song have been sounding around the world ever since, bringing hope and encouragement wherever it is heard and believed.

> Still through the cloven skies they come
> With peaceful wings unfurled,
> And still their heavenly music floats
> O'er all the weary world.
> Above its sad and lowly plains

They bend on hov'ring wing,
And ever o'er its Babel-sounds
The blessed angels sing.

Yet with the voice of sin and strife
The world has suffered long;
Beneath the heavenly strain have rolled
Two thousand years of wrong;
And man, at war with man, hears not
The tidings that they bring,
O hush the noise, ye men of strife
And hear the angels sing!
                    *(Edmund Hamilton Sears, 1846)*

True peace can only come as men's hearts are in tune with the heart of God. Jesus said, "Blessed are the peacemakers, for they shall be called children of God." We bring that quality of peace of which the angels sang when we are "men with whom he is well pleased." That means that with every little sacrifice of self we make, every step we take along the road of obedience to Jesus, every small area of control we give up to him, we bring his peace to that extent to the world. We can be peace-bringers by living our lives in harmony with him.

1. In what way has your life come into greater harmony with God in these last few weeks?

2. How has the "God of Love and King of Peace" brought more hope and encouragement in your life?

# HIS MERCY ENDURES

*For by grace*
*you have been*
*saved by faith;*
*and this is not*
*your own doing,*
*it is the gift of*
*God—not because*
*of works, lest*
*any man*
*should boast.*

*Ephesians 2:8, 9*

## DAY 1 • ALL OF GRACE

Daily Reading: Ephesians 2:1-10

*For by grace you have been saved through faith; and this is not your own doing, it is the gift of God—not because of works, lest any man should boast. (vv. 8,9)*

The theme of grace has ever been a favorite of those who have found favor in the sight of the Lord. After an elderly woman had heard a famous preacher preach the Gospel, she said to him as she came out the church door, "I'll tell you one thing: if Jesus Christ saves me, he'll never hear the end of it!" And that's the way we should feel. Our works, our efforts, our prayers—what are they, or what would they avail, if God were not gracious toward us? Grace is the unmerited favor of God—the undeserved, unearned favor. He loves us because of who he is—not because we are good. Knowing that should make us so firmly grounded in him that we can get on with all that needs to happen to make our lives what they ought to be. We have far to go, even though we may have come a long way. But what of it?

> Through many dangers, toils and snares
> I have already come.
> 'Tis grace that brought me safe thus far,
> And grace will lead me home.
> *(John Newton)*

Today, do not forget to be thankful for that grace—which is greater than all your sins, failures, mistakes. Grace that covers as a garment all the scars of your past. God looks upon you and me in his Son and finds us beautiful. That is grace.

1. Why is it hard for us to accept the fact that we are saved by God's grace alone?

2. It has been said the "good" people have more difficulty recognizing the role of grace in salvation than notoriously "bad" people. Why is this?

## DAY 2 • MERCIFUL AND GRACIOUS

Daily Reading: Psalm 103:1-22

*The Lord is merciful and gracious, slow to anger and abounding in steadfast love. (v. 8)*

This psalm is a great cure for down times, for times of self-pity, or discouragement. "Bless the Lord, O my soul." And no one can obey that injunction for very long without having his or her spirits lifted. So when you feel down, try blessing the Lord. It really does work!

It is useful to remember the ways God has shown himself in your life. It would be well if we kept some kind of diary or journal, because we do tend quickly to forget the things he has done.

"Bless the Lord, O my soul, and forget not all his benefits."

The Israelites fled from the Egyptians, and found themselves trapped between the oncoming army of Pharaoh and the Red Sea. They were terrified. They cried to the Lord, and complained to Moses, and Moses went before the Lord with the complaint. Then God told them to "go forward," and, as we know, the Red Sea waters opened, and they passed over dry-shod. The Egyptians pursued them, but were drowned in the sea when the waters came roaring back in, catching them unawares. The Israelites had a great celebration, and you can read their victory song in Exodus 15. But hardly have the strains of the victory song died away when we read, "They went three days in the wilderness and found no water" (15:22). What did they do? "And the people murmured against Moses." They had forgotten the merciful and gracious hand of God which had led them forth out of bondage. "Forget not all his benefits!"

Today, as you go about your activities, seeing familiar faces, doing familiar and ordinary things, remember, "The Lord is gracious and merciful, slow to anger and abounding in steadfast love." Look around you for the evidence that this is so for you!

1. Look back over the last few days and see the places where you lost your grateful heart and began to murmur and complain. Ask God's forgiveness for this.

2. Make a list of some of the ways God has been merciful and gracious to you recently.

## DAY 3 • ON THOSE THAT FEAR HIM

Daily Reading: Luke 1:39-56

*And his mercy is on those who fear him from generation to generation.* (v. 50)

We have here in Mary's Magnificat an interesting combining of two thoughts: the mercy of the Lord and the fear of God. It is significant that these two concepts are tied together in this way because they give us a clue to the way God's mercy operates.

First, for those who have no fear of God, there is a negative aspect to this mercy. Both his kindness and his severity are meant to bring those who do not fear him to their senses, so that they will have a proper, healthy fear, or reverence, for God. For a person who does not have these, God's mercy cannot be seen or understood, even though, as Jesus taught us, the Father causes the sun to shine and the rain to fall on the just and the unjust. What is operating in the lives of those who do not fear God is a series of circumstances designed by Providence to bring them to repentance and faith. Whether they will let those circumstances work for them or not is up to them.

Second, for those who do fear God, mercy is evident, and far from removing their healthy fear or reverence, it increases it. The more we truly understand the love of God, the more we are afraid of rejecting and refusing it.

Third, for those who fear God there is a multiplication of mercy from generation to generation. The prayers of the forefathers, the mercies shown to them, and their dealings with God are remembered by God himself. (Mary speaks of this in v. 54.) So those who fear him are blessed in their own time, and can confidently expect that God will remember his mercy to their children and to their children's children. That seems to be the clear message of this passage, and what hope that should give every parent and grandparent who longs to see spiritual blessing come to their progeny!

1. It is difficult to fully understand and explain the "fear of the Lord," yet it is talked about frequently in Scripture. What does the fear of God as talked about in today's devotion mean to you?

## DAY 4 • DELIVERED TO SERVE HIM WITHOUT FEAR

Daily Reading: Luke 1:57-80

*Blessed be the Lord God of Israel, for he has visited and redeemed his people . . . that we, being delivered from the hands of our enemies, might serve him without fear, in holiness and righteousness before him all the days of our life.* (vv. 68, 74-75)

These canticles or songs in the early part of Luke's Gospel are packed with spiritual truth and insight. Yesterday we thought about "the fear of the Lord" and how it is related to the enduring mercy of God. Now we see the whole matter from a slightly different perspective. As Zechariah spoke or sang his prophetic word, he again saw everything that was coming to pass as a part of God's performance of "the mercy promised to our fathers" (v. 72). In the reverent fear of the Lord, Zechariah and his wife Elizabeth had lived their lives, and now, in their old age, they were seeing that God is able to do beyond all that we ask or think.

> E'en down to old age, all my people shall prove
> My sovereign, eternal, unchangeable love;
> And when hoary hairs shall their temples adorn,
> Like lambs they shall still in my bosom be borne.

The fear of the Lord—the healthy, wholesome reverential awe before the almighty Creator and Maker of all things—dispels the "fear of our enemies." When our hearts are completely wedded to him, given to him without reserve, what can man do to us? Pioneers, saints, missionaries, martyrs—all have testified that they found in serving him a freedom from the fear that enslaves.

What does that mean to you today? Of what do you find yourself afraid? Loss of a friend's favor? The anger of someone with whom you should be honest? Rejection by others? These little fears can control us, if we do not see the tremendous power of God's deliverance and the freedom to be ourselves that Jesus has brought. Day by day, bask in the enduring mercy and the reality of the love which sought you, found you and is bringing you back to the fullness of God's creative purpose for you. What a Savior we have! How great this salvation!

1. Most of us are troubled by fears—often little ones. Of what do you find yourself frequently afraid?

2. How can you keep from allowing these fears to control you?

## DAY 5 • THAT HE MAY HAVE MERCY ON ALL

Daily Reading: Romans 11:1-36

*For God has consigned all men to disobedience, that He may have mercy upon all.*
(v. 32)

As we think this week about the enduring mercy of God, it is well to recall how we came to know it and to receive it. St. Paul, a Jew, is concerned here that Gentile Christians appreciate how God had dealt with his people through all the ages, and how he had used even their disobedience as a way of opening the door of salvation to others (vv. 30, 31). It is part of the holy mystery of our faith that God chose the Jews, and in their rejection of the Messiah opened the door that all might come in. We do not have to understand or explain this, even to ourselves, but it is important to know the truth of it. It was God's way, not man's! And God's ways often astound us and make little of our human reasoning.

Paul is eager for all to understand that God still remembers his mercy towards Israel, "beloved for the sake of their forefathers." A part of the wonder of God's mercy is his remembrance.

Since this is the way God is, and since he has proved himself faithful in the past, we have a solid foundation for our life in him today. Are you facing problems, fears, anxieties about yourself or someone you love? Remember God's mercy. God remembers. He forgets not his own, and his own are those who seek his face in every age and place. He looks at all of us, so far from all that he intended us to be, and declares us all in need of mercy. The grace of God which was revealed in the face of Jesus is directed towards us all—"whosoever will."

1. In what areas are you facing problems or anxieties about yourself or a loved one?

2. How best should you handle these concerns?

# Day 6 • Grace, Mercy and Peace

Daily Reading: 1 Timothy 1:1-20

*To Timothy, my true child in the faith: Grace, mercy, and peace from God the Father and Christ Jesus our Lord. (v. 2)*

Someone has described "grace" as pertaining to our sins, and "mercy" as pertaining to our misery. "Paul's sense of his need of 'mercy' had deepened the older he grew" *(Fausett)*. The same should be true of us. The more we go on with the Lord, the more experiences which challenge and defeat all our efforts, the more we should be deeply aware of our constant need of God's mercy. The prayers of an old minister I heard years ago seem to be especially fitting: "Yesterday's mercies are all used up. We are in need of new mercies every day."

But what a heartening prayer this is, prayed in the full confidence of one who has stood in the battle of life, one who has known almost every conceivable hardship and setback a Christian can expect: "Grace, mercy and peace." With an abundant supply of these, what can life bring which can defeat us? Our God is *gracious*. He bestows his loving favor on the undeserving, on those who did not and cannot earn it because of who they are. He bestows his loving favor on sinners, wrong ones, people who have negative thoughts and hateful feelings. He does not wait until we have achieved victory over all that keeps us from being like him in order to love us. He is *gracious*.

And he is *merciful*. He is moved with compassion at our condition. He does not despise us because we are weak and wrong and needy! That is his nature. So we can rejoice in who he is, and expect a daily supply to meet our needs. And because he is this way, are we not encouraged to "follow his example"?

1. When do you have difficulty showing mercy to others?

2. How can you cultivate a more merciful heart toward others?

## DAY 7 • HIS MERCY IS OVER ALL

Daily Reading: Psalm 145:1-21

*The Lord is good to all and his tender mercies are over all his works. (v. 9)*

In this song of praise, we are encouraged to "rehearse" the characteristics of God as he has revealed himself to us. Here are some of them:
"Great . . . and greatly to be praised" (v. 3).
"Mighty" (v. 4).
"Majestic" and "wondrous" (v. 5).
"Terrible in might" (v. 61).
"Abundant in goodness" (v. 7) and, in the same verse, "righteous"
"Gracious, merciful, slow to anger" (v. 8).
"Abounding in steadfast love" (v. 8).
"Faithful" (v. 13).
"Just" and "kind" (v. 17).
He is the upholder of the fallen, the giver of food in due season, the One who is near when called, the savior of those who cry to him, the preserver of those who love him, the destroyer of the wicked.

Just to read over these attributes or descriptions of what God is like should bring a lift to the heart and encouragement to our souls!

But for me, the most beautiful verse in this entire psalm is verse 9. In the RSV it reads, "The Lord is good to all, and his compassion is over all that he has made." How different is that attitude from ours! Whereas we demand perfection, or something that approaches it from our point of view, God is compassionate. He is patient in working with us, leading us out of what and where we have been, into what his goodness and kindness plan for us.

> We are his people, we his care,
> Our souls, and all our mortal frame:
> What lasting honors shall we rear,
> Almighty Maker, to thy Name?
>
> We'll crowd thy gates with thankful songs,
> High as the heav'n our voices raise;
> And earth with her ten thousand tongues,
> Shall fill thy courts with sounding praise!
> *(Isaac Watts, 1719)*

1. Where do we demand perfection of ourselves and of others?

2. How can we begin to put a stop to these impossible demands?

# WHERE DO WE GO FROM HERE?

*Guard the
truth that has
been entrusted
to you by the
Holy Spirit
who dwells
within us.*

2 Timothy 1:14

## Day 1 • Let Us Go On to Maturity

Daily Reading: Hebrews 6:1-20

*Therefore let us leave the elementary doctrines of Christ and go on to maturity. (v. 1a)*

Peter Pan, you remember, was a boy who didn't want to grow up. Some people are "Peter Pan Christians"—they simply refuse to grow up. Have you found that Jesus has answered your cries for help, and that you have been graced to make it through the hard places over and over again?

The letter to the Hebrews was written when many Christians were paying for their faith with their very lives. It was a dangerous time to be a Christian. They needed all the help they could get!

It is quite clear, reading the New Testament, that if a person was not willing to "go on to maturity" in that early day, he or she would have a difficult time even remaining a follower of Jesus. In our day, however, it is easy to "hide in the woodwork," so to speak, because there is enough strength in the Church to carry us along, at least outwardly, even if we are not growing spiritually. We are the losers, however, for in Christians an arrested adolescence is never a satisfying, fruitful way to live.

Check out before the Lord any areas in which you are holding back, not wanting to go on to maturity, wanting to avoid responsibility, letting others bear the brunt of battle. Christ gives us new birth, and God gives the increase and growth, but it requires our steady cooperation for us to become mature, stable soldiers of the Cross.

1. There is a strong warning in Hebrews 6 against turning away from the truth and light we have. Where does this passage (vv. 4-9) tell us that we find the strength and grace to do what God calls us to do?

2. What does verse 19 say to you about your prospects for the future of your life as a disciple of Jesus Christ?

## DAY 2 • LOOKING TO JESUS

Daily Reading: Hebrews 12:1-11

*Looking to Jesus, the pioneer and perfecter of our faith, who for the joy that was set before him endured the cross, despising the shame, and is seated at the right hand of God. (v. 2)*

We began our Christian walk looking to Jesus. Overwhelmed with our sense of wrong and need, we turned inwardly to him, and found his grace sufficient. The cross before our eyes became our hope—he died that we might live!

Jesus is pictured here, not only in his saving, substitutionary work, but as a "pioneer of our faith." A pioneer is one who blazes new trails, explores new terrain, opens new territory—he is a pace-setter for others to follow. In what sense, then, was Jesus the pioneer of our faith? He taught us how to obey, how to submit our wills to the Father's will, how to trust beyond sight and reason, and how to suffer in hope. As we read of his life, all these things come out of the way he lived, and who he was. Day by day he sought not his own will, but the Father's. In the great temptations in the desert, he showed us how to battle Satan's tempting thoughts and pictures. He showed us how to resist friends when they tried to dissuade him from God's chosen path. He taught us how to stand against the onslaughts of lies and calumnies, without flinching or running away. He taught us how to put family in proper perspective, asking, "Who are my mother and my brothers?" On and on we could go, showing how Jesus is the trail-blazer, and how he calls us to "follow in his steps."

As we keep looking to Jesus, his example inspires us. Moreover, the glorious reward with which God crowned his life—his resurrection from the dead and his exaltation to the Father's right hand—should help us to get our eyes off immediate things and consider eternal things! "For the joy that was set before him." His joy is still set before us, and we can only receive it as we, too, endure the cross, and go on with him. Let us, without fail, keep on keeping our eyes on Jesus.

> Turn your eyes upon Jesus,
> Look full in his wonderful face.
> And the things of earth will grow strangely dim
> In the light of his glory and grace.

1. Jesus taught us by example. Today's devotion gives us ways in which he was a pace-setter for us. What lessons do you learn by looking unto Jesus?

2. Name some of the most important truths you have learned in 3D.

## DAY 3 • TESTING PRODUCES STEADFASTNESS

Daily Reading: James 1:1-27

*Count it all joy, my brethren, when you meet various trials, for you know that the testing of your faith produces steadfastness. And let steadfastness have its full effect that you may be perfect and complete, lacking nothing. (vv. 2-4)*

New ventures are often begun in enthusiasm. We catch a gleam, a spark of hope is ignited, and off we go on a new thing. But if any venture is to succeed, there will be trials and testings that must be overcome. We may see the mountain top, but find that the path upward leads through much undergrowth, with rocks, insects, uneven ground, and a lot of other things that did not appear in the lovely distant view.

We have looked to Jesus, the pioneer and perfecter of our faith, and we have engaged ourselves to follow him. Hallelujah! We have met the internal and external temptations that would keep us from our goal of becoming "perfect and complete" in him. There are the daily temptations that would keep us from our discipleship commitments, lure us away from the disciplines we have accepted, and send us scurrying back down the mountain away from the vision which had seized us in the beginning. Don't give up! Even at the eleventh hour, there is need for persevering on. Otherwise the joy of his "well done" will not be ours.

When I was small and trying to learn to tie my shoes, I can remember how very impatient I became when the laces would not stay together! First I had to learn "patience," and then the knack of tying the shoe laces. Years later, I saw my own children go through the same frustration, and watched their impatience with amusement and understanding. It does not do for the adult to "do it for them," but one must allow through trial and error the miracle of growth, patience, and learning to take place. In our spiritual life can we see that God lovingly allows the trials to produce steadfastness and maturity as a result of the whole process?

> I follow where Thou leadest, what are bruises?
> There are cool leaves of healing on Thy tree;
> Lead Thou me on. Thy heavenly wisdom chooses
> In love for me. . . .

All unafraid, so I will fearless follow
For love of Thee.
*(Amy Carmichael)*

1. Trials can produce steadfastness and maturity. What trials have produced the most maturity in you?

2. What daily temptations give you the most trouble?


## DAY 4 • STIR UP THE GIFT WITHIN YOU

Daily Reading: 2 Timothy 1:1-18

*Hence I remind you to rekindle the gift of God that is within you through the laying on of my hands: for God did not give us a spirit of timidity but a spirit of power and love and self-control. (vv. 6, 7)*

Paul regarded Timothy as his spiritual son, and was very concerned that, as a young minister of the gospel, Timothy should keep alive in himself that which God had planted in his heart. The faith had been first evidenced in his mother and grandmother, so Timothy had had a good start. Paul had great hopes for him, as he indicates in these two letters. But he knew that, apart from the "stirring up," the lamp would burn low, and faith would become weak.

It is important not to look for a let-up or a let-down in your walk with Jesus. This is not something for a season but for a lifetime. It is the thing that lifts life out of the dumps and the dregs, and lets it soar with meaning and hope.

You have a gift from the Lord within you. He has placed within you—a child of God—the gift of his very presence, in the person of the Holy Spirit, the third person of the Trinity. By this gift, Jesus Christ himself dwells in you, and you are a "temple," a dwelling place of the Spirit. What happens as a result of that gift, how brightly you manifest the reality of God, how much you allow it to change your life—is really up to you; he will never leave you nor forsake you. He is always faithful, and what he has begun in you, he will carry through. But you must do your share—your allotted part, in cooperating with him, and in walking daily in the way he leads. Apart from that, you will experience a diminishing of the sense of his presence. Let it be your daily care to "rekindle the gift of God that is within you."

Jesus, confirm my heart's desire
To work, and speak, and think for thee;
Still let me guard the holy fire,
And still stir up the gift in me.
*(Charles Wesley, 1762)*

1. What can you do daily to continue what God has begun in you through 3D?

2. There is a "quitter" in each of us. How can you overcome the desire to quit or give up?

## DAY 5 • IF WE ENDURE

Daily Reading: 2 Timothy 2:1-13

*If we endure, we shall also reign with him. (v. 12)*

Look at the encouraging words in this Scripture: "Be strong in the grace that is in Christ Jesus," "Take your share of suffering," "No soldier . . . gets entangled in civilian pursuits," "An athlete is not crowned unless . . . ," "It is the hardworking farmer who ought to have the first share of the crop." All of these are meant to spur young Timothy on in the course he has set for himself. All of them imply that the labor is not in vain, the effort is not lost, the struggle is worth it!

Jesus is faithful. Jesus calls us to walk after him and with him on a way that seems narrow and strange to the world. "The gate is wide and the way is easy, that leads to destruction, and those who enter by it are many. But the gate is narrow and the way is hard, that leads to life, and those who find it are few" (Matthew 7:13, 14).

Keep on the way! It leads to greater joy, greater freedom, greater peace. He can never fail you. "If we endure, we shall also reign with him."

1. What changes have taken place in your life that have brought you freedom and satisfaction?

## DAY 6 • DO YOUR BEST

Daily Reading: 2 Timothy 2:14-26

*Do your best to present yourself to God as one approved, a workman who has no need to be ashamed, rightly handling the word of truth. (v. 15)*

When you were young, your parents probably often counseled you with that phrase, "do your best." Whether it was in school, in sports, at home, or church or wherever, they wanted you to "do your best," in whatever you had set out to do.

In writing to young Timothy, Paul urges him to keep his eyes on the heavenly Judge, and to do his best to appear before God as one who has proved himself. Having God's approval must mean more to him than the praise of men. In that way, keeping his goal clearly before him, Timothy would have no reason to be ashamed in the "great day."

Doing our best is all that God requires of his children. "My yoke is easy and my burden is light," said Jesus. He does not ask of us anything that he does not give us the grace to carry out, but he does ask us to do our best. As we read in yesterday's Scripture, "It is the hard-working farmer who ought to have the first share of the crop." Seeking God's "well done" is a motive well worth cultivating, to offset the desire for instant approval and instant satisfaction which compete so strongly with that motive in all of us!

Today, "Do your best," to live for Jesus Christ instead of self. In the small decisions (and the big ones)—eating, sleeping, talking, working, playing, resting—"do your best to present yourself to God as one approved, a workman who has no need to be ashamed."

Notice, too, the admonition, "rightly handling the word of truth." When you hear that word of truth from another, especially if it is a hard, difficult, painful word, handle it rightly. Go to God with it and pray for ears to hear what he is saying through another person. If the Holy Spirit impresses a word of truth on your heart, do not handle it lightly or despise it, but act upon it as one who must give an account before God. It is the way to growth and maturity in Christ.

1. "Having God's approval means more than the praise of men." Comment on this and give an example of the truth of it from your own life.

2. When someone has shown you where a change is necessary in your life how have you reacted? What is the best way to accept a word of truth?

## DAY 7 • I HAVE FOUGHT THE GOOD FIGHT

Daily Reading: 2 Timothy 4:1-22

*I have fought the good fight, I have finished the race, I have kept the faith. Henceforth there is laid up for me the crown of righteousness, which the Lord, the righteous Judge, will award to me on that Day, and not only to me but also to all who have loved his appearing. (vv. 7, 8)*

Paul was nearing the end of his course when he wrote these words. His was a life-course, in which he suffered many hardships and troubles, and experienced many miracles and joys. Ours has been a mini-course in the Christian life, preparing us for daily living on a different level, for a more serious pursuit of our high calling of God in Christ Jesus.

"I have fought." The apostle knew what it meant to fight the world, the flesh and the devil. We don't always know what it is we are fighting when we are in the midst of a spiritual struggle. Read in the story of *Pilgrim's Progress* how the enemy attacked Christian in various ways—through personal encounter (the Valley of Humiliation); through subtle suggestions of others—Worldly Wiseman, Atheist, etc.; through discouragement (Doubting Castle). By making these experiences visible, Bunyan is seeking to help us know, as Paul did, what it means to fight the good fight!

"I have finished the race." Each year in a nearby city, a famous marathon is run. Not everyone wins. Only one can be first. But it is quite a challenge to finish the race. Many do not. In our Christian life we may know some who fall by the wayside, who drop out of the race. Look again at the victory in those words: "I have finished the race!" And hear again the call of the writer to the Hebrews, "Let us run with patience the race that is set before us, looking to Jesus."

"I have kept the faith." Thank God for those who have kept it, preserved it, treasured it for us. We will forever be in their debt. We can keep it for others—our children, grandchildren, people we may know and love, or people we will never know this side of eternity. But we can, by God's grace, keep faith and go from strength to strength in the Lord.

1. Paul knew what it was to fight temptation of all kinds. We all need to battle also. What are the temptations you are going to have to fight most?

# ALONG THE KING'S HIGHWAY

———&

# BABY STEPS

*Like*
*newborn*
*babes. . . .*

*1 Peter 2:2a*

## DAY 1 • FOLLOWING THE TRUTH

Daily Reading: 3 John:1-12

*No greater joy can I have than this, to hear that my children follow the truth. (v. 4)*

We are fellow pilgrims on the King's Highway. Life is not a resting place; it is a journey, and it can be likened to a road. Going down (or up) this road, there are always changes, always new experiences, new challenges, new opportunities for learning and growth. We may not always think about life this way, for it has the capability of a very strange illusion: that things stay the same.

A young woman recently said, "I don't like changes." An older person replied, "Then you are avoiding the reality of life, because life is made up of changes. The illusion that things stay the same is just that: an illusion." If we are not prepared to accept change and to work *with* change for the better, we are actually choosing to stay in unreality.

The aged John, writing the short letter we call Third John in the New Testament, made this beautiful statement: "No greater joy can I have than this, to hear that my children follow the truth." I do not think he is just talking about mental truth, or propositions that are true, or doctrines that are beyond doubt. Those things are important, of course. But even having the most unimpeachable, orthodox theology, we can still choose to live in unreality—ignoring the unpleasant things we don't like to face. And following the truth means ridding ourselves of as much of that unreality as possible.

These weeks will help us along that line, if we let them. They will help us look at things from some different perspective, perhaps to *hear* the truth inwardly in a fresh and helpful way. Although the truth is not always pleasant, it is always healing. When Jesus said, "I am the way, the truth, and the life," he surely meant that his way is the way to life, and his truth is the key to life. Since he came that we may have life in all its abundance, to walk in his truth is to enter more deeply into the life he came to give.

Truth is not to be feared. It is to be sought, for it is the key to freedom. The burden of unreality is really a heavy one. Jesus says his burden is light. So truth frees us to inner lightness and freedom in a way that no self-concocted "realism" can.

Baby Step #1: Choose to live in as much truth as possible—TODAY.

1. What new challenges or new opportunities for growth have you experienced lately?

2. Describe briefly how you met this (these) challenge(s). Can you see how you might meet such challenges better?

## DAY 2 • FIRST OF ALL

Daily Reading: 1 Timothy 2:1-8

*First of all, then, I urge that supplications, prayer, intercessions, and thanksgivings be made for all men . . that we may lead a quiet and peaceable life, godly and respectful in every way. (v. 1, 2)*

When Paul wrote his young protégé Timothy, laying down wise and experienced instructions on how to live and work as a servant of God, he begins with this counsel. Why? Because Paul knew that no effort would succeed if it is done without the power of God in it and behind it. Too often we make up our minds about what to do—perhaps go ahead and do whatever we've chosen—and then ask God to bless it. "Establish thou the work of our hands upon us" (Psalm 90). Then we feel quite pious and godly about our decision. But Paul reverses the order, and says, "First of all. . . ." Before we set out or undertake anything, we need to recognize that without God's blessing it is going to turn to dust and ashes. Isn't that the story of so many of our endeavors? I don't know about yours, but it certainly is true of mine.

And, if we could carry this concept a little farther, I would suggest that it might be well to take the last word in Paul's list and put it first: "thanksgivings." Before we lay our shopping list of needs before the throne of grace, it would be well to return thanks for those already fulfilled! And what a list it would be if we could recall all the ways we have been blessed.

Let us "raise our Ebenezer," as the old song puts it, saying, "Hither by thy help I've come." Make a list of the blessings that come to mind, large and small, for the more we remember and rehearse these gracious gifts, the more our faith is strengthened to go on.

Do you have a regular prayer time each day? Do you make it a priority to faithfully keep that appointment with God? If not, are you willing to start? Even if you fail, and have to start over and over again, it is worth the try. These little meditations and prayers are meant to be starters. They are not the whole thing. For that you must branch out on your own. You must try your wings if you haven't already done so, and trust that God will bless your efforts. All the manuals on spiritual growth recommend having a regular time and place for prayer. I hope you can find one and commit yourself to it. I know it will pay great dividends.

Baby Step #2: Make prayer and thanksgiving "first of all" today.

1. List some of the ways you have been blessed recently.

2. Write a prayer of thanksgiving and begin to use it with your thanksgiving list.

## DAY 3 • STEP BY STEP

Daily Reading: John 16:1-12

*I have yet many things to say to you, but you cannot bear them now. (v. 12)*

One of the most encouraging examples of God's love and mercy to us is that he doesn't dump everything on us at once. Not even every good thing. He observes the law of growth and change. We are being *formed* in his image. We do not, like the Greek myth, spring forth like Athena from the head of Zeus full-grown.

The disciples were facing a difficult time, and Jesus was concerned to give them everything they would need to see them through. So we have this beautiful discourse with them, recorded in the 14th, 15th and 16th chapters of John's Gospel. These chapters contain a wealth of encouragement for the disciples. It's no wonder they were treasured and read again and again after his resurrection. And we have here in today's text that little indication that they would be learning new things, that they would face new challenges and new opportunities after he was gone from them. I suspect that many of us who are parents would have done well to learn from him the principle of letting life teach many things, trusting God with our children. Instead, many of us tried to cram in every kind of instruction and warning, often to minds unwilling or unable to hear and receive the wisdom we thought we had for them. Jesus shows more patience and more understanding in dealing with us.

Do we see some important things about life more clearly than we did, perhaps even a year ago? As the road of life moves on, do we allow the Holy Spirit to drive home the lessons that he is teaching us? Learning needs not only an able teacher but a willing learner.

The very fact that you've embarked on this little journey says that you want to learn. You will not learn the whole thing during this brief period. You won't arrive at the end, and when the weeks come to an end, there will still be a way to go. But that is all right because Jesus understands the process and is involved in it. He wants you and me to be *whole* persons, integrated in body, soul and spirit. He wants to see his image emerging from the brokenness that is in all of us. And it will happen. We have his assurance. He has many things to teach us and is in the process of teaching us, even now.

Baby Step #3: Seek to be open to something new from God today.

1. What do you see about life now more clearly than you did a year or two ago?

2. Name three areas where you feel a need for personal change.

## DAY 4 • HELD BY THE HAND

Daily Reading: John 14:25-27; 16:13-15

*When the Spirit of Truth comes he will guide you into all the truth. (v. 13a)*

Jesus promised that the Holy Spirit would guide us into all the truth. It would be presumptuous to say we know just what he had in mind, for we have only partially seen and known his truth. We have enough to enable us to walk with him. We have enough to enable us to make the next step he calls us to make. We have enough to assure us that his is the right way. But we still have much to learn.

In these sessions, we are not just learning "facts," not even "Bible facts." The truth into which the Holy Spirit is guiding us is an experiential truth about who we are and about who Jesus is. Those things are not learned in books any more than we learn to swim by reading about swimming. The way we learn to swim is to get into the water and begin to follow instructions. And the way we are guided "into all the truth" is by facing what the Lord asks us to face.

Being guided into the truth will mean facing some things about yourself you would rather not look at. We cannot see ourselves as we are by ourselves. There is something in us that is so resistant to the ugly truth about us that we need help. God provides "mirrors" in the person of people and circumstances.

A friend of mine just today asked for help in facing a situation in which he had been seriously wrong. He was supposed to be representing Christ (as a Christian "ambassador") in a business situation, and instead had lost his temper and said some very unkind things. As the conversation began, he was still "right" in his mind because the other person had been so obviously wrong and had failed to do what he should have done. But when it was suggested that my friend's failure was more basic than any business arrangement, that he had failed to be a good representative of Jesus Christ, he was able to see, repent, and ask forgiveness. This was a good example of how we sometimes have to struggle to see our wrongness in order to receive the blessing the Lord has for us.

There will be many such lessons as life goes along—if we are willing to let others show us about ourselves what we seem unable to see alone. Our worst hindrance to being guided "into all the truth" is this deep resistance to anything that crosses our good image of ourselves.

Baby Step #4: Listen for truth about yourself today—from someone else's lips!

1. How has someone else tried to cross your good image of yourself, and how did you respond?

2. Have you had the experience of trying to tell someone else something he or she had a hard time receiving? How did you respond to that?

## DAY 5 • NO SMALL OBEDIENCES

Daily Reading: James 2:8-17
*Whoever keeps the whole law but fails in one point becomes guilty of all of it. (v. 10)*

Jesus says that those who love him will keep his commandments. The way to express our love for him and our gratitude for all he has done for us is to obey. Obedience is an expression of love.

More often than not, however, we think of obedience as earning a reward. "What a good boy am I," said little Jack Horner. And that's the way we're tempted to feel when we obey. Jesus told about the servant who came in from work and then prepared the master's meal and served him before he himself ate. "Likewise," said Jesus, "you ought to say, we are unworthy servants. We have only done our duty."

One of the discouraging things about any kind of discipline we undertake—whether it is diet, exercise, or spiritual exercises, is that results do not come as quickly or as dramatically as we'd like. The discouragement grows out of our wrong attitude towards obedience. We assume it will have a speedy and commensurate reward. And when it doesn't come, in our discouragement we may slip, rebel, give in to the easier way of self-indulgence, all under the rationalization that "it isn't working anyhow."

On the other hand, having said all that, we need to add this: there are no small obediences (or disobediences). The widow's mite was "small," but for her it was a great sacrifice. Just staying on our little discipline may seem a small thing (it probably will to others) but the Lord sees and knows how much of a struggle is involved to be faithful to it. And seeing it, he always honors it. The "pay-off" comes in the strengthening of our inner spiritual muscles, our ability to stay on course. If we persevere, those small obediences can add up to a big plus—even a big step forward.

So do not overlook the little obediences he calls for. Listen to what he says in your heart, the little impulses you get to do something that may cost you a little inconvenience. Listen and obey, for there is blessing in obedience. Each obedience says, "Lord, I love you and I thank you for all you are doing in my life."

Baby Step #5: Attempt some small but difficult obedience today.

1. Describe the "small obediences" that have been asked of you this week and how you have responded to them.

2. How is obedience an expression of love?

## DAY 6 • EXERCISING THROUGH BABY STEPS

Daily Reading: Hebrews 12:7-13

*Therefore, lift your drooping hands and strengthen your weak knees. . . . (v. 12)*

Yesterday we talked about "little obediences" and their importance in our spiritual journey. Today's text carries this thought a little further.

We know, do we not, that even a few days of bed rest can cause our muscles to begin to atrophy. Then when we get out of bed, we feel weak, unstable and shaky. The writer to the Hebrews was aware that the same thing could happen to us spiritually and emotionally. If we are "bed-ridden," passive, inactive, lazy, then our spiritual muscles will atrophy just as our physical ones do when they are not used.

What does it mean, then, to "lift drooping hands" and to "strengthen weak knees"? Does it not mean taking hold of today, of the situations we face in our ordinary life, and, although we feel weak and inadequate, to face them in the strength of Christ? That means facing the little irritations, the interruptions, the unplanned demands that confront us in an ordinary day. That means confessing our failures, finding forgiveness, and resolving to go on in spite of them. It means allowing what comes into the day to make us stand instead of encouraging us to collapse.

There are no problems in our day that are too hard for God. "Drooping hands" can be raised in praise and thanksgiving, and in so doing they will be better able to tackle the things that we need to do. Thanksgiving is a great way to strengthen wobbly knees. We know what fear can do. It can drain the strength right out of us. But when we are armed with even a *little* faith, we can move mountains—mountains of seemingly impossible magnitude.

A friend of mine takes exercise regularly with a group. He is older than most of them, and a little more overweight than most. As a result, when they go "power-walking" down the street, he is several yards behind the group, struggling to keep up. But his determination is paying off. His faithfulness to the routine is having its effect. Little by little you can see that he is "catching up." That's a picture to me of all of us in our walk with Jesus. At the present it may be a big effort just to do the little things we've committed ourselves to. But as we exercise in these little obediences, we begin to feel and to see the results.

Baby Step #6: Thank God today for one hard thing in your life.

1. Describe places where you feel your spiritual "muscles" are weak.

2. For what can you lift your hands and praise the Lord?

## DAY 7 • DON'T GET DISCOURAGED

Daily Reading: Galatians 6:1-10

*Let us not grow weary in well-doing, for in due season we shall reap, if we do not lose heart. (v. 9)*

Probably no temptation we will face in this journey is more deadly than discouragement. Discouragement has meant the wreck of many a well-intentioned starter. When I typed the text for today, I inadvertently typed "wearing" for "weary." That's what happens. Spiritual discipline can be "wearing." And something in us wants to break the fetters.

The adversary knows this is about us, and plays on our impatience. Discouragement is one of the main weapons in his bag of tricks. After all, we cannot hasten the results; we can only trust that God will bless our efforts. We cannot even be sure that the results will be exactly what we had envisioned. Only God knows. The writer of Proverbs says, "Many are the plans in the mind of a man, but it is the purpose of the Lord that will be established" (Prov. 19:21).

A friend said recently, "Years ago, I went to a retreat with one thing in mind: I wanted my marriage to be 'fixed up.' But God had something far greater in mind, and that retreat led to a complete life-change for me and for my family." Looking back we can often see how limited our vision is compared with what God has in mind, and how small our faith was when we took that first step of obedience. But that's the glory of it! God does not wait for us to see the whole glorious plan. He gives us enough light to take the steps *today* that lead us along the road in the right direction. It doesn't really matter how far we have to go as long as our steps are in the right direction!

Discouragement is the temptation to quit. To give up the fight. When such thoughts come, we can remember the immortal words of John Paul Jones, the great Revolutionary patriot: "We have not yet begun to fight!" Jesus' word to us should enervate us and give us the determination not to give in to feelings of self-pity and discouragement. Recognize the enemy and put him to flight. He has no power over us except that which we allow by listening to his smooth and beguiling lies. One week is ending. Praise God, and take courage for the remainder of the journey.

Baby Step #7: Spend some time praising God!

1. In what disciplines have you experienced discouragements?

2. Name some of the ways in which you have experienced encouragement from God and from others.

# SIDE STEPS

*O foolish
Galatians!
Who has
bewitched you?*

*Galatians 3:1*

## DAY 1 • THE LURE OF THE WAYSIDE

Daily Reading: Deuteronomy 5:28-33

*You shall be careful to do therefore as the Lord your God has commanded you; you shall not turn aside to the right hand or to the left. (v. 32)*

If you were plotting how to turn a Christian from the right way, would it not seem logical to place something alongside the right road that looked similar, but more alluring, more inviting? Sin, as someone has said, has its pleasure "for a season." If there was nothing attractive in it, sin would have gone out of business a long time ago!

When God called his people out of their Egyptian slavery, he was leading them toward a land where they would know freedom and responsibility. Their main business as slaves had been to stay alive and obey their masters. Here in this new land, they were to be guided by the Law, the expression of God's concern and God's wisdom for a life that was to be fulfilling and freeing. But the Bible makes it plain that freedom was not to be interpreted as self-indulgence. There were limits, good limits. Beyond those limits was not freedom but a new kind of slavery.

As Christians we are called to be a free people. "For freedom Christ has set you free." We are called to develop the fullest extent of our created potential. We are called to claim a heritage which can never be adequately expressed in words. None of us has fully possessed that heritage *yet*. It still awaits us.

But the tempter always suggests that the wayside is a better place than the road. It is a place of self-indulgence, of forgetting our goals, of letting down our guard. The wayside is soft, whereas the road may feel hard. The wayside seems wide, while the road *feels* narrow. And so its lure.

What does the wayside mean to you? How are you tempted to turn aside? This week we will be talking about these sidesteps that are so easy to choose. The writer of today's text says simply, "Be careful to do as the Lord has commanded you; turn not aside to the right or the left." The path you have chosen, walking with the Lord, may be hard at times. Keep your eye on the goal: to become what God created you to be!

1. What goal or goals have you set for yourself in this present 3D series?

2. In what ways have you been tempted to turn aside already? How did you deal with the temptation?

## DAY 2 • DISTRACTIONS

Daily Reading: Psalm 119:33-48

*Turn my eyes from looking at vanities; and give me life in thy ways. (v. 37)*

Do you recall when bedroom "suites" had something called "Vanity Dressers"? They were very popular back a generation or so ago. They had triple mirrors that moved, so that Milady could see herself from several different directions. They made entertaining diversions for children!

What was entertainment for children, however, was often serious business for grown-ups who took their vanity seriously. Looking good is one of the main goals of life for many people. They worry about what people will think of them, of their hair, of their skin, of their figure, etc. And they may spend a lot of time, effort and money trying to make sure that people think as well of them as possible.

The psalmist may have had something altogether different in mind as he wrote these words, for concern about the way we look is only one of the vanities with which we entertain ourselves, or worse, vanities for which we drive ourselves. Popularity with friends is only one of them.

The sad thing about vanities (the word "vanity" really just means "emptiness") is that they distract us from the really important things in life. It is not that they are intrinsically evil in themselves, but that they serve an evil purpose. They take our attention away from the things that really matter, and we may spend our lives in things that don't really matter, only to find out, looking back, what a waste they were.

We've all spent a great deal of time being distracted from the real purpose of life. Wasting time can be a way of life, unless we begin to take seriously this warning and this prayer: "Turn my eyes from looking at vanities." The thing about vanities is that they are entertaining. They are distracting. Sometimes they are fascinating. But when all is said and done, they are "emptiness."

1. What distractions see to trouble you most?

2. What ways have you found best in dealing with distractions?

## DAY 3 • LOOKING FOR AN EASIER WAY

Daily Reading: Isaiah 30:8-18

*They are a rebellious people. . . who say to the seers. . . "Speak to us smooth things, prophesy illusions, leave the way, turn aside from the path. . . ." (vv. 9-11)*

Ours is a supermarket age. We're used to looking for bargains in almost every area of life. We want to get the best product for the lowest price.

Unfortunately, some Christians have adopted this same attitude toward their spiritual life. And it seems (without being unduly judgmental) that many churches have tried to accommodate this demand: the most satisfactory product for the lowest price. By this I mean that it is easy to turn away from a message that seems too hard, too demanding, and listen to someone who seems to be demanding less and promising more. Dietrich Bonhoeffer called it "cheap grace," meaning the kind of message that is all promise and no demand.

Isaiah indicted his people as being caught up in this search for "cheap grace." They wanted, nay, demanded, that the prophets bend and shape their message to suit them. "Speak to us smooth things." We can sympathize with the people who made these demands, because there is something in us all that would prefer the easier way if we had our choice. It is only when the easier way turns out to be dust and ashes, or when it runs into some impossible situation and has no answer for it, that we are willing to hear the call to the harder way.

I know of no "easy" way to discipline myself to daily prayer and meditation, to put first things first, even when they are not the things I want to do. It is much easier to let our feelings at the moment rule over us, and make us slaves of the passing moment. But when we look at the accomplishments of people we admire, we know that they made hard choices. When we look at the people we admire for their generosity, loyalty, cheerfulness and love for others, we know, *we know* that this did not come easily. It was not handed them "on a platter." They had to make choices against sidestepping to the easier way.

There is one very basic thing about "the easier way" that lures us from our path. *It does not go where we want to go!* Its destination is not what we've chosen. So if we're going to get to our chosen destination, we must follow the path that leads to it. And that path is *not* the "easier way."

1. Name some of the ways that seem easier to you.

2. Can you describe an "easier way" that turned out to be a harder one?

# DAY 4 • OTHERS CAN—WHY NOT I?

Daily Reading: Psalm 73:1-14

*I was envious of the arrogant. (v. 3)*

One of the most dangerous temptations we face as we go along the King's Highway is that of being envious of others who don't seem to have as hard a time as we do. This is such a common malady that we may not even be aware of how dangerous it is.

The psalmist stepped aside in his own spiritual life and observed how easy some people seemed to have it. He was indignant. No matter what they did, they seemed still to prosper. And the more he looked, the more discouraged he became. "They come into no misfortune like other folk; neither are they plagued like other men" (v. 5). "They prosper in the world and these have riches in possession" (v. 12). So discouraged was he that he said, "I have cleansed my heart in vain and washed my hands in innocency" (v. 13).

I've known people who expressed almost the exact same thought and feeling. Somehow they expected that God was going to make it different for them, and even that he "owed" them a different treatment. A friend recently talked about his relationship with God, and his attempts at being obedient. As it turned out, he was on a *quid pro quo* relationship with God. When he did something "good" or something "right," he expected *as a deserved return* that God would bless him with material blessing. This wasn't happening in his life, and he was very angry about it. As we talked, however, he began to see that there was another way of looking at the situation. Do you remember the once-popular song, "I'm looking over a four-leafed clover that I overlooked before?" Well, this man's situation was something like that. As my friend began to remember and rehearse the blessings that God had given him—blessings that were not bought but freely given—his attitude began to change.

All you have to do to get over envying the arrogant, to stop looking at others who seem to have it better, is to begin to remember the untold blessings you have been given. Gratitude and envy cannot live in the same heart. Gratitude builds up strength in the heart. Envy corrodes like acid and destroys.

1. What are some of the situations or people of which you have been envious?

2. Name one or more difficult experiences for which you were eventually thankful.

## DAY 5 • SLIPPERY PLACES

Daily Reading: Psalm 73:15-28

*My steps had well-nigh slipped. (v. 2b)*

Have you ever been walking along and stepped into a slippery spot? If so, you know how sudden and how dangerous slippery places can be. Every winter we hear of people who hit ice patches on the road and end up in serious accidents. Slippery places are dangerous places.

They are also unnoticeable. They can be places that look like the other parts of the road or walk, but conceal their deadly power to harm. That is a parable, I think, of what happens in our spiritual life. Things are going along relatively smoothly. We may even be a bit cock-sure about how things are working. Our confidence is high. Then, all of a sudden, something happens. Someone says something that hurts our feelings. A disappointment comes in some important area. Or any number of things could happen, and we find ourselves literally "off our feet." This has happened many times to all of us, I suspect.

What can we do when we hit these slippery places that cause damage to our walk with Jesus Christ? First, we can pray to become more alert and not quite so careless about them. That is something we all need to take seriously. Since we have an adversary we can expect that these places are going to appear in our path from time to time!

Second, when we do hit one of these spots and go into a tailspin, we can refuse to waste time lying there discouraged and berating ourselves for having been so foolish, and we can get up. When this happens, survey the damage and let it humble you. Repent of whatever you have done that you can take responsibility for. The psalmist says that his steps had well-nigh slipped because of his envy of the arrogant. Accept the forgiving mercy of God, who is not interested in condemning you and leaving you in the mud, but bids your rise and go on. And resume your walk!

1. What slippery places in your life are you aware of? Discuss them.

2. How have you avoided or overcome some slippery places in your life?

# DAY 6 • THIS ONE THING I DO

Daily Reading: Philippians 3:7-16
*But one thing I do. . . . I press on. (v. 13b)*

I don't know anyone who has attempted disciplines of any serious sort who hasn't made some sidesteps in the process. Diets are not "fun." Disciplines are sometimes hard to stick to. And so the sidesteps come easy.

Paul, in talking with the Philippians about his own experience, freely acknowledges that he has not yet arrived, has not yet attained what he is aiming for. This is a great word for anyone who wants to follow Jesus, because Paul was completely honest about the nature of the struggle and the battle. When all was said and done, however, he said these words: "This one thing I do. . . . I press on."

Think of the sidesteps you have taken in your life. Have you made excuses for yourself and blamed others for the things that go wrong? Have you often viewed yourself as a victim, and chosen to think that it is just *too* hard to carry on a disciplined life in Christ? Have your sidesteps been in the form of indulging yourself when you could have been harder on yourself, and allowing the self-deluding thought, "It doesn't matter that much"? All of these add up to failure and self-condemnation if they are repeatedly indulged.

So what can be done? We can look back at our call to be whole persons in Christ. He died and rose again to defeat the enemy of our souls, and to make us new people in him. He lives and cares about us where we are—even when we are "down for the count" momentarily. And I think his word to everyone of us to press on. Paul says, "This one thing I do." He could have done many other things, but he made the right choice. He chose to press on. So can we!

1. What has been required of you that you felt was too difficult for you? How have you handled these requirements?

2. What commitments do you need to make to go on with your journey?

## DAY 7 • WHAT IS THAT TO YOU?

Daily Reading: John 21:15-23

*[Peter said] What about this man? Jesus said, "What is that to you? Follow me."*
(vv. 21, 22)

In this incident which John relates in his Gospel we have two things: jealousy and curiosity. Both are equally effective in getting us to sidestep from the right way. As soon as we get too curious about other people, about what makes them tick, about what their plans and provisions are for their lives, we are getting into dangerous water. It's one thing to be interested in people. It's quite another thing to be driven by curiosity. Curiosity breeds gossip. And gossip lives on other people's misfortunes. We don't really "gossip" about the good things that are happening to friends and fellow Christians. It's the tragedies, the failures, the compromises that feed the gossip machine.

Peter has just been told by the Lord that when he is old, others will lead him about and he will not have control over his own life. It must have been a hard word to accept at that point. Immediately Peter turns to John, who is much younger than he, and asks, "What about this man?" And the reply is stunning. Jesus says, "If it is my will that he should remain until I come, what is that to you?" Right here is the core of a right relationship with Jesus. If we are receiving our life from him day by day, if we are looking to him for the grace and strength we need, learning and leaning, trying and trusting, what does it matter to us how he is dealing with our sister or brother? That distraction is a sidestep from the real business of discipleship. "What is that to you?" Or better, we should turn this saying in our minds to say, "What is that to me?" So many questions will simply fade away and disappear if we can ask this one and mean it!

How much the Lord loves us! His word to us is the same one he spoke to Peter that day by the seashore: "Follow me." He wants us to be with him. He wants to be with us. There is companionship in our struggle, and he is our ever-present help. "Follow me" is a word of great love, and of great encouragement. Each day, the Lord asks us to make the simple choice to follow him.

1. Name some ways others seem to be "getting away with things" that you cannot.

2. In what way does God's dealing with you seem unfair?

# BACK STEPS

*No one*
*having put*
*his hand to*
*the plow and*
*looking back*
*is fit for the*
*kingdom of*
*God.*

*Luke 9:62*

## Day 1 • Stepping Backwards

Daily Reading: John 6:51-69

*Many disciples drew back. . . . (v. 66)*

One of the saddest things I have ever seen is a person who starts a walk with Jesus Christ but draws back and drops out. I have known young people who were enthusiastic about their newfound faith, testifying of the change that God had brought in their lives, only to see them drawn inexorably back into the world.

Jesus witnessed the same thing in his ministry. We know he cared deeply for the people who listened to him, and desired to see them come into a vital and living relationship with God. Here in this sixth chapter of John's Gospel, he spoke of the need to be fed and nourished by his Body and Blood. This was an offensive thought, and many of the disciples said, "This is a hard saying. Who can abide it?"

We've talked about sidesteps, in which we may wander off the main course of our lives and get seriously separated from the right path. What we are facing today is an even more serious possibility: that of being so deluded or discouraged that we become dropouts. So today's text becomes an important warning. Even when we do not realize it, we may be entertaining thoughts or indulging in actions that so dull our spiritual awareness that we become capable of turning into spiritual dropouts. And anyone who has ever tried to "re-convert" or re-convince a spiritual dropout into rejoining the ranks, knows what a difficult task that is. Judas stepped backwards after the months and years of being in the choice fellowship of the disciples. We cannot analyze his motives, but it is not unlikely that the fatal decision to betray Jesus to his enemies came about as a result of many *little* decisions. The deadly work was done in his heart before he made his deadly move to betray his Master.

The lesson is this: do not let the hard sayings, the hard times, harden your heart and prepare you to make a spiritual "back step."

1. In what way or ways are you tempted to "drop out" or draw back in your Christian walk?

2. What "hard sayings" (difficult truths) seem to bother you most?

124

## DAY 2 • HESITATING

Daily Reading: 1 Kings 18:17-39

*"How long will you halt between two opinions? If the Lord is God, follow him."* (v. 21)

Are you a hesitater? Do you find it hard to make up your mind when faced with choices? This writer sometimes hesitates several minutes comparing items on a supermarket shelf, trying to decide between two brands of cookies or some other goody!

Israel was having a hard time making up its mind. In spite of the fact that a famine had been going on for several years, the people still couldn't decide whether to put all their faith and hope in the Lord, or whether they should pay some worship at the shrines of Baal. Their hesitancy was rooted in their lack of faith and in their rebellion against what God had required of them. Baal was an easier taskmaster (or so it seemed) than the Lord God of Abraham, Isaac and Jacob. And so they hesitated. They "halted." Such a delay was not neutral. It was a form of rebellion.

That says to me that our hesitations are not neutral! They are rooted in our fear of obedience and our lack of faith. So, knowing that, we should be able to "press through" and cease our haltings.

1. Describe some of the ways you have "stood still" instead of moving on in your Christian walk.

2. Respond to Crashaw's line, "A slow and late consent was a long No."

## DAY 3 • OLD THOUGHTS DIE HARD

Daily Reading: Luke 5:36-39

*As he thinks in his heart, so is he.* (Prov. 23:7)
*They will say, "The old is better."* (Luke 5:39)

It is certainly true that the thought is the father of the deed. Temptations begin in our thoughts, sometimes so unconsciously that we do not even know that we have already given in to a course of action before we begin to think much about it. You might call that thinking "in the heart." It is the inmost thoughts that are most important, because when "the rubber hits the road" (as the saying goes), it is those inmost thoughts that control our behavior.

In the June 1992 issue of *Reader's Digest* there is an article entitled "Pastor, Father, Addict." It tells the chilling account of a dedicated minister who overworked himself and got hooked on prescription drugs. The chilling part, however, is that, after he was free of them, he went back on them again and again until his life was ruined. There was a consistent theme each time he started back on the deadly drug: "I am in control; I can stop whenever I choose; I deserve this little lift, because I work hard and mean well." It was not until his *thinking* changed and he made a deeper commitment of himself and his problem to God that he began to get free.

Any change in behavior must be rooted in a change in thinking, but if our old way of thinking did not seem good and right, we would have changed it long ago. A man I know is constantly getting into conflict with people he works with. The reason? He cannot stand the thought of being wrong when he is confronted about anything, and so an argument ensues. Several times he has almost lost his job, but he still *thinks* he's right in his way of thinking. It is almost ludicrously easy to see the flaws in such thinking in other people. It is much, much harder to see it in ourselves.

Jesus addressed this problem in terms of new and old wine. The new wine represents a new way of looking at life, at ourselves, at God's place in our life. The old wine is the way we've always thought—a more comfortable way, one we've gotten used to. And he is saying that although the old *seems* better, the life we seek is in the new. Today he is offering every one of us *new* ways of thinking—small ways, no doubt; baby steps, as we talked about earlier—but important new ways of looking at ourselves and our lives. Don't be afraid of them, for they open up the possibility of healthful, rewarding change into the people God intended us to be. And he said in the Bible, "Behold, I make all things *new*." That includes us!

1. What "old habits" of yours have the 3D disciplines crossed?

2. What old thinking pattern do you feel it is important to change?

## Day 4 • The Race Goes On

Daily Reading: 1 Corinthians 9:19-27

*So run that you may obtain [the prize]. (v. 24)*

The 1992 Indiana 500 was (I am told) one of the most exciting races in the history of that event. One of the things that made it exciting was the number of cars that could not make it to the end. Sadly, one person was killed, and several others required hospitalization as a result of injuries sustained. I'm not a fan of auto racing, but one thing seems clear: it is no sport for the weak-hearted.

Neither is discipline of any serious nature. The weak in heart grow weary. The day wears on and other interests crowd in, and it's all too easy to decide that discipline just isn't worth what it's costing.

Paul was concerned that the people of Corinth should not fall prey to such faulty thinking. He knew that if they did, they would become "back steppers." As in all of his letters, Paul is struggling to keep Christians "in the race." He warns us that "every athlete exercises self-control in all things. They do it," he says, "to receive a perishable wreath, but we an imperishable." (vv. 25–26)

You could wonder how those people in the Indy 500 felt, whose cars had failed them, or who had made a serious mistake in their driving and were disqualified for the remainder of the race. The race went on without them. And the truth about life is just as stark: whatever decision we make, the race goes on. Some will continue and reap the reward.

The reward we seek is not just some physical improvement. It is a spiritual condition, an inner life that is more closely attuned to God's will, more attentive to him and better able to obey. That's not a "perishable wreath," but an imperishable one. It's well worth continuing in the race!

1. What are some difficulties through which you have pressed on and for which you have become thankful?

2. Name some of the times you have faltered, and tell what happened as a result.

## DAY 5 • WASTING TIME

Daily Reading: Exodus 14:5-18

*Why do you cry to me? Tell the people of Israel to go forward! (v. 15)*

The people of Israel were in a tight spot. The Egyptian army was close behind them, and they knew that if it caught up with them, they would not fare well. After all they were technically "runaway slaves." But before them there seemed to be no way of escape. The Red Sea blocked their path to freedom. And so they did what we so often do when we are confronted with tight spots: they stopped and waited. Moses, their spiritual leader, went before the Lord in prayer.

Now, there are times when it is absolutely right to wait on the Lord, waiting for a signal to move in one direction or another. It is never wise to run ahead of his leading. But this was not the time. Their waiting was not for direction. It was even fraught with the danger, I think, that they might decide to give up and go back to Egypt voluntarily. So their delay was not one of waiting humbly to see what God would have them do. It was one of wasting time, refusing to go forward as they had been instructed from the first to do.

God sounds almost irritated when he responds to Moses' prayer. "Why do you cry to me?" There are times when even prayer is an excuse to keep from doing what we know we must do. Years ago, someone described a certain kind of Christian who spent much time early in the morning praying about what she should do. And the speaker said, "While she was praying and waiting on the Lord, the unmade beds cried out, the unwashed dishes cried out. The mundane duties cried out. But she wasn't listening!"

We can be quite sure that God will expect us to fulfill our little, uninteresting duties, day by day. Spiritual disciplines are no escape from such earthly responsibilities. It is really a "back step" to shirk the humdrum duties for a more "spiritual walk." Such a course can lead to disaster sooner or later, because we have substituted our time-wasting "super-spirituality" for the realities of life which have been given to us. Never confuse such super-spirituality with obedience. It is a short-cut to disaster.

1. Which is easier for you—waiting or rushing ahead? Why?

2. How are you tempted to use "spiritual disciplines" as a way of escaping ordinary duties?

## DAY 6 • DISCOURAGEMENT

Daily Reading: Deuteronomy 31:1-8

*Be strong and of good courage. Do not fear or be in dread of them. For it is the Lord your God who goes with you. (v. 6)*

Israel faced an uphill battle in occupying the land the Lord had given them. There would be moments of bitter defeat. There would be pain, uncertainty, even facing times when the fault lay completely in themselves. But this word for them was intended to gird them up to carry on.

Many of our problems in the spiritual life would be solved if we remembered that we are in a battle against a real enemy. The natural tendency is to forget this, and to assume that everything is just "normal." If we could sensitize ourselves to realize that the random thoughts and the recurring feelings have in them the ability to discourage us to the point that we give up, we would be ready to fight them harder and find ways to defeat them. In the letter to the Corinthians Paul said, "No temptation has overtaken you that is not common to man. God is faithful and he will not let you be tempted beyond your strength, but with the temptation will also provide the way of escape, that you may be able to endure it" (1 Cor. 10:12, 13). That's the same thought that today's text is voicing: "Be strong and of good courage, for it is the Lord God who goes with you."

When you are tempted to get discouraged about yourself, remember these words. The enemy would like nothing better than to see you so disheartened that you just stop trying. His work is easy then. And think of it: his whole victory would be built on the lie that God had failed you or that his grace and strength are not enough. Away with such thoughts! Be strong and of good courage as you continue on the King's Highway!

1. Name some of the ways in which you get discouraged about yourself.

2. Name some of the ways in which you get discouraged about others.

## Day 7 • Living in the Past

Daily Reading: Genesis 19:15-26
*But Lot's wife behind him looked back. . . . (v. 26)*

Why was Lot's wife "behind him?" Was she reluctant to leave her old life, even with all the tragic discoveries of the night before, when she and all her family were in danger of losing their lives in the wicked city of Sodom? Why did she look back? Was it her fatal fascination with "the way things used to be"?

I think there's a place for looking back, recalling the past and rehearsing the mercies of God through the events of our lives. But doing so can also be dangerous. The Israelites had hardly gotten across the Red Sea before they began to accuse Moses of bringing them out into the desert to perish, and, forgetting the whips of their taskmasters, they remembered the leeks, the garlic, and the other tasty foods of their former life.

Memory can do very tricky things, straining out the difficult and leaving the pleasant memories larger than life. This is particularly true when we meet a hard place in our pilgrimage. We can begin to think, "Things were much better before I started this." I've heard people say that their lives were more tranquil before they surrendered themselves to Jesus!

Lot's wife was turned into a pillar of salt. Somehow her final condition seems expressive of her longing and weeping for what she felt had been. She had fixed her eyes on earthly things and had forgotten that she was being saved from utter destruction by fleeing from all that the past represented.

As we go through these weeks, let the Holy Spirit separate in your life the good things of the past from those which, however good they may have seemed, had evil or negative consequences. We must not cling to the past, for it is no more. Nor must we live simply for the future, which is not yet. Jesus calls us to live in the Now of Today. Here is where we meet him in all his graciousness. Here is where he meets us in all our needs. Don't miss out by taking a "back step" into the past!

1. What are some of the good memories you have of the past?

2. How do these memories trip you up in your present life?

# TRAPS AND PITFALLS

*Your adversary*
*the devil prowls*
*around seeking*
*someone to devour.*

*1 Peter 5:8*

## DAY 1 • A PLAIN PATHWAY

Daily Reading: Psalm 27:1-14

*Lead me on a level path because of my enemies. (v. 11)*

The 27th Psalm was written against a host of conflicts with adversaries and enemies. David is affirming the trustworthiness of God and reminding himself that he has nothing to fear with God on his side. "I believe that I shall see the goodness of the Lord in the land of the living."

It is hard to imagine what life would be like if we did not have that same faith. Not only for the life that is to come are we to trust God; by faith we shall see and experience "the goodness of the Lord in the land of the living." Day by day he unfolds his purpose and leads us along his chosen path, if we but choose to follow.

It is not always possible to walk a level path, because sometimes the King's Highway goes upward. Yet it is all right to pray for that level path, for sometimes we need its relative ease, its smoother going. God gives us the courage and strength to press on when the way becomes rocky and the path uncertain. There is always enough light to take the next step, however dim the distant goal may seem.

Today you are making decisions along the journey of your life. Today God is in your life to encourage and strengthen you in your desire to obey his will. The path is plain enough for you to see what he would have you do today. Tomorrow and its problems will wait. Today's obedience will make them more manageable when you arrive. But tomorrow's problems can be unnecessary encumbrances along today's path. The level path is the path of the Now. "Sufficient unto the day is the evil thereof," said our Lord.

Our psalm ends with these great words: "Wait for the Lord, be strong and let your heart take courage; yea, wait for the Lord!" (v. 14).

1. In what ways have you seen God's purposes for you unfold?

2. How is God strengthening and encouraging you to choose his will for your life?

## Day 2 • Trap #1: "I Have Arrived!" (Overconfidence)

Daily Reading: Romans 12:1-13

*I bid every one among you not to think of himself more highly than he ought to think. . . . (v. 3)*

There are traps along our journey. The enemy of your soul and mine lays them wherever he can, and he tries to figure out which kind will work best for each of us. The one we're looking at today is a well-covered one, and many souls have fallen into it. It may also be said that it is a favorite one used on new Christians or those newly awakened to the supernatural dimension of their Christian faith. The excitement and thrill of knowing Christ in a personal and vital way are certainly blessings for which we should ever be grateful. But excitement can easily spill over into a kind of unrestrained "enthusiasm" which lacks restraint and wisdom, and fancies itself as being much farther along in the spiritual life than is actually the case.

Overconfidence often shows itself in an unwise zeal to get other people to share our experience. Many of us look back regretfully at having "turned people off" in our foolish assumption that we were changed creatures. While we saw the "new" in our lives, others continued to see evidence of the "old," and were less impressed than we were!

Overconfidence can easily breed a self-righteous, judgmental attitude toward those we deem less spiritual. This is a deadly development; it breaks fellowship, it fosters a spiritual elitism and brings disrepute on the very things we are trying to uphold.

Sadly, overconfidence often precedes dismal failure. Unaware of the weakness and vulnerability of the flesh, Christians can go quickly from the heights of overconfidence to the depths of self-indulgence. So, no matter how good overconfidence feels, we should be aware of this trap. Sooner or later, we all meet it, and have to deal with it. Honesty about what we really think and feel is one of the best safeguards against it.

1. Name a situation in which you were "overconfident."

2. Why do you become overconfident in certain areas?

## Day 3 • Trap #2: "I'll Never Make It!" (Overrating Satan's Power)

Daily Reading: 1 Peter 5:1-11

*Resist him [Satan], firm in your faith. . . . (v. 9)*

The "flip side" of overconfidence is what we might term "undercon-fidence." Not that we should have confidence in ourselves, if we know ourselves at all, but what it really is is underconfidence in God! We can easily overrate the power of our adversary and attribute to him more power to spoil our spiritual walk than he actually has.

First, we should remember what the Bible tells us about temptation, so that we are prepared to take responsibility for resisting it. Temptation is not sin. The sin comes when we toy with the idea and walk around entertaining it in our minds until we give into it. We are promised that God will "with the temptation make a way to escape, so that you may be able to bear it." Getting off the path, going into self-indulgence of any kind, begins in the thought process. The more we have given in to these thought patterns, the harder we are going to have to fight and the more repeatedly we are going to have to "resist him, firm in your faith." "Each person," says James, "is tempted when he is lured and enticed by his own desire," (James 1:14). When we become aware of the old desire, we need immediately to run to the Lord with our prayer for help, knowing that we are now in a crucial spiritual battle.

Second, the real object of the enemy is to lead us into further discour-agement and passivity. "I'll never make it" is something he delights to hear, because it means that we are ready to "throw in the towel" and give in. His final object is not to tempt us to this or that particular disobedience, but to cause us to leave our Christian walk, to stop taking part in the spiritual warfare to which we are called. If we know this, we can avoid the second stage or aftermath of any failure—the further temptation to give up.

Third, we never have to fight this battle alone. "If it had not been the Lord who was on our side, let Israel now say—if it had not been the Lord who was on our side, when men rose up against us, then they would have swallowed us up alive . . ." (Psalm 124:1, 2a). But as the psalmist went on to say, the Lord *was* on their side, and he delivered them. And he is on *your* side in this battle. So there is every reason to have confidence in his ever-present help.

1. Where have you given the adversary more than his due in your life?

2. How does unforgiveness of yourself contribute to "under-confidence" in God?


## DAY 4 • TRAP #3: "IS THIS REALLY THE RIGHT WAY?" (DOUBT)

Daily Reading: Psalm 119:17-32

*Put false ways far from me; and graciously teach me thy law! I have chosen the way of faithfulness. I set thy ordinances before me. (v. 29, 30a)*

Sometimes the Highway becomes an uncertain path. We simply do not know which way to go, and the path seems obscure. It may be some difficult decision we have to make, not knowing beforehand what the outcome will be. In such case, Doubt looms large and Faith grows small (for most of us!). Do you have a hard time making such decisions? The question as we've posed it for today has an element of accusation in it: "Is this the right way?" It is an accusation against the King himself. We are saying, in effect, this way is not as clear as it should be, and it is wrong for me. Now I'm left in doubt as to which way to go, and that's not fair!

I once expressed some concern about a decision I had to make, to a dear friend much farther along in her spiritual maturity than I, and her reply was, "Remember, we walk by faith, and not by sight. It is a *faith walk*." That reminder was helpful, because it encouraged me to give up my demand to *know* the outcome of any specific decision beforehand.

Just today a young husband came to talk about a serious situation which he and his wife are facing. They have prayed and committed the whole circumstance to God, but he is still fearful that things may not work out as they had hoped and expected. As we talked, he came to see that although the way at present is uncertain, he knows enough about God to know that God can be trusted, and this time—this time when Doubt and Fear are trying to be foremost in their hearts and feelings—this time is a very important time for both of them. They must affirm God's goodness and put their trust in him to carry them through.

And so must we. Whenever the question arises, with whatever overtones of self-pity, fear or uncertainty, we can say, "I walk the King's Highway. The Way is the right way and God is for us. Who can be against us? He will not fail—even if we make a wrong decision!"

1. Name some difficult but important decision you have had to make without knowing whether or not it was the right one.

2. Where are you tempted to doubt and accuse God because of uncertainty in your life at this time?


## DAY 5 • PITFALL #1: "OOPS! I'VE BLOWN IT!" (PRIDE'S FALL)

Daily Reading: Proverbs 29:15-27

*A man's pride will bring him low, but he who is lowly in spirit will obtain honor. (v. 23)*

We have lived to learn of some very sad and tragic falls from high places on the part of spiritual leaders. It is plain that pride had begun to cloud the sensitivity of conscience which could have been a safeguard against their falls. In some cases, prison sentences were added to the disgrace and stumbling-blocks which their moral and spiritual failure had occasioned.

One does not have to be in such a public or high place for this warning to be relevant. One does not have to be in the public eye to let pride begin to take control of one's life, and in the spiritual life, this is surely one of the most deadly defects. Pride of accomplishment is serious, because it denies our creaturely dependence upon God who is our Enabler. But spiritual pride, pride that we've overcome certain defects, that we've overcome temptations, that we've reached a certain goal that we set for ourselves—such pride is sure to bring us to a great fall if we do not recognize it and do something about it

You cannot help feeling the swelling of pride when something is going well. There is even good reason to feel a sense of satisfaction, gratitude, and joy. But pride slips in unbidden and takes credit to itself. Then we have to recognize that we are usurping what belongs only to God. He is the Source and Creator of all good, and he cannot allow us to steal his place. That's what happened in the fall of Lucifer eons ago. Only God is qualified to be God. Pride vies for his place and his honor.

So, in his great love and mercy, God lets us stumble and fall. He doesn't *cause* us to fall, but he refuses to *prevent* the fall, which is our own doing. Then, if we have any kind of healthy sense of humor, we can laugh at our foolishness, ask forgiveness for taking the honor to ourselves, and acknowledge, as the saints have done, that without his help, we'll keep making fools of ourselves! Then we can dust ourselves off and continue our journey. The fall is not a place to rest. It is a place to learn, and having learned, to be left behind.

1. Name the accomplishments of which you are most proud.

2. What is the pitfall that pride leads you to in these accomplishments?

## DAY 6 • PITFALL #2: "WHY DO I KEEP DOING THESE THINGS?" (CONFUSION)

Daily Reading: Romans 7:7-15

*I do not understand my own actions. . . . (v. 15)*

You do not travel far along this road until you meet this riddle wrapped in a conundrum: Why do I do the things I do? Why do I keep disappointing myself? Why do I not live a more consistent and victorious life?

If it is any comfort, Paul the Apostle, who wrote a great portion of the New Testament, had the same question. He confronted the battle that went on inside himself and says quite frankly in the letter to the Romans, "I do not understand my own actions."

It has been estimated that most of what we do comes out of our subconscious—that part of our thought processes that we cannot immediately get hold of. We may be acting out something that is rooted in very early childhood experiences, hurts, rejections, fears, loss of one kind or another. But as we talk about what we're doing with others we can trust, oftentimes the Holy Spirit throws light on our hidden motivations that helps us understand ourselves a little better.

It is a mistake, however, to think that all the mysteries are going to be cleared up. When all is said and done, we're still going to be living with this mystery we call "self." And we are going to be disappointed in ourselves from time to time. Out of this confusion we can go either of two ways: we can become despairing of who we are and what we are, or we can let ourselves be pressed to God, who already knows us and has not rejected us. The choice is ours. If we take the former route, we will be led off the King's Highway. We'll decide that the struggle just isn't worthwhile, since absolute victory is going to evade us. But if we let our inner conflict drive us closer to our Heavenly Father, we will find that his love and mercy cover us, even as we struggle to know ourselves better and to be more faithful.

As in every aspect of our Christian walk, the crucial choices are ours.

God has so honored us that he allows us the freedom to choose obedience or disobedience, hope or despair. In spite of any confusion we may feel at any given moment, we can choose to go on with him.

1. How does discouragement about yourself lead you away from God?

2. Write a prayer confessing any discouragement and accepting God's forgiveness and love.


## DAY 7 • PITFALL #3: "I HATE MYSELF!" (DESPAIR)

Daily Reading: Luke 22:24-34

*Simon, Simon, behold Satan has demanded to have you, that he might sift you like wheat, but I have prayed for you that your faith may not fail. . . . (v. 31)*

These are Jesus' words to Peter before Peter's great denial. Peter did not understand at that time how weak and unstable he was. He insisted that, though all the others should desert his Master, he, Peter, would be steadfast. But Jesus knew human nature better than Peter did! He knew that there would come a time when the pressure to deny Jesus would be greater than the loyalty that could cause Peter to risk all to stand with him.

The encouraging thing here, I think, is that Jesus had foreseen all that would happen and had pre-prayed for his friend. He loved Peter and he knew that Peter loved him. But Peter's love was imperfect. It was a mixed love, and there was much self still in it. The test that lay ahead would show him the difference between the two.

Did Peter despair of himself after the crucifixion? I think he came very close to it. He went fishing, his old trade. To do so was tantamount to saying, "Why go on? I'm an utter failure anyway." And then Jesus reappeared to him (in the last chapter of John's Gospel) and asked him three times, "Do you love me?" All Peter could say was, "Lord, you know everything. You know that I love you." Jesus was inviting Peter to give up his despair and get on with his divinely given task.

Despair is a pitfall—it is kin to self-PIT-y. It's no place to linger. Jesus knows who and where you are. Never, never forget that. And he bids you and me to get on with our appointed way!

1. How is despair related to our refusal to change?

2. What steps can you take to get out of the pit of self-PIT-y?

# WAYWARD WANDERINGS

*If anyone is
overtaken in any
trespass, you who
are spiritual
should restore
such a one in a
spirit of
gentleness. Look
to yourselves,
lest you too be
tempted.*

Galatians 6:1

# DAY 1 • PRONE TO WANDER, LORD, I FEEL IT (INCONSISTENCY)

Daily Reading: Romans 7:15-25

*I see in my members another law at war with the law of my mind. . . . (v. 23)*

Are you an inconstant person? Most of us are, internally at least. Our moods swing from one extreme to another, our interests wax and wane, our "staying power" is definitely limited.

The title of today's meditation is taken from a hymn by Robert Robinson (1757). The full stanza reads like this;

> O, to grace how great a debtor
> Daily I'm constrained to be.
> Let that grace, Lord, like a fetter,
> Bind my wandering heart to Thee.
> Prone to wander, Lord, I feel it;
> Prone to leave the God I love;
> Here's my heart, Lord, take and seal it,
> Seal it for Thy courts above.

The writer acknowledged (as have the countless thousands who have sung his words) that his human condition was full of inconsistency. Just acknowledging that fact can help take some of its strength away. Pretense and denial are of no help here at all. Freely admitting what we are inside, to ourselves and, when it is right and prudent, admitting it to others as well, helps rob the inconsistency of its power over us.

The inner struggle, the challenge of our life in Christ, the challenge of any discipline, however mild it may be—these are necessary expressions of our desire to belong to God, to grow in grace and likeness to Jesus. We will not experience instant achievement, and the fact of our inner consistency is one of the arenas where the battle must go on.

Do not be afraid of your own inconsistency. God is faithful. He is *consistent.* So there is no reason not to do battle, and to expect that, in the end, he will prevail.

1. What are some of the place in which you find yourself being inconsistent?

2. How do you find the most help in fighting your inconsistencies?

## DAY 2 • TOO MANY GOALS

Daily Reading: James 1:1-15

*That person must not suppose that a double-minded man, unstable in all his ways, will receive anything from the Lord. (vv. 7, 8)*

There are two ways (at least) of thinking about double-mindedness. One is to see it as an basic indecision about following Jesus. The double-minded person tries to keep one foot in the world and the other in the Kingdom. That just won't work, and sooner or later a decision has to be made. Which one? Which way?

There's another kind of double-mindedness, and I think this kind may be more applicable to many of us. It comes from having too many goals.

Someone I know has a habit of facing almost any day with a full agenda. The agenda is so full that it not only takes in the day, but it takes in the week, and many weeks ahead. If there is something planned ahead in which that person is involved, the agenda tends to become a heavy burden, a cause of worry and anxiety, and a drain on energy. Peace of mind flees and tension can be felt wherever that person goes. I think the problem is "too many goals."

Life is not meant to be made up of anxiety-producing goals. When we allow our goals to dominate us, control our waking moments, our prayer time, our worship—even our sleep—then something is out of kilter, out of proportion. We need to simplify. We need to find out what these goals mean to us and why we are letting them come between us and the simple walk of faith to which we are called.

Double-mindedness cuts us off from the grace which is sufficient for each moment. The fact that we insist on keeping these multiple goals as *the* important things in our lives prevents us from the moment-by-moment blessing he wants to give. As we let "his kingdom and his righteousness" take first place, other goals will take their rightful place. Having first one main goal— to walk with God daily—in the practical little things of our lives, keeps us from the folly of seeking too many things at once.

1. What are some of the "other goals" you find appealing and attractive?

2. How have you dealt with any of these goals that conflict with your 3D goals?

## DAY 3 • LOOKING FOR INSTANT RESULTS

Daily Reading: Galatians 5:1-15

*For you were called to freedom, brethren; only do not use your freedom as an opportunity for the flesh, but through love be servants of one another. (v. 13)*

We are a part of the microwave oven generation. No more do we want to take time to put food in pots or pans and warm them over a burner or in an oven. We prefer the magic of microwaving. Or we make our instant coffee from water which comes steaming hot out of a special faucet. The computer on which this is written is almost obsolete, because later generations of the same brand deliver the letters on the screen, or do other functions, even more rapidly than this one. Such is our drive for "instant results."

The same malady is seen in our desire to have news fed us in "sound bites." We want short, simple statements that we can grasp easily without much thought. When issues get complicated, we become irritated! We are all looking for instant results.

This attitude carries over in our spiritual life. Many, many people are genuinely confused and bewildered when they find that there are no instant results in this life. Somehow we got the idea that if we heard the gospel's joyful sound and responded, then all would be taken care of. The idea that there might have to be struggle, warfare, self-discipline, had somehow escaped us. We didn't know it was going to take so long or be so hard!

If we look back at the heroes of the past, the spiritual lights who left the world in their debt, we find a constant testimony: steadfastness in the face of hardship. God has entered our lives with his saving grace. He has transferred us from the "kingdom of darkness" into his own Kingdom of Light. That is an accomplished fact, a gift that costs us nothing because we have nothing to pay, but now he asks our cooperation, our willing steadiness in the process of formation. We are not yet what we should be. We are not yet what we want to be. And there are no easy shortcuts, no instant results.

But there is hope. And there is his promise that if we persevere, we will not have labored in vain. That is enough, and we must allow it to be enough.

1. Where have you become impatient in reaching your goal?

2. What seems to help most in re-focusing on your goal?

## DAY 4 • LOOKING FOR A FRIEND

Daily Reading: Matthew 6:25-34
*But seek first his kingdom and his righteousness. . . . (v. 33)*

This question comes up in our minds as we read those hard words of Jesus: What does he mean by that term "hate"? Does he not tell us to love one another?

Today we've combined that word with the First Commandment given to Moses for God's people. It was a commandment against idolatry, putting *anything* ahead of loyalty and faithfulness to God. That, I believe, is what Jesus is talking about when he uses that strong word of warning. Human loves can become competitors for the love we should have for God.

How does this work out in our lives in practical ways? Is it not in our striving and energetic efforts to have people think well of us? Is it not in the compromises we make in order to (as we think) secure friendship? A little girl I know was confronted recently about something wrong she had done wrong with her friends. After a long discussion, she said that the reason she had done it was to have friends. At eight years old, she is already well on her way to let "looking for a friend" run her life in the wrong way.

Our motivations need to be exposed to the light so that we can make choices against wrong motives and in favor of good ones. If it is our desire above all else to be loved and to feel acceptable to others, we will miss the blessing God has for us. Friendship with the world, says St. James, is enmity with God. Sometimes rejecting this kind of temptation to idolatry is very difficult. The goal we seek does not seem evil. It may even have the temporary rewards of good feelings that we like very much. But if we have allowed "looking for a friend" to become an expression of idolatry, we are off the Highway and on dangerous ground.

1. Who in your life do you rely on—perhaps more than on God?

2. What relationship do you need to place on the altar in order to put God first?

## DAY 5 • SEARCHING FOR SATISFACTION

Daily Reading: Luke 15:11-24

*The younger son gathered all he had and took his journey into a far country, and there he squandered his property in loose living. (v. 13)*

Life at home was too boring for the younger son. He wanted more thrills. So he talked his father into giving him his inheritance and off he went in search of satisfaction. Apparently this worked for a while, because he squandered everything before he had second thoughts.

Why do we think that we should always have to be "satisfied"? Have we lost our sense of duty, of responsibility, of sacrifice and honor? Many people say that our generation has gone far down that road, and they are not particularly hopeful about the future—especially the immediate future. We have sown the wind and now we are reaping the whirlwind.

We know, of course, that much of our present *dissatisfaction* comes from having been barraged with advertisements that fill our minds with foolish delusions about what this or that product will do for us. We have become a pleasure-oriented people, and the old standards by which our forebears lived are in short supply. When satisfaction eludes us in one area, we are tempted to begin looking for it in another.

Jesus carried his parable to an end, showing the younger son in his reduced straits, coming at last to his senses, and deciding to make that difficult trip back to his father's house, to offer himself as a servant, since he had forfeited his right to be a son. And we know how generous and merciful the father was in welcoming his son back. All this is a picture of God's graciousness to us. Our little satisfactions dim before the joy of being rightly related to our Creator and Redeemer. His love and his presence make sacrifice not only endurable, but full of joy.

1. How do you deal with the areas of dissatisfaction in your life?

2. How has your dissatisfaction been used to turn you toward true satisfaction in God?

## DAY 6 • WHAT'S WRONG WITH WANDERING?

Daily Reading: Ephesians 2:1-10

*You were dead through the trespasses and sins in which you once walked, . . . the spirit that is now at work in the sons of disobedience. (v. 1, 2)*

Make no mistake about it: the world does not consider wandering wrong! More and more we are subject to a concerted campaign to convince one and all that there are no standards except those you wish to create for yourself. The landmarks are being destroyed. Moral standards are now (according to what one reads in newspapers or sees on television) entirely irrelevant.

In such a time as this, it is not unexpected that we would ask the same question: Why stay on such a disciplined course when there are so many other options? Paul called it "the spirit now at work in the sons of disobedience."

Here are some thoughts in answer to this question:

First: Wandering from God's ways dulls and deadens the conscience. More and more we lose the ability to discern between what is good and what is evil. The end result is evil in its grossest and most hideous expression—and this possible because little steps have killed our ability to choose between light and dark.

Second: The dulled, deadened conscience is a prelude to the deadening of the very things that are most fulfilling and joy-bringing in life. Instead of being happy (because of the removal of restraint) we are actually more miserable, and may end up desperately seeking to satisfy ourselves, as did the prodigal, "with the husks that the swine did eat." It's a picture of human disobedience "gone to seed." The end is not a pretty one.

Finally: Because we do love others and do feel a desire to be faithful, it is important to remember that wayward wanderings do affect others, and can cause real harm. That harm may not disappear even when we repent and return to the right Road. Knowing that can be a safeguard against the temptation to self-indulgence.

1. Where are you prone to wander—in your thoughts or actions?

2. Why are wandering thoughts more dangerous than they seem?

## DAY 7 • ONE WAY, ONE DOOR, ONE LIFE

Daily Reading: Ephesians 4:1-16

*There is one body and one Spirit, just as you were called to the one hope that belongs to your call, one Lord, one faith, one baptism, one God and Father of us all. (v. 4)*

We know it by now, do we not? There is only one hope for us who have come to know Jesus Christ as Lord and Savior. Other ways may appeal, and we may wander from the path in our foolish self-centeredness. But when all is said and done, we know that he is the way and there is no other.

He was the Door by which we entered into a life that has promise beyond the present difficulties and circumstances. He met us in our need, in our brokenness, in our rebellion, and said to us, "Here is life. Choose life. Why will you die?" Our hearts responded out of their tired weariness. If there is hope for me, I do choose it. As the Father welcomed his wayward child in the parable of the prodigal son, we were welcomed, not as renegades at last coming home, but as beloved children. George Herbert, the seventeenth-century English poet said:

> Love bade me welcome; yet my soul drew back,
> Guilty of dust and sin.
> But quick-ey'd Love, observing me grow slack
> From my first entrance in,
> Drew nearer to me, sweetly questioning
> If I lacked anything.

Jesus is the Way by which we return to the Father. His life is our pattern, from which we can learn how to live. The things he taught are meant to be our guidelines—we are to live in the same pattern of obedience he showed, if we wish to taste the fruits of full fellowship and fulfillment. He did not prefer himself. He allowed the Father's will to be his will, and we can follow that blessed example. "If you love me," he said, "keep my commandments."

He is the Life. His life is a daily source of life and strength and guidance for those who walk with him. He is the Way. Our way without him brings defeat, discouragement and discontent. With him even rough ways are brightened and made sources of blessing.

1. Describe the condition in which Jesus met you and began to change your life.

2. Write a prayer of renewed faith and commitment to Jesus.

# ROAD BLOCKS

*I hold my*
*feet back from*
*every evil way,*
*in order to keep*
*thy word.*

*Psalm 119:101*

## DAY 1 • ROAD CLOSED

Daily Reading: Deuteronomy 28:58-68
*Thou shalt not. . . . (Exodus 20, 9 times)*

What a suggestion! That the King's Highway is closed! As I write this I think of two separate attempts our family made, many years ago, to travel along the Blue Ridge Parkway. We went up to the entrance in Virginia, only to see the sign: "Road Closed." It was because the weather was too bad to allow safe travel. The road was fogged in and visibility was too poor to allow traffic on it.

This question then comes up: Why would our way, as we walk along with the Lord, have such a sign? In practical terms, I see it like this: the King's Highway is not some artificial path going in a straight line from this world to the next. Life is not like that. And as we go along, thinking we are going in the right direction, sometimes we do meet a block, making forward movement in that particular direction an impossibility. At this point we may have to take stock, reassess what we were trying to do, and ask God, "Why?" What is he saying to us by placing a block in the way? A Bible story comes to mind of a very rebellious prophet named Balaam, who was, after several attempts, persuaded to go with some emissaries of the king of Moab, who wanted him to curse Israel. On his way to the rendezvous, Balaam's donkey saw an angel standing in the road "with a drawn sword in his hand." When Balaam's eyes were finally open, the angel said, "I have come forth to withstand you, because your way is perverse." Balaam acknowledged his wrongness and was allowed to go on. Sometimes the "Road Closed" sign is God's way of keeping us from making a serious mistake or committing a serious sin.

There are other uses of these "Road Closed" signs. The Ten Commandments give us ten of them, indicating that there are paths along the way that are definitely closed to us if we want to walk on with God. They are not to be taken lightly, for they are "Signs of Life." To ignore them and walk on past the "Road Closed" sign is to do so at great peril and with the most serious of consequences. That's why God has placed them there.

1. Name some of the "Thou shalt nots" God has placed in your life.

2. What are your reactions and responses to these prohibitions?

## DAY 2 • DETOUR

Daily Reading: Exodus 15:19-27

*When they came to Marah they could not drink the water of Marah because it was bitter. (v. 23)*

The forty-year journey through the wilderness between Egypt and the Promised Land was made up of many twists and turns. It was not a straight line, plotted out to be the shortest and most efficient route. It was a journey which included many detours. The people of Israel were not free to choose when to move, when to stay. They had to follow the command of Moses, who was responsible for following God's directions for them.

There is a very graphic account in the books of Numbers and Deuteronomy of God's wrath at the Hebrews' lack of faith and obedience. Their fear had kept them from going courageously forward, in spite of all God had already done for them in leading them out of Egypt. In response to the situation, the people decided to take matters into their own hands and make a second attempt at tackling their adversaries. The battle was a disaster, because they went on without the blessing and help of God. That can serve as a useful example to us. We must be willing to accept the "detours" which God indicates by circumstances beyond our control. We can choose to see them as irritating and annoying delays, or we can follow where he leads, or wait as he indicates we should wait, and see what blessings he has for us in the detour.

An artist writes that years ago she decided to switch from flat brushes to round brushes in her painting. "I felt as if I had taken two steps backward!" she writes. But she persevered, because she had been persuaded that this "detour" would be ultimately for the best. And she goes on to say that, although she saved two flat brushes, in case she should need them later, she has never used them at all. Sometimes the detour which seems to delay or even to hinder our walk with God is adding a new, permanent dimension to our lives for which we will ever be grateful.

Don't be afraid of God's "detours."

1. What unexpected detours have you encountered in your life?

2. Can you name some detours which turned out to be blessings?

## DAY 3 • SUBJECT TO CHANGE WITHOUT NOTICE

Daily Reading: Job 1:1-22

*In all this Job did not sin or charge God with wrong. (v. 22)*

None of us has had the "changes without notice" to the extent that Job did. But Life does not always notify us of what lies ahead. Sudden news, even tragic news, can catch us unawares.

What gives the greatest difficulty in accepting an unforeseen change of circumstance? Is it not our demand to stay in control of our lives, and the feeling that we have the right to know what is going to happen? Yet it doesn't work out that way. And God must have known what he was doing when he refused to draw the curtain of the future aside so that we could tell just what was coming. I think he was very wise and very merciful in planning life that way. One of the most pernicious evils about the whole matter of fortune-tellers and prognosticators is that they feed our inordinate curiosity and our illusion of being in control if we know (or think we know) what is going to happen.

Job's three blows came as successive waves of tragedy: first losing all the cattle, the source of his wealth; then losing his children, the source of his hope for the future; and finally, losing his own strength and health, and living in pain. To make matters worse, it seems, there was no good explanation as to why all this was happening. His three "comforters" insisted that he must have done something wrong, because God would not treat a righteous person like this. And we have much the same attitude when sickness or tragedy comes. Or we turn the situation around, and ask angrily, accusingly, "Why is this happening to *me?*"

God did have a purpose in allowing all this; it was to deal with Job's own "rightness," which was deeper than his outer righteousness. When God was through, Job repented, not of what he had done, but for who he was. No longer did he expect to be justified, but simply acknowledged that God is God. Then God, in his love, restored Job's fortune, family and health. But the main part of the story is Job's deepened understanding of himself and his newfound willingness to accept "change without notice."

1. How do you respond to the unexpected and unpredictable things that come in your life?

2. Are there circumstances in your life now that tempt you to murmur against God as the Israelites did?

## DAY 4 • INNER BLOCKS (CHANGES OF MOOD)

Daily Reading: Psalm 43:1-5

*Why are you cast down, O my soul? And why are you disquieted within me? (v. 5)*

The greatest hindrances to our full life as Christians lie within us, not outside. And this matter of mood swings can be quite a problem for many of us. It can be a serious swing from heights to depths, and may even require professional help in some cases. A friend who is a psychologist terms these swings "bi-polar mood swings."

In another psalm, the writer describes his own feelings like this- "As for me, I said in my prosperity, I shall never be moved" (Psalm 30:6). Things were going well, and he felt good about himself. Does that sound familiar? In that euphoric state, it was easy to say, "I shall never be moved." But then something happened. "Thou didst hide thy face, I was dismayed" (v. 7b). It sounds as though this happened in an instant, for no particular outward reason.

I have found that when this kind of mood change comes, it is important to look to see where I have buried some reaction. It may be that I have been disappointed in something I wanted to do, and I just tried to forget it instead of praying about it and turning it over, *really* turning it over to God. Or it may be that my ego was wounded by some supposed slight or rejection. Most of us are much more sensitive to such things than we like to admit! And if I do not really face that, confess my hurt pride, ask for and accept forgiveness, a whole day (or more) can feel "blah," and "down."

If you allow such mood changes to come and go at will, you can be unrealistically positive or unnecessarily negative. In either case, your walk with Jesus can be hindered by such mood changes.

One final word: we do not always *need* to feel "on top." Most of our spiritual work must be done in the valley, where things are perhaps less exciting but more productive. There is a false spirituality which tries to always be "up." That can also be a real road block, not only to ourselves but to those close to us. True spirituality is *reality*.

1. What kind of experiences usually get the best of you?

2. In what ways have your "down" times or "valley" walks brought you closer to the Lord?

## DAY 5 • IS THIS THE KING'S HIGHWAY?
## (IS GOD REALLY IN CHARGE?)

Daily Reading: Psalm 40:9-17

*Evils have encompassed me without number; my iniquities have overtaken me till I cannot see; they are more than the hairs of my head; my heart fails me. (v. 12)*

The psalmist is in trouble. He honestly lays out his case before God, and describes a situation that is too hard for him to handle alone.

Any honest person who walks this path has occasions sooner or later to ask that question: Is God really in charge? Something happens in spite of everything we could do or think to do. The situation is serious; it may even involve life and death. We pray. We cry out for help. We rehearse all that we know and believe about God's goodness and mercy. The problem is still with us. I suspect that everyone who reads these words could cite situations that seem intractable, that simply do not yield to any known remedy.

Then we may ask, "Is it all in vain? Is this the King's Highway, or am I living in some kind of unreal fantasy?" This must have been in the mind of the psalmist when he said, "All in vain have I kept my heart clean and washed my hands in innocence!" (Psalm 73:13). He had begun to wonder if it was all worthwhile.

But these psalms show us the way out of such thoughts. In Psalm 40, while acknowledging his neediness, David nevertheless rehearses what God has done for him. "He drew me up from the desolate pit . . . and set my feet upon a rock . . . He put a new song in my mouth. . . " (vv. 2,3). When we begin to wonder why things are not easier, and begin to ask, "Is God really in charge?" we can *all* remember where we have been blessed. And that new song can rise again from our hearts.

1. What experiences have you had that were too hard for you to handle alone?

2. Where have you found that your impossibilities became God's possibility?

## DAY 6 • DON'T IGNORE THE WARNING

Daily Reading: Hebrews 1:1-4, 2:1-4

*Therefore we must pay the closer attention to what we have heard, lest we drift away from it. (Hebrews 2:1)*

Using this metaphor of the Highway, we can think of some of the warnings we are familiar with. There are signs that warn us of unsafe shoulders, where moving off the road will create an immediate hazard. There are signs that warn us when the road changes from four lanes to two, indicating that we will face oncoming traffic. (Could we dare say that such a traffic pattern represents those who have turned back and are going another way?)

A couple was traveling in England, and in addition to having to drive on the left side of the road, they found it sometimes very confusing to follow the English road signs. On one occasion they were going to visit a friend in West Yorkshire, and following his directions, found the road number and managed to get the car around the "roundabouts" and on the right route. Several miles later, however, they realized they were going away from their destination instead of toward it. This can be a reminder that, even though we are moving "on the right road," we can still be heading in the wrong direction—especially if we are not paying "closer attention to what we have heard."

It is very important when traveling to make sure that we are still on the route that leads to our desired destination. God has clearly marked the road, and it is up to us to make sure we are following the signs.

The warnings are put there out of his great love for us. They may come in the form of a waning of enthusiasm, a coldness of heart, a lack of zeal. It may involve conflict with others, an inability to relate to them as we know we should. Those warnings are meant to awaken us to return to our first commitment, seek divine help, talk with others if possible, and awaken to what is at stake. Christian commitment is no light thing. It is the most important thing in our lives, for it involves not only our immediate desire to be closer to Jesus, but it involves our eternal destiny. Whatever the warnings along the roadside, let us pay heed to them and continue on our way!

1. What guidelines do you use to discern and then follow God's will?

2. How do you get back on the track once you discover you have missed God's way?

## DAY 7 • THE OPEN ROAD

Daily Reading: Hebrews 2:14-18; 4:14-16

*Let us then with confidence draw near to the throne of grace, that we may receive mercy and find grace to help in time of need. (Hebrews 4:16)*

I find the image of the open road particularly appealing. It suggests that there is life, spread out before us, welcoming us. James Herriot captures this feeling in his book, *James Herriot's Yorkshire*:

"I recall one Autumn day among the awesome vastness when I had the wonderful feeling of being on the roof of England. Gazing at the enormous grass-clad bulk . . . I looked over to where the whole landscape falls away. . . . There, countless centuries had carved out gullies where unseen streams played and waterfalls splashed among their rocks."

God in his goodness to us allows us to come to the "open roads" in our lives. These are times when there are no road blocks to stop or slow us down. They are times of grace, when we can proceed, seeing the goodness and vastness of God's love to us and to others. What graced times they are indeed! And we all need them. They are given as encouragements and refreshments along our journey, and they are not to be despised!

Our confidence all along this road is in his ready and immediate help. He does not make passive weaklings of us, and like a good parent, insists that we walk rather than be carried through life. This reflects his respect for what he has created us to be and is a part of the process by which he helps us become what we are not yet. But he is never far from us, and the throne of grace is always open to us. So, enjoy the open road!

1. What does the idea of the "open road" mean to you?

2. Find a psalm that expresses how you feel when everything is going well, and read it as a prayer of gratitude to God.

# GROWING WEARY
# ON THE ROAD

*Do not*
*grow weary in*
*well-doing,*
*for in due*
*season we*
*shall reap*
*if we do not lose*
*heart.*

*Galatians 6:9*

## DAY 1 • OFF TO A GOOD START

Daily Reading: Galatians 5:1-11
*You were running well. . . . (v. 7a)*

A good start is important in any undertaking. When we decide to follow Jesus, or ask him to be our Lord and Savior, or have some specific goal to which we commit ourselves as Christians, there is grace abounding. It may even seem easy for quite some time.

Apparently this is what had happened to the Christians of Galatia. They had heard the gospel which Paul preached, their hearts had been moved, and they turned from their old ways to the new life in Christ. It was a good start. Then things happened. Other people came with slightly different messages. They began to get confused. Some of the things suggested may have been even more demanding than the message Paul preached. But they were confused enough to begin to waver in their commitment, and Paul was greatly concerned about them.

A good start is important, but it is only the beginning. The fresh energy, spiritual and emotional, which is given to us at the beginning will not last. Sooner or later we will notice that our zeal is flagging a little, our enthusiasm which seemed boundless is now running down. This is the real test of our sincerity. Do we really want to go all the way with Jesus? All these questions will help us sort out where we are on the Highway and why.

Someone has come up with the term "dazzle drooper" to describe those who start with great enthusiasm, but fade quickly into ineffectiveness. "Dazzle Droopers" can be very frustrating if you are depending on their support or help! Jesus talked about the seed which sprang up quickly but had no depth of earth, and therefore faded and became useless. His warning is meant to strengthen us to let the "good start" carry us on through the more difficult hours and days.

1. What "ordinary" tasks do you undertake with a sense of enthusiasm? Do you find your enthusiasm fades quickly, or do you sustain it over a long period?

2. What do you think your basic motives are for undertaking the 3D disciplines?

## DAY 2 • LOSING FRESHNESS

Daily Reading: Galatians 1:1-9

*I am astonished that you are so quickly deserting him who called you in the grace of Christ, and turning to a different gospel. . . . (v. 6)*

What causes flowers and plants to wilt as the day progresses? Heat and drought, especially the lack of sufficient water. And those two conditions certainly meet every one of us who walk the King's Highway. Heat and drought.

In a sense, however we can't do much about the heat. I take that to represent the pressure that comes from the outside. President Truman made famous the remark about the pressures that a president must endure. He said, "If you can't stand the heat, stay out of the kitchen." In life we don't have the choice of "staying out of the kitchen," because in every life the "heat" comes in one form or another. Sometimes it is pressure to conform to what we know to be wrong. It may come in the form of temptations to be dishonest with ourselves or with others; or to get caught up in the pressures of "duties" and "responsibilities." Whatever it is that "turns up the heat," it can cause a loss of freshness in our walk with Jesus.

The drought, I think, is a different matter. "He shall be like a tree planted by the rivers of water," says the psalmist of the godly person. The answer to the dry season is having our roots "planted in the rivers of water," in our vital, life-giving relationship with our Lord. He compared himself to the vine and called us the branches. That's another picture of how we avoid losing freshness—a vital connection with his life. These daily disciplines of Bible reading, meditation and prayer are given to help us maintain that connection. If we "lose freshness" as life goes on, we must take responsibility for it and get back to him who is the source of life, Jesus Christ our Lord.

1. Discuss places where you find it difficult to be honest with others about your feelings.

2. How can you maintain a vital connection with the life of Jesus?

## DAY 3 • THE HEAT OF THE DAY

Daily Reading: Matthew 20:1-16

*You have made them equal to us who have borne the burden of the day and the scorching heat. (v. 12)*

Jesus told this parable of God's mercy, which is not based on merit but on his own nature and grace. In the process of the story, however, he also shows us something about *human* nature. Our great zeal for fairness is usually directed at our own interests. We get much more indignant when we think we are being treated unfairly than we do at the sight of others being treated unfairly.

In this parable the workers were being treated *fairly*, according to the agreement into which they had entered at the beginning of the day. Their reaction shows how far off we can get when we start looking around us to see how other people are faring. Comparing ourselves to others, measuring how hard we have it as compared to how easy they have it, can cause us much grief. Unnecessary grief.

Why is it that some of us seem to have a harder time than others? Only God knows, but he does know, and, "he does all things well." An aged Christian mother spoke of her daughter who had a debilitating stroke and was left partially paralyzed. She said of her daughter, "She knows the Lord and she knows he knows what he is doing!" And that was that. It would be so much to our advantage if we would cultivate that attitude. What difference does it make to us if other people's children turn out "so well," and ours seem to give us a disproportionate amount of concern? Our main concern should be to do the best we can with the burdens we have been asked to bear. After all, Jesus has assured us that we do not carry any burden alone.

It is an important truth to remember, that since God knows all about us, and knows what we need to make us into his image more perfectly, the burdens we are given to bear and the trials we are asked to face are part of his merciful design. We are products not only of our inheritance from our particular family line, but of decisions and reactions of our own since our earliest days. In working with us, the Holy Spirit asks us to struggle against the wrong patterns and habits we have developed. That is work, but it is redemptive, productive work, as we are in a healing, growing process, leading to yet undreamed-of freedom and wholeness in Christ. The "heat of the day" is part of that process, and we must not despise it!

1. How do you compare yourself unfavorably with others?

2. What burdens do you think you are perhaps unnecessarily bearing "alone"?

## Day 4 • The Midday Demon

Daily Reading: Psalm 91:1-16

*You will not fear . . . the destruction that wastes at noonday. (v. 5a, 6b)*

In the 91st Psalm, the writer mentions several ways in which the soul is attacked: (1) the terror of the night; (2) the arrow that flies by day; (3) the pestilence that stalks in darkness, and (4) the destruction that wastes at noonday.

Perhaps we are all familiar with "the terror of the night," either as children or as adults. It can be frightening indeed to be faced with a sudden emergency in the dark of night. Fear of the unknown is always a challenge to us mortals.

What is the arrow that flies by day? I think it could refer to those calamities and adversities which we see clearly, yet have to deal with. They do represent the "unseen" attacks, but I think the daytime reference means we know the nature of the enemy.

Pestilence refers to the natural ills that beset and plague us from time to time. They are the common lot of humanity, and in spite of all the medical and scientific advances, they sometimes still "stalk in darkness," and cause us worry and alarm.

But what of this "midday demon," the destruction that wastes at noonday? Here is a problem of quite a different order. The noonday of our lives is that period when we have reached some measure of maturity, perhaps some symbols of success, some weight of responsibility. The destruction can come at this very point: getting our eyes on the wrong things, forgetting our "first love," growing too satisfied with ourselves, or too discouraged with our lack of success. It is the destruction that seems peculiar to life's prime.

Yet the psalmist says that those who "dwell in the shelter of the Most High" will not fear, because "his faithfulness is a shield and buckler." We do not have to fear failure or success. We have only to fear disobedience and its inevitable consequence!

1. Which motivates you more: fear of failure or striving for success?

2. How can you become freer of that motivation?


## DAY 5 • RATHER SWITCH THAN FIGHT?

Daily Reading: 1 Timothy 6:1-12

*Fight the good fight of faith; take hold of the eternal life to which you were called when you made the good confession in the presence of many witnesses. (v. 12)*

The presence of "many witnesses" is sometimes a real safeguard when we are tempted to let down! That must have been what Paul had in mind when he wrote these words to young Timothy. Somehow, having made a commitment to a certain course of action in the presence of others seems to give added strength.

Years ago, a certain man attended a retreat in which he was confronted with his need to listen to what others had to say. In particular, he was told, "You should really listen to your wife, because she speaks the truth to you." He thought quietly, "That is true, and when I leave the retreat, I am going to turn over a new leaf. I will listen to what my wife says when she corrects me, instead of arguing with her." He had not been home very long when some subject came up, and his wife suggested that his attitude was wrong about it. Immediately, everything inside wanted to defend his rightness and explain that his attitude was correct. At that moment he had a choice. He made it by arguing, saying to himself, "I'm glad I never told her that I was going to listen to her and not argue back!"

In that case, it would have been helpful if the husband had made his intention known "in the presence of many witnesses." If we do not take measures to "nail down" our good intentions, it is very easy to "switch" rather than fight. The fight must be done within ourselves, fighting all that would lure us off course, and fighting against the self-love that wants an easy time of it. The Lord is calling us all to fight the good fight of faith, which is often done in small, practical, everyday, down-to-earth decisions.

1. When someone confronts you with the idea that you are wrong, how do you handle it?

2. Where have you found it helpful to let others know your desire to deal with some troubled area or problems?

## DAY 6 • LOOKING FOR A SPIRITUAL LIFT AS THE DAY WEARS ON

Daily Reading: Psalm 42:1-11

*My soul thirsts for God, for the living God. (v. 2)*

The English people have a wonderful "institution": afternoon tea. If you have spent time in England, you may have seen strong, rugged men go into a tea shop and enjoy a "cuppa" before going on home. Or, going into an old-fashioned hotel, you may have found a beautiful tea, complete with pastries and sweets, all set up and waiting for people to enjoy. It makes a wonderful "lift" in midafternoon.

We talked earlier this week about the "midday demon." Years ago, a minister and his children were "brainstorming" possible sermon titles, a kind of game. Someone came up with the title "Matinee Idle," with the emphasis on this part of life, when things begin to slow down a little, and we begin to look around for other interests. Today we have such terms as "mid-life crisis" to cover that same phenomenon, when we begin to ask questions that had not ever seemed relevant earlier in our experience.

What is true of life can also be true of a period of intense commitment. We may need a "spiritual lift" as the day wears on. Where shall we find it? How shall we make sure we do not run down before the race is run?

(1) Keep up your prayer, especially confessing any failure you know about, and accept the forgiveness of God.

(2) Whenever you find you've missed something or neglected something, get back on track as quickly as possible.

(3) Make an effort to reach out to someone else, and get your mind off your own problems. They can be too great a burden if you allow them to be.

1. How have others reached out to help you along your journey?

2. List some people you can reach out to and ways you might help them.

## DAY 7 • NOT THE START, BUT THE FINISH!

Daily Reading: 1 Corinthians 9:19-27

*Do you not know that in a race all the runners compete, but only one receives the prize? So run that you may obtain it. (v. 24)*

What the Apostle is saying about earthly races is true. The wonderful thing about this "race" is that we can all be winners. We have to remember, however, that we must run according to the rules if we want to win.

There is a wonderful story in Greek mythology about an argument between two goddesses over a certain young man. One of the goddesses was renowned as the fastest runner in the universe, but her rival pitted the young man against her on a wager. Confident that no mortal could possibly compete with her, the foolish goddess took on the challenge. The older goddess was depending on wiles rather than innate speed for the success of her wager.

On the appointed day, the race began, and the goddess shot forward, leaving the mortal "speedster" lagging behind. He was good, but not *that* good. Then, the rival goddess took a golden ball and rolled it gently in front of the leading runner. She knew that the young goddess had a fatal weakness: her love of gold. Confident of her speed, the goddess paused long enough to scoop up the ball and ran on, still leading. At an opportune moment, her rival rolled a second ball across her path. Again, looking back, she saw that she could retrieve that ball also, and so she did.

As they approached the finish line, a third ball rolled temptingly across the path. Glancing back, the goddess hesitated, unsure about her lead. But the temptation was too much: she picked up the ball, only to have the mortal dash past her and finish first!

Do we see any truth about ourselves in that ancient story? It really is the finish, not the start, that determines the winner.

1. What are the most tempting distractions at this point in your journey?

2. Write a prayer for grace to keep on course to the finish line.

# RESTING PLACES

*Rest in*
*the Lord and*
*wait patiently*
*for him.*

*Psalm 37:7*

WEEK EIGHT

## DAY 1 • GOD'S RESTING PLACE

Daily Reading: Isaiah 25:1-12

*Thou hast been . . . a shelter from the storm and a shade from the heat. (v. 4)*

No doubt this verse is part of the inspiration behind the familiar hymn, "Beneath the Cross of Jesus." The poet calls the cross "the shadow of a mighty rock within a barren land." The prophet here reminds us that God provides that shelter and shade we need along life's way. And he reminds us that not only does God provide that shelter and shade, but that he is that shelter. "A mighty fortress is our God, a bulwark never failing!"

It seems very fitting at this point in our journey to reflect a little on the fact that God knows our strength and weakness, and is mindful of our need for rest. He never puts on us more than we can bear, and Jesus says, "My yoke is easy and my burden is light." Jesus called his disciples apart from their ministry saying, "Come apart and rest awhile."

Some of us have a hard time resting. There is a certain uneasiness in just *being*, and we take refuge in doing "good things." It is as if we cannot allow ourselves to be indebted, even to God. We insist on earning our right to be, and then (if we are not very careful) fall into the trap of thinking that we've paid our dues and have a right to expect some return from God.

Rest counters all this. God's rest takes into account that we are mortal, that we have only limited endurance, and that we need to be cared for. So, he does the caring. We do not have the right to demand that others care for us, but God cares without our demand. We have only to accept, to be humble enough to *let* him give us his rest.

So if the storm is howling or if the heat is burning—go to him for his rest. "Come unto me, all who labor and are heavy laden, and I will give you rest." He never fails to keep his word.

1. Where do you try to earn your worth by doing something?

2. Why do you think you resist "just *being*" without having to accomplish something?

## DAY 2 • MY RESTING PLACES (SELF-LOVE)

Daily Reading: 1 Kings 19:1-18

*But he himself [Elijah] went a day's journey into the wilderness, and came and sat down under a broom tree; and he asked that he might die, sayings "It is enough; now, O Lord, take away my life; for I am no better than my fathers." (v. 4)*

If ever anyone *deserved* rest, from a human standpoint, Elijah did. He had faced the 450 priests of Baal and the treacherous king Ahab and his wicked wife, Jezebel, and had supposed that he was alone standing for God through those three years of drought. But the pressure finally got to him, and he wanted out. So, running miles and miles away from Jezebel's threat, he "asked that he might die." It wasn't that he wanted to die. Jezebel would have taken care of that very neatly! But he was hurt, discouraged, and tired.

At this point, Elijah was full of self-love and self-pity. He had found his own resting place, a place of refuge of his own making. He had declared himself "off limits" to everyone, including God.

We can be very foolish in trying to insist on making our own resting places. God's plans and ours are not always the same. He may be asking something more of us than we find comfortable, or he may be asking us to rest when we want to run. In either case, insisting on having things our way can lead to a lot of conflict and wasted energy.

Several ministers were talking about what they did on Sunday after their church service. One of them said, "I feel I need a rest, and I insist on being able to watch a ball game. If something comes up of an emergency nature, I find I get angry about it." Another said, "I think you are trying to carve out your own 'Sunday rest,' and it won't work."

Look for the places where you are insisting on having the pressure taken off *before* God is ready to have it removed. Look for the places where you demand that others give you space, or understand your need for special care. These can be places where self-love is reigning, and taking rest will not bring renewal. Elijah had to learn that, and then he was ready to carry out his next assignment. So can we.

1. Where have you carved out a place of rest that is not of God?

2. How can you distinguish between resting places of your own making and those which God provides?

## DAY 3 • CARELESS REST (TOO BUSY FOR GOD)

Daily Reading: 1 John 2:15-17

*Do not love the world or the things in the world. If anyone loves the world, love for the Father is not in him. (v. 15)*

Here are some words I ran across recently: "Busyness is the enemy of spirituality. It is essentially laziness. It is doing the easy thing instead of the hard thing. It is filling our time with our own actions instead of paying attention to the Lord's action. It is taking charge."

This set me thinking about how easy it is to postpone our prayer time in the interest of reading, watching television, doing chores, or any number of other activities. Somehow, for many of us, quieting ourselves down and "getting down to business" with God is harder than it seems.

It is ironic to think of the way Christians have talked about and sung about prayer, and how little we have actually used it aright. Years ago there was a popular gospel song entitled "Sweet Hour of Prayer." For many years it seemed hypocritical to sing that hymn, because it did not correspond to my own experience or that of anyone I knew. What was the problem? Why did not our experience of prayer correspond to that of the song writer's? Perhaps because we were too busy for God. We were too "work oriented," "achievement oriented." And prayer is remaining in a state of need before God. It doesn't *do* anything.

The last part of the story however, is meant to encourage you. For some years, now, my prayer time has become a joy and a privilege. Beginning the day before the Lord in quiet prayer and reading has assumed an important place for me. The careless rest I used to take, avoiding the hard work of prayer and concentrating on easier tasks, did not bring about the much-needed spiritual rest, the lift I needed along the road. But I find, as have countless other pilgrims along the way, that the work of prayer does bring needed refreshment and renewal.

It was not by accident that Jesus taught us that "men ought always to pray and not to faint."

1. Do you feel you spend enough quiet time with the Lord? If not, why do you think you avoid it?

2 What do you find the most difficult in your "work of prayer"?

## DAY 4 • FAITHLESS REST (DISOBEDIENCE)

Daily Reading: Hebrews 3:7-19

*So we see that they were unable to enter [God's rest] because of unbelief. (Hebrews 3:19) Let us therefore strive to enter that rest, that no one fall by the same sort of disobedience. (Hebrews 4:11)*

Putting these two verses together, it is easy to see that the author of this letter identified *unbelief* with *disobedience.*

How do you handle your doubts—your doubts about God, about the sufficiency of Jesus—about your own relationship with him—your doubts about the efficacy of prayer? Do you regard doubt as unbelief? Do you see yourself as a kind of "victim" of your doubts, and think there's nothing to be done about them? Or do you, as do some, actually take pride in your doubts, saying to yourself, "It shows I'm a thinking person that I doubt so many things and have such a hard time accepting things on faith."

Unbelief is tied to two very dangerous things: disobedience and hardness of heart. Disobedience can be said to usher in doubt. It opens the door to darkness. When we violate our conscience and go against the prompting of the blessed Holy Spirit, we open ourselves to the kingdom of darkness. The adversary then has a "right" to harass and plague us. Doubts may come across our minds, but we do not have to believe them, talk with them, entertain them. They are often rooted in our demand to know, to be in charge of our lives, to control. When we see we're losing control of circumstances, doubt is one of the options we are offered—questioning God, questioning our direction, etc.

After a time, unbelief can lead to hardness of heart, a kind of crust over our feelings that makes us insensitive to God's will or to the needs of others. Hardness of heart can make us passive, resigned in the wrong way, "enduring" rather than accepting each day as a gift from a loving Creator and Father.

1. How do you handle your doubts about God and your relationship with him?

2. How are disobedience and unbelief connected in your own life?

## DAY 5 • DEMANDING REST (THIS IS TOO HARD!)

Daily Reading: 2 Timothy 4:1-5, 9-10

*Demas, in love with this present world, has deserted me and gone. . . . (v. 10)*

We do not know how many times the apostle Paul found himself deserted by someone he had trusted and depended on. We know that John Mark left him and Barnabas on their first missionary journey. Mark found the going "too tough" and left for home.

Here in one of Paul's last letters, we get a glimpse of another "deserter," Demas. He was enrolled among those who were standing with Paul in his great work. In Paul's letter to Philemon (verse 24) Demas is listed as a "fellow worker." He is also mentioned in Colossians 4:14 as sending greetings along with Paul to the Christians at Colossae. But now he has left Paul and gone to an easier place. We don't know why, but this is the last we hear of him.

Reading this verse makes one ask, "How willing am I to desert my post in favor of an easier way?" Surely we all know how strong the temptation can be. Most of us are creatures of comfort, and we have not put our body under enough discipline to convince it that it doesn't *have* to have the rest it craves.

Even more important, many of us have not hardened our spiritual muscles enough to endure hardship inwardly without flinching. So when difficulty arises, we are apt to find ourselves *demanding* rest, feeling that it is unreasonable to expect us to bear something that difficult and painful.

A young man was called to make a certain move in his life. He was very fearful about what the move might mean, and what responsibilities he might be asked to carry. Although he would agree that the move was full of many good possibilities, he was harassed by the old pattern of fear, of demanding that others make life easy for him. He was *demanding rest* from the very challenge God was placing before him.

It is important to remember that God never asks too much of us.

1. Where do you feel at the present time that you are "stretched to the limit?"

2. What one thing can you do to make sure you do not give up, but keep on doing what you feel God wants of you?

## DAY 6 • BREAKDOWN AND BURNOUT (THUS FAR AND NO FARTHER!)

Daily Reading: Acts 12:25–3:13

*And John [Mark] left them and returned to Jerusalem. (Acts 13:13)*

Yesterday we mentioned John Mark's decision to leave the missionary journey of Paul and Barnabas. Many people believe this is the same "young man" who is mentioned in the Gospel as having followed behind when Jesus was arrested in the Garden of Gethsemane. When the soldiers seized him, he fled from them naked, leaving behind the linen cloth in which he was wrapped.

It seems, then, that Mark had a history of running from difficult situations!

People experience what is now called "breakdowns" and "burnouts." A lot is written about these experiences and what to do about them. One thing, however, we might remember: sometimes it's easier to "break down" than to press through.

Have you given yourself an order, "Thus far and no farther?" Have you set yourself certain limits beyond which you will not go? If so, you may be "programming" yourself to miss some of the best and most profitable experiences God has in store for you. If we have said in our hearts, "Thus far and no farther," we are serving notice that if things get too hard, or if we decide we've had enough, we'll find some way to abort the process.

Don't do it! Don't cheat yourself out of what God designs and desires to bring into your life. Try to stay open, flexible, trusting that he knows best. Give over the control of your circumstances to him, who sees all and knows the end best.

1. Where have you set limits on what you will do?

2. What things are overburdening your plate, and what things need to be added to it? How can you distinguish one from the other?

## DAY 7 • GOING PAST THE STOPS (YET I WILL FOLLOW THEE)

Daily Reading: 2 Timothy 4:6-11

*Get Mark and bring him with you; for he is very useful in serving me. (v. 11)*

In spite of all our good intentions, good resolutions, and fierce determination, we sometimes stop to rest at the wrong places. We disappoint ourselves and others by our lack of firm resolve, and we may even have a very hard time forgiving ourselves.

Perhaps that is why the conclusion of the story of John Mark is such an encouraging one. Yesterday we read about his desertion of Paul and Barnabas on their first missionary journey. That was a serious mistake, and Paul had difficulty giving Mark a second chance. Barnabas, however, insisted that Mark should be allowed to go on the next journey, and so sharp was their contention that the two men split, and Paul took Silas with him when he left.

Now years have passed; we don't know how many. But there have been many experiences in the lives of both Paul and Mark. Writing from prison, in this second letter to Timothy, Paul asks him to bring Mark with him, "because he is very useful in serving me." There is a wealth of feeling, experience, reconciliation and restoration in that little phrase.

All of us have to go past these stops. When we find that we have failed or fallen, when we have disappointed ourselves and perhaps others, there is one thing to do: get up and keep going forward. "Yet I will follow thee!" We are not pilgrims who are building up great rewards for ourselves with our heroic achievements. We are needy people who live day by day by the grace of God. His strength is made perfect in our weakness.

Never let this be an excuse for easy self-indulgence. Never let it be a subtle temptation to give in to the blandishments of the enemy and of the flesh. But always remember that Jesus is ready to receive our heart's desire to follow faithfully. It was so with Mark. It was so with Peter after his great denial. And it is so for us.

1. Write a prayer of acknowledgement of your own stopping to rest at the wrong place. Accept forgiveness and ask for grace to "go past the stop."

2. What will this mean practically in the next few days?

# HEEDING THE SIGNS

*How great*
*are his signs,*
*how mighty*
*his works!*

*Daniel 4:3*

## DAY 1 • SIGN #1: STRAIGHT AHEAD, NO TURNS

Daily Reading: Luke 9:51-62

*No one who puts his hand to the plow and looks back is fit for the kingdom of God.*
*(v. 62) (RSV)*

Life moves forward, not backward. And, strange as it may seem, it does not stand still. We are always "on our way." The fleeting moment of the present is wedged between what is no longer and what is not yet. The Now is life, and we must be prepared to live in it if we are to find what life is about.

Looking back can be fun if it is held in check and not allowed to become "a way of life." It can, upon reflection, show us some things about ourselves which we would rather not remember. We made mistakes, chose wrong paths, turned into counter-productive ways. Remembering them may cause us pain, but they can be instructive in how to make better choices in the present.

But looking back, as Jesus speaks of it here, is a different matter. It is to look back with unreality, with a kind of nostalgia that covers over what really was. It is looking back as an escape from the present. Looking back in this sense is not an innocent past-time. It is rebellion against moving with God in the present.

When the people of Israel stood at the edge of the Red Sea with the Egyptians in hot pursuit, they paused and cried to the Lord for help. His word to Moses was, "Speak to the people and tell them to go forward." That is the word we need to remember as we move along this great and wonderful Royal way. What lies ahead is better, far better than what lies behind. God is leading and guiding and training us. The first sign for us all is: Straight ahead! No turns.

1. To what are you tempted to look back, with the result that you hesitate in moving on with God?

## DAY 2 • SIGN #2: SPEED LIMIT

Daily Reading: 1 Thessalonians 5:1-22

*Encourage the faint-hearted, help the weak, be patient with them all. (v. 14)*

Sometimes we get so caught up in our own spiritual agenda, our desire to make "progress" in the particular discipline we have undertaken, that we forget our obligation to others who may be having a harder struggle than we are. Christians who take their faith seriously, (and especially those who undertake some serious form of discipline), run the risk of "spiritual elitism."

Today's text is written to counteract such elitism. It is good to read it in conjunction with the great chapter on "Love" or "Charity" in 1 Corinthians 13. There love is described in its humility, its tolerance of others' weaknesses, its undaunted faith and trust that God will ultimately have his way.

Do you ever wonder why there are people in your life that try your patience? Do you find yourself failing on this point, feeling irritated at their lack of understanding or lack of commitment to what is good and right? Paul says, "be patient with them all." Their presence in our lives is both a test of the genuineness of our own love for God and our willingness to be trained in the way of Christ, and is a gift in that very training. The way to grow in patience is to live with people who arouse our impatience!

Much as we would like to speed along the way, untrammeled and undisturbed, that is not God's way. The Royal Road is a way in which every person, every event, every circumstance, is intended to perfect the work God has begun in us. What a heartening thought! Nothing that irritates me or brings out the ugliest reactions in me, is accidental. God means it for good, and intends that I learn from my reaction how far I still have to go. That produces humility—or at least it *can* produce humility if we let it.

So heed the sign: Don't run too fast down this road. You'll miss something important if you do!

1. Is there someone in your life whom you are tempted to judge as unspiritual or less serious in their commitment to God?

2. What steps can you take to be merciful to the people you have judged?

## Day 3 • Sign #3: Bumps Ahead

Daily Reading: John 16:1-11, 29-33

*In the world you have tribulation, but be of good cheer. (v. 33)*

How loving of our Lord to warn us ahead of time that we will be meeting bumps on this King's Highway! It is not all "smooth sailing," and there are both high places and low ones which have not been cleared by the time we get to them. So the warning is intended to help us to get ready for them, so we will be able to deal with them constructively when we meet them.

Bumps are uncomfortable. They may be small ones or large. In either case they interrupt the normalcy of life. So we are apt to resent them. Jesus says, "Be of good cheer." Recently, a friend told of a little incident which illustrates the kind of bumps we all experience. Late one evening, he decided to mow his front yard. He had been away from home for several weeks, and others had been tending the yard in his absence. One gasoline can was empty, and another can still contained last year's gas. He was beginning to feel irritation, but decided to try the old gas. Then he discovered that the lawnmower handle was broken, so the front of the mower could not be raised as it cut. He had to take the time to repair the handle temporarily. More irritation. When he finally got the mower ready, it was almost dark, and he was only able to cut a small section of his yard.

Sound familiar? It is such "bumps" as this that we all experience and, believe it or not, our reaction shows a great deal about where we are with God!

Then there are more serious bumps. Unexpected sickness—in ourselves or in those we love. These are sources of anxiety and "tribulation." But again, Jesus warns us ahead of time, and says, "Be of good cheer."

Why can we be of good cheer about these bumps that await us all? Because he who is in us is greater than he who is in the world. Because Jesus Christ truly is the answer in the midst of tribulation. Because there is a reality here that the world knows nothing of, but which is promised to those who love him.

The bumps will probably always upset us. That is all right. But if we are learning when they come to turn quickly to Jesus, so that bitterness and fear will not prevail, then we do not have to fear them. In the meantime, this advance warning is a gift of his loving care.

1. What does your reaction to "bumps" show you about yourself and your attitude towards God?

2. Tell of one place where a serious "tribulation" turned into a blessing.


## DAY 4 • SIGN #4: VIOLATORS WILL BE CAUGHT

Daily Reading: Galatians 6:1-10

*Do not be deceived; God is not mocked, for whatever a man sows, that he will also reap. (v. 7)*

Recently a newspaper article described a situation in which highway patrolmen were able to outwit the so-called radar detectors some people use to protect themselves when exceeding the speed limit. As I understood the article, the patrolmen were able to make the detector inoperative so that the driver was not aware that radar was in use.

The incident shows two things: the desire to violate the speed regulation and the determination of the police to enforce it and exact a penalty from violators.

The Word of God warns us in many places that we cannot with impunity ignore and violate God's laws. There are, for instance, physical laws that operate, and we "break" them at our own peril. Someone has said, "You don't break the Law of Gravity. If you violate it, it breaks you." The same could be said of the "laws" that pertain to health. If we ignore them, we have to live with the consequences. Too little sleep, too much food or drink, too much indulgence—these all exact their penalties, sooner or later.

Paul was anxious to have the new Christians understand that what he was saying about freedom (and he says a lot about it in this Letter to the Galatians), it did not mean that we are free to violate God's laws. We sow and we reap. If we sow bad thoughts and attitudes, we reap certain results within ourselves. Medical and psychological therapists now agree that much physical pain and suffering is ultimately rooted in unresolved inner conflicts and attitudes.

It is important to remember, however, that God does not "catch" the violator in order to punish and exact some equal amount of suffering. His intention is always for good and healing. His revealed purpose is to save, not to destroy. So at whatever stage we may find ourselves to be reaping what we have sown, we can absolutely depend on God's active participation in the healing process.

1. Where are you now living through consequences of wrong decisions you made in the past?

2. Where is God working for good in this situation?

## DAY 5 • SIGN #5: TURN ON THE LIGHT (DARK PLACES NEED LIGHT)

Daily Reading: John 12:20-36

*Walk while you have the light. (v. 35)*

Jesus says in that passage from John's Gospel, "Walk while you have the light, lest the darkness overtake you; he who walks in darkness does not know where he goes. While you have the light, believe in the light, that you may become children of light" (John 12:35, 36).

A woman said that she first joined 3D in order to lose five pounds. She was a conventional churchgoer, but avoided anything that looked "spiritual." A friend had recommended 3D as a good program for losing weight, and that was about all she knew about it. She signed up for the twelve-week period, only to find out that there was a lot more to it than weighing in and staying on a diet! She said, "I was furious! I felt I had been tricked. But because I had signed my name, I stuck with it." And then she added, "It was an absolutely life-changing experience for me."

That 3Der walked while she had the light. She could have chosen to rebel and give in to her feelings that this was "too much." But she chose to stay.

Turning on the light means allowing yourself to see what may have been hidden heretofore. "He who walks in darkness does not know where he goes." And when we live in self-chosen darkness, we do not even know who it is who is going! We don't know ourselves well at all. So walking in the light means allowing dark places to be exposed to the truth.

One of the most difficult areas to get into the light has to do with our hidden negative feelings, such as jealousy, envy and resentment. "Walk while you have the light," says Jesus, and that means letting the light shine into those dark places we would rather keep hidden.

1. Can you identify places where you are still hidden or afraid to look at the truth?

2. Can you identify any particular places where jealousy is a problem for you?

176

# DAY 6 • SIGN #6: BRIDGE OUT (NO WAY ACROSS)

Daily Reading: Acts 16:1-10
*But the Spirit of Jesus did not allow them. (v. 7)*

How many times have you been frustrated when you tried to do something "good" and were not permitted to carry it through? We have all had such experiences and perhaps have been confused by them. Our text today concerns Paul and Silas on their missionary journey. It was Paul's great ambition to carry the gospel of Christ into new areas where the name of Jesus had not been heard. He had a great sense of urgency which characterized his whole life. Here at this point, however, he and his companions were not allowed to go in the direction they would have chosen. "They attempted to go into Bithynia, but the Spirit of Jesus did not allow them."

The sequel to this story is that Paul saw a Macedonian in his dream, saying, "Come over to Macedonia and help us." He took this leading as the new direction for the mission, and turned west. The course of history was affected by this as the gospel was then carried to Europe rather than Asia. We do not realize how sometimes a seemingly small decision can affect the entire direction of our lives.

What do we do when the sign faces us, "Bridge Out, No Way Across"? We can sit down and get angry, and lose a lot of time and energy in vain regret that the course we had thought was good is not open to us. Or, on the other hand, we can seek guidance as to how to proceed with our life, knowing that God does not play tricks. If one road is closed, another will open. The self-chosen roads are dangerous. They may even contain washouts that are not labeled. But when God puts this sign across the road, we can be sure that he means to lead us in a better way.

1. Where have you seen God closing one road and opening another in your life?

2. How can that experience help you to handle "closed doors" when you encounter them?

## DAY 7 • SIGN #7: CHECKING YOUR DESTINATION

Daily Reading: Matthew 7:7-20

*The gate is narrow and the way is hard that leads to life, and those who find it are few. (v. 14)*

It doesn't matter how easy and pleasant the road is, if it is going in the wrong direction. You cannot tell by the quality of the way itself just where it is leading. So it is important from time to time to "check your destination." Are you still on the right road?

Jesus warned specifically that the way to life is hard and many would miss it. That's a hard saying, and none of us enjoys hearing it. But it is a warning of reality and a warning of love. Not all roads lead to the same place.

A wife asks her husband from time to time, when they are traveling in unfamiliar territory, "Why don't we get on such and such turnpike and go that way?" The husband answers, "Because it doesn't go where we want to go." It matters not that the turnpike is a pleasant, fast road on which to travel. It ends up at the "wrong place." In life, many people have decided to settle for the quality of the road, ignoring its direction. Then there are always those siren voices that assure us that all roads are the same, and they all end up equally true. What folly! Common sense tells us that there are different qualities of life, that there are different standards, different goals. You do not become a pianist by practicing baseball in the sandlot. You cannot become a star athlete by sitting in front of a television set. Some things have to be sought.

You have wanted a fuller life, a more abundant life, a closer walk with God. Keep seeking it. Check your destination. Get rid of whatever would hinder you in this walk, and keep your eyes forward. "The gate is narrow and the way is hard"—but remember what Jesus said: "It leads to *life*."

1. Have you chosen an easier road lately?

2. If so, what steps can you take to make sure you are on the right road again?

# UPHILL, DOWNHILL

*I have learned, in*
*whatever*
*state I am, to*
*be content.*

Philippians 4:11

## DAY 1 • WHEN WE REACH THE HILLS

Daily Reading: James 1:2-8, 12-15

*Count it all joy when you meet various trials. (v. 2)*

Some people love climbing mountains. There is a challenge that meets some inner urge and fills some need in the very difficulty of it. We are probably all familiar with the famous answer as to why someone attempted to climb Mt. Everest: "Because it is there!"

Life was not meant to be lived without challenge. Our human nature needs to be tried and proved at many levels. We do not understand ourselves easily, and in these trials and testings we learn some important truths about ourselves. Peter thought he was loyal and "true-blue" until he failed to meet the test when Jesus was being dragged through the mock trial. Judas apparently miscalculated both what Jesus was doing and his own involvement, because after his betrayal, he went out and killed himself, saying, "I have betrayed innocent blood." Trials bring out what is hidden.

James tells us to "count it all joy" when we reach these hills of difficult trials. The flat plains may make walking easier, but it is the hills that invigorate the heart. They call for the best we can have, and they offer their ample reward when we meet the test. None of us can meet the test successfully alone, however. We are in constant need of divine help, and if we forget that, we are sure to fall. "I need thee every hour" is more than a pious line in an old hymn. It is a very practical prayer. Awareness of our need can help us "count it all joy" when we meet various trials, because in each of these trials, we encounter the sufficiency of God and the adequacy of his grace overcoming our own weakness and failure.

So joy can abound!

1. What have you learned about yourself from the trials in your life?

2. What trials or challenges are you facing this week?

## Day 2 • Hairpin Turns and Dangerous Drops

Daily Reading: 1 Corinthians 10:1-13

*If anyone thinks he stands, let him take heed test he fall. (v. 12)*

Driving in hill country can be exhilarating. Sometimes one can find roads that go dizzyingly up, without rails or walls to keep motorists from going over the side. Coupled with this, there may be hairpin turns, showing the breathtaking distance one would fall if the car went over the side.

Life has its hairpin turns, too. These turns may give the impression that we're actually going backward instead of forward. If we are not aware of what's going on the situation can be confusing.

The reason the road turns in this twisting fashion is that otherwise it would be too steep for us. So it is God's mercy that the road is bent to accommodate our need and weakness. So many things in life, if we look at them rightly, have been made to accommodate our need and weakness. Even the Incarnation, the appearance of God in the flesh, is an accommodation to our need. "No one has ever seen God; the only Son, who is in the bosom of the Father, he has made him known" (John 1:18).

There are dangerous turns in all our lives. There are places where we need to be particularly watchful and prayerful. Looking to them, "taking heed lest we fall," is a way of continuing on in our lives. Each of us knows some of these places because of past falls and past experiences. Other places may become clearer to us as we allow God to show us more of our nature. But it is important to remember, the road leads upward and onward. These turns are not dead ends. They are simply places where we may have to go a little slower, a little more carefully, and a little more humbly.

1. Name some of the places where life seemed to be going "backward" for you, and turned out to be God's way of leading you forward.

2. Where are some current hairpin turns in your life where you are liable to leave the way of obedience?

## DAY 3 • DOWNHILL—EASY DOES IT

Daily Reading: Psalm 30: 1-12

*As for me, in my prosperity, I said, "I shall never be moved." (v. 6)*

Sometimes life seems to coast. The weather is great, our family and friends are agreeable, and things just "go well." You might call it a "downhill" period.

It is very, very easy to get deceived, however, when such a period comes. The psalmist writes about such a time in Psalm 30. In his prosperity, he felt he was well-established. "I shall never be moved," he said. Many, many professions of faith and loyalty have been made in such circumstances. And sometimes these continue for a considerable period, even for years for some people.

Then the rains and floods come, to use another metaphor. The storm blows against the life and tests its foundation. That's when we find out whether we have enough strength to survive the easy "downhill" period. The tricky part of this easy period is the ease with which we deceive ourselves into thinking we are "more spiritual" or "more mature" than we actually are. Even our spiritual reading and exercises can become a part of that deception, and we can think ourselves to be on par with what we are reading.

The easy time is a gift of God. It is a time of encouragement and respite from the struggle; it is an accommodation to our need. But only if we use it rightly can it remain the blessing God means it to be.

If you find yourself in an easy, "coasting" time, give thanks to God, and ask for the discernment not to be fooled by it.

1. Name some of the "easy times" you have experienced in your Christian journey.

2. What dangers did you face as a result of these easy times?

## DAY 4 • HILLS, THRILLS AND SPILLS

Daily Reading: Psalm 69:1-18

*I sink in deep mire where there is no foothold! (v. 2)*

How many children have found it so! "After the thrill, the spill!" So many times that which seems so easy, so delightful, so wonderful, is followed by a serious spill—even an injury. That's what the psalmist was writing about: the aftermath of a spiritual and emotional spill. "The waters have come up to my neck. I sink in deep mire where there is no foothold." And a little later he adds, "O God, thou knowest my folly; the wrongs I have done are not hidden from thee" (v. 5).

Probably nothing is more discouraging in the life of a serious Christian than finding oneself in "deep mire," knowing that, in part at least, it is one's own fault. That is why the Church has encouraged a regular confession of sin, to keep us from being surprised at ourselves. If we are aware of our own nature and our proclivity to disobedience, independence and rebellion, we will not be so shocked when we discover that nature expressing itself in one way or another. If, on the other hand, we insist on believing only the best about ourselves, if we are in a kind of denial of the dark part of our nature, we will be surprised, even overwhelmed, when confronted with its fruit. All of us, without exception, can be guilty of doing unkind things without consciously planning or intending them. But we have to take responsibility for them, or we will get locked into this "deep mire where there is no foothold." If, however, we are willing to take responsibility for what comes out of us, then we have a forgiving Savior whose steadfast love rescues us "from the stinking mire" (verse 14).

It is true that in these lowest depths we often find out the most about ourselves and about the love and mercy of God.

1. What "dark part of your nature" do you have the most trouble accepting?

2. What steps can you take to be more accepting of yourself, including that dark part?

183

## Day 5 • Thanksgiving in Tough Times (Energy for the climb)

Daily Reading: Psalm 34:1-10
*I will bless the Lord at all times. (v. 1)*

There are few things we can do that will renew our energy for our Christian walk more readily than thanksgiving and praise. Thanksgiving is the root motive for our praise and worship of God, because we are people who have received untold blessings. One hymn says, "Eternity's too short to show thy praise."

It is especially important to *practice* thanksgiving during tough times. When the road gets steep, rocky, uncertain; when we're tempted to sit down, give up, turn back; when we grow so unsure we don't even know if we're on the right road at all—then it is time to thank and praise the Lord.

Israel is a good example of people who forgot to be thankful. Hardly had they crossed the Red Sea under the mighty miraculous hand of God than they ran into a little difficulty and began complaining that Moses had brought them out to perish in the wilderness. Thanksgiving can help prevent that kind of blind forgetfulness. This is obviously one of the important functions of the Eucharist, or Lord's Supper: recalling that for which we must be eternally thankful. The ancient church called that meal "Eucharist," which is the Greek word for "Thanksgiving."

The great hymn, "Onward, Christian Soldiers" reminds us that "Hell's foundations quiver at the shout of praise!" We have a mighty weapon in our spiritual warfare, a source of energy for the tough climbs that life brings: our thanksgiving. Make it real; make it specific; make it regular; make it intense and personal; make it your weapon of victory. "I will bless the Lord at all times. His praise shall ever be in my mouth!"

1. Write a prayer of thanksgiving for the ordinary blessings of today.

2. Name as many things as you can remember for which you should be thankful today.

## DAY 6 • LOOKING BACK AND TAKING COURAGE

Daily Reading: 1 Samuel 7:1-13

*Hitherto hath the Lord helped us. (v. 12)*

Everyone of us has a story to tell. It is a story of great need and great mercy. Some of us have stories that have elements of drama, even tragedy in them. Most of us have stories with quite a little comedy in them, when we get to the point that we can laugh at ourselves. All of us have a story of Jesus' love and sufficiency for our need. "The Lord is *my* Shepherd. I shall not want."

We've talked earlier in these weeks about the danger of living in the past, of gazing back at time that is no more, so that we lose our forward movement toward our goal. Looking back can be tricky, and can be a real hindrance to us. But there is a place for looking back in the right way. Samuel wanted Israel to remember that "hitherto," "up to this point" the Lord had helped them. They would face new challenges. There would be new obstacles. There were still enemies to be fought. But "hitherto" the Lord had not failed them, and there was no reason to suppose that he would fail them in the future.

That's where looking back can be a means of catapulting us forward. Seeing how faithful God has been, in spite of our own foibles and failures, we can go forward with confidence. "My God has delivered me, and will deliver me," said Daniel. And that is the faith that helps us press on.

We need new courage every day. Like leaky vessels, we allow ourselves to lose some of the spiritual strength we've been given, and easily slip back into old patterns of thought, feeling and action. So we need often to "look back and take courage." There is nothing awaiting us that is too hard for God. There is nothing in this day that we cannot face with his divine assistance. "Hitherto the Lord hath helped us!"

1. Make a list of specific ways in which God has helped you through difficult times in the past.

2. On the basis of those ways, what affirmation can you make about the future?

185

## DAY 7 • "ABOVE THE LOW LEVELS OF LIFE"

Daily Reading: Philippians 4:4-13

*Whatever things are pure . . . lovely . . . of good report . . . , think on these things.*
*(v. 8)*

We do choose where we live mentally, emotionally, and spiritually. Our outward circumstances are not nearly so important as the inner world we choose. Here are some choices we make:

(1.) We choose whether to carry grudges and resentments against those who have hurt us, or whether to forgive them. If we carry the "root of bitterness" in ourselves, life will take on that kind of bitter tone. Things will look gray, cloudy, perhaps even hopeless. And all because we have chosen a cloudy inside.

(2.) We can choose fear or faith, hope or despair. It truly is a choice. A certain man had made bad choices much of his life. He was basically negative, and in his heart he accused God of being unfair. Then news came that he had a serious illness, probably fatal. The most amazing thing happened. He began to look at life differently. He began to emphasize the goodness of God. He began to rehearse the many miracles that happened in his life—miracles that showed without any question that God loves and cares for him. And another thing happened—he began to improve physically. It was an impressive display of this point: we can choose the level of life we want to live on.

Where are you choosing to live this week? Life goes uphill, and life goes downhill. There are, for every one of us, days of sun and days of cloud. But in and through them all the sunshine of God's love never goes out. We are still his children, the objects of his love and mercy. New every morning, God's love and mercy invite us to live "above the low levels of life." They invite us to remember who we are, a people greatly loved and redeemed by the precious blood of Christ. Struggles, to be sure, are part of our pilgrimage. But we are on the King's Highway!

1. Where have you chosen to be fearful or despairing?

2. Write down where you are choosing to live mentally, emotionally, and spiritually this week.

# TRAVELING LIGHT

*My yoke*
*is easy and*
*my burden*
*is light.*

*Matthew 11:30*

## DAY 1 • TOO MUCH LUGGAGE?

Daily Reading: Matthew 13:1-7, 10-23

*But the cares of the world and the delight in riches choke the word and it proves unfruitful. (v. 22)*

If you have ever hiked up a mountain, you know how important it is to carry as little as possible. People who have been in military service tell hair-raising tales of marches with heavy packs on their backs. Unnecessary weight can be a terrible burden.

Our text today suggests that life, too, can be overburdened with unnecessary luggage. "Cares of the world." What a thought that phrase invokes! Are you one of those people who cannot let go of such cares? Or, better said, are you one who *thinks* you cannot let go of such cares? Responsible people, like Martha of Bethany, may allow such cares to spoil their disposition and steal the enjoyment they are meant to have in simple pleasures.

A mother labored hard and long each Christmas to make Christmas what it should be "in her eyes." It meant baking special cookies, cakes, and the like. It meant making sure that the Christmas tree was nicely trimmed and presents properly placed under it. But in the process, her overburdened spirit began to cry out. Something was wrong. So when Christmas itself came, she felt hurt and disappointed, and ended up being unpleasant to others. Such was the effect of carrying too much luggage.

There are other, more serious elements to this problem. If we focus our attention and our love on outward things, we starve the inner spirit. One of the results of these weeks of discipline can be and should be to strengthen the inner life. It will mean lightening our luggage—letting go what is unnecessary for our journey, "laying aside the weight and sin which so easily clings to us."

1. What unnecessary "luggage" are you carrying in your life at this point?

2. Which of these do you think you can let go?

## Day 2 • Spring Cleaning

Daily Reading: 1 Thessalonians 5:12-24

*Examine yourselves, to see whether you are holding to your faith. (2 Corinthians 13:5) Test everything; hold fast what is good. (1 Thessalonians. 5:21)*

It seems that no matter how faithfully and carefully the house is kept, there comes a time when a "spring cleaning" is necessary. Spring cleaning can be arduous if it has been neglected for a long time.

A gentleman had lived alone in a small apartment for many years. Like many unmarried men, he had neglected to keep "short accounts" on the things that collected in his living space. Little by little the space had grown smaller and the things being saved grew more numerous. Finally the day came when the gentleman had to move to a nursing home. He could no longer maintain himself without help. Friends went in to help him move, and found that the entire apartment had now grown to paths only wide enough to allow movement from one area to another. Everything else was filled with boxes, papers, magazines, Christmas gifts (carefully wrapped in newspapers), unused clothing, and so on. His treasures had choked his living space.

Life can become so full of "undigested" matters that we are seriously hindered in our ongoing spiritual progress. We have mentioned some of them several times, but it is important for us to remember that they are serious handicaps: resentments, guilt over unrepented sin, jealousy, greed, and ambition, to name a few. A "spring cleaning" can help us deal constructively with some of these things. It may involve private confession to a minister or priest. It may involve writing down the memory of such problems, offering them to the Lord, possibly taking them to Communion and symbolically "leaving them on the altar." Above all, it means taking such things honestly to God, seeking and accepting forgiveness, forgiving others, and forgiving ourselves! That is the essence of "spring cleaning," which can be very helpful in setting us afresh on our path.

1. What jealousies do you need to deal with in your life?

2. What resentments can you get rid of today?

## DAY 3 • ITEM #1: UNNECESSARY GUILT

Daily Reading: Psalm 32:1-11

*I said, "I will confess my transgressions to the Lord"; then thou didst forgive the guilt of my sin. (v. 5)*

If we are going to travel light, we must unburden ourselves of some specific unnecessary weights. The first one many of us need to deal with is unnecessary guilt.

Are you one of those people who automatically respond in guilt if accused directly or indirectly? Guilt can be a very controlling emotion. People will sometimes do unwise things, and put themselves in very difficult situations, in an effort to avoid this feeling of condemnation. It can even reach sick proportions to the point that a person needs professional help to "get it out" so that it can no longer control behavior from its subconscious base.

We are all guilty because we are all sinners. We are guilty of betraying the creative intention of God in allowing us to be. We are guilty of betraying the redemptive purpose of Jesus who died to set us free and make us new creatures. "We have left undone those things which we ought to have done, and we have done those things which we ought not to have done, and there is no health in us." Those words from the Book of Common Prayer are down-to-earth and realistic. They describe our human condition. But the prayer goes on to ask forgiveness, and it is followed by words of assurance and pardon. We are not left in hopeless guilt, but as "guilty but forgiven sinners." The criminal who is pardoned is still guilty, but he is free because the pardon sets him free. It is the same with us. And we do not, once we have repented and confessed our sin before the Lord, need to live in false guilt. Forgiveness is a reality to those who "with true faith and hearty repentance" turn to him.

The way to get rid of unnecessary guilt is through honest repentance and the humility to accept forgiveness *with thanksgiving*.

1. Are you aware of any place in your life where you have not accepted the forgiveness of God?

2. What steps can you take to accept the forgiveness of God and to forgive yourself?

## Day 4 • Item #2: Unforgiveness

Daily Reading: Matthew 6:7-15

*But if you do not forgive men their trespasses, neither will your Father forgive you your trespasses. (v. 15)*

After any war there are old mine fields which must be cleared and undetonated bombs which still endanger the unsuspecting and unwary. They may lie out of sight and forgotten for years, but still have the potential of doing great harm.

This is a picture of unforgiveness carried in our hearts. We would not think of carrying an unexploded bomb around with us, with the knowledge that it might be set off accidentally at any point. But we are less afraid of an even more deadly weapon: unforgiveness toward others.

Sometimes this unforgiveness grows out of great and terrible wounds that have been inflicted in childhood. No one who has counseled people who have been abused as children would take lightly the difficulty of arriving at full forgiveness toward the abuser. Or, it may be that a person has witnessed great wrong being done to someone they love, and carries the bitterness of unforgiveness toward the wrongdoer. But the Lord has not made any exceptions to our need to forgive. He has not left any situations that are so hard that we are not expected to come to forgiveness. And why? Because he loves us, and because unforgiveness is so destructive to our spiritual life. It is like acid that eats away the soul, and leaves it shriveled and deformed. The real and greater harm from the great wrong or wound comes when unforgiveness is allowed to remain intact.

Forgiveness is not excusing the wrong. It is refusing to harbor hatred of the wrongdoer, and a desire for revenge. It is allowing God to be the judge, and refusing to play God in the situation. Unforgiveness binds. Forgiveness sets free.

1. Whom do you need to forgive at this point?

2. What steps can you take to forgive in this case? (or these cases?)

## DAY 5 • ITEM #3: JEALOUSY AND ENVY

Daily Reading: 1 Peter 2:1-10

*So put away all malice and all guile and insincerity and envy and all slander. (v. 1)*

    The fact that Peter mentions all these sins indicates that they are not isolated or unusual. From the first century to the present they are the "little foxes" that destroy the good vine of Christian fellowship and Christian victory. They are sins that easily hide beneath pleasant surfaces, and therefore can go unconfessed, all the while doing a deadly work.

    We are told to "put away" these things, and it is significant to see the order the apostle uses. First, we are to put away malice. That is, actually giving up the ill will we feel toward a person or a group. Do you have someone for whom you actively *feel* ill will? Recently a minister attended a conference where another minister was being lauded and praised lavishly. In addition to being a highly gifted person, the minister being lauded was "wrong" in his theology and thinking. Our friend who was observing the scene says that he felt personal "ill will" toward the other man (ostensibly because of his wrong theology). Finally, however, he had to confess his jealousy of his brother, and ask forgiveness and a change of heart. That is really the only way to deal with these malicious feelings that arise in our hearts. We cannot change them by our own strength, but with the power of Jesus Christ in us, we can "put away" malice.

    The second things we are to give up are "guile and insincerity." Too much of our surface friendliness is made up of these two elements. They are simply ways of denying or avoiding facing the darkness in our own hearts. So by *acting* friendly, we delude ourselves that we *are* friendly. That is guile and insincerity. The way to deal with this is to avoid pretending that we love someone "to death," when we couldn't care less. In the meantime, we must go back to step one, and "put away malice."

    "Slander" is the fruit of envy and jealousy. So the key here is to guard our tongues from speaking evil, telling little negative things about someone of whom we are jealous or envious. Getting rid of these burdens can make the trip *so much more enjoyable!*

1. Discuss any situation in which you feel ill will toward another person.

2. Why is it important to get rid of this ill will?

## DAY 6 • ITEM #4: IDOLATRY

Daily Reading: Exodus 20:1-17
*You shall have no other gods before me. (v. 3)*

It comes as a distinct shock to many of us to learn that idolatry is alive and well. We had comfortably placed it in the dark ages of the past, or in those areas where the gospel has not yet penetrated.

It comes as an even more distinct shock to learn that idolatry is alive and well *in us*. That is an unwelcome addendum to the Good News that we would just as soon forget. For idolatry, as we are talking about it here, lives deep in the heart, and is not ready to leave willingly.

Idolatry is, as our text suggests, putting any god before God. Now we know that there is but one true God, the God and Father of our Lord Jesus Christ. The old pantheon of gods and goddesses faded away under the light of the gospel, and the light of the gospel has been carried to the ends of the earth. But the real idolatry is not just in the figures made out of wood, stone or metal. Real idolatry is the creation of the heart. It is lodging our affections on someone or something in such a way that God is crowded out, set aside, disobeyed or defied. When it is all boiled down to "the bottom line" (as the current phrase says it) it means worshipping ourselves and holding on to what makes *us* feel good.

Probably the most frequent choice of an idol is a person. Someone to love us as we wish to be loved. Someone to fill our lives with meaning. Someone for whom we will forsake the truth and build a dishonest relationship. Someone whose favor we will do almost anything to keep. (Perhaps you can add your own list of identifying characteristics of this malady.)

Idolatry disguises itself as a necessary feature to give life zest and joy. Fearing the loss of a person's favor can be one of the most crippling and irksome burdens we try to carry with us. If we are walking in dishonesty and self-blindness, sooner or later the truth will come out, the light will come on, and we will be devastated to see how our idolatry has betrayed us. Good relationships are built on honesty and truth, openness and sincerity. Idolatry is built on "what will keep the relationship going." We have the choice. No one can make it for us.

1. Ask God to show you any idolatry in your life, and discuss it here.

2. Compose a prayer to get free of all idolatry.

## DAY 7 • GAINING BY LOSING

Daily Reading: Luke 9:18-27

*Whoever would save his life will lose it, and he who loses his life for my sake will save it. (v. 24)*

Did Jesus know, when he spoke those words, how hard it would be to make the choice he is asking for? I think he did. I think first of all, that he had made the choice himself, and would continue to make it. We do not do him credit if we think that all his choices were easy and automatic. He had to choose the Father's will, and only by aligning his own will with that of his Father could he perfect the work he was sent to do. So, tasting human nature and "being tempted in all points as we are," he knew the difficulty of making hard choices.

We are all, by nature, "life savers." We do not want to lose our lives, even when they seem drab or boring. The will to live is very strong in us all. Paul says, "No one ever hates his own flesh, but nourishes and cherishes it . . ." (Eph. 5:29a). And so, when we are asked to lose our life for any cause, it gives us pause, to say the least. But Jesus here states a life principle. The very thing we want comes only by giving it up. The effort to save our lives by refusing to give them up for his sake is a losing proposition. We will end up losing the thing we're trying to save.

You can illustrate this in your own experience. As children, we often made ourselves unhappy by being selfish. Many, many conflicts between children grow out of a refusal to share what they have with another. Jesus calls us to "give up" what seems "life" to us—whatever that may be, "for his sake," and in so doing, he promises that we will find life. He never disappoints or cheats one who dares to take him at his word. It is safe to travel light.

1. Where are you trying to "save" your life?

2. Where are you willing to "lose" your life?

# WALKING WITH JESUS

*So that . . .*
*we too might*
*walk in*
*newness of life.*

*Romans 6:4*

## DAY 1 • I AM WITH YOU ALWAYS

Daily Reading: Matthew 28:1-10,16-20

*And lo! I am with you always, to the close of the age. (v. 20)*

This *is* the King's Highway. This life to which we are called, this life we are given by grace, this pilgrimage which is ours to follow—all this is his royal gift. Many generations ago, John Bunyan wrote of a pilgrim who fled from the City of Destruction and found his way to the Celestial City. This was an allegory of the Christian life, in which Christian met with many adventures and many dangers.

A later pilgrim, John Newton, the former slave-trading sea captain turned Anglican minister, wrote his famous hymn, "Amazing Grace." In it he summed up the way God had led him in these words: "Through many dangers, toils and cares I have already come; 'Tis grace has brought me safe thus far, and grace will lead me home." He, too, knew that he was traveling the King's Highway.

We Christians often forget that we have a Companion along this way. We are tempted to think that we are traveling alone, with the burden of every circumstance and trial resting entirely on our own shoulders. We can become quite weary with such thoughts, forgetting that Jesus Christ has committed himself to going with us. When he spoke to his disciples before his glorious ascension to the Father, he assured them that he was not sending them out alone, that he would be with them.

In the great conversation recorded in John's Gospel, chapters 14-17, Jesus promised that the Comforter, the Paraclete, the Holy Spirit of Truth will abide with his people forever. That promise is still in effect. Quiet as the light at dawn, still as the dew of evening, the blessed Spirit is present with us. The only problem is that we often ignore his presence and act as though he had forgotten us.

As we come to this week of our little journey, it is a comfort and a challenge that this text leaves with us. Jesus is with us by the Holy Spirit. He is indwelling every one of us who love him, and "nearer than breathing, closer than hands and feet." We can talk with him, give him our fears and burdens, and *believe* that he hears and cares, even when our feelings tell us otherwise.

He has never taken back his promise. It is still ours today. "Lo! I am with you always, to the close of the age."

1. What does it mean to you that Jesus is always with you?

2. What separates you from being always "with Jesus"?

## DAY 2 • DEEP WATERS

Daily Reading: Isaiah 43:1-13

*When you pass through deep waters. . . . (v. 2a)*

It is no surprise that one of the hymns that remains a favorite, generation after generation, is "How Firm a Foundation." It is based on this 43rd chapter of Isaiah, and expressed in practical and poetic terms, it is a reassurance of God's presence in all circumstances. No matter how advanced we may get in medicine, psychology or technology, we still, all of us, have to go through deep waters at times.

Here is what the hymn says: "When through the deep waters I call thee to go, the rivers of woe shall not thee overflow. I'll strengthen thee, help thee and cause thee to stand, upheld by my righteous, omnipotent hand."

When I read those words I recall some of the times when the waters were deep in my own life—the life-threatening illness of one of our children when he was four years old. I recall the nights I sat by his hospital bed, praying and asking God to spare his life. I am happy to report that God brought us through and he is now a minister of the gospel. Then I remember another child who did not survive birth. This was a dark and difficult time for both mother and father. The waters were deep. But God did not fail. You who read these words have your own stories and your own testimonies of God's faithfulness!

What do you do when you realize that you are in deep waters? I think you and I must let those times make us newly aware of how dependent we are on God and how trustworthy he is. This is not to minimize the difficulty or to brush lightly over it. To do so would be to choose an unreal, super-spiritual approach which will betray us sooner or later. We cannot live in denial that trouble is trouble, and that difficulty is difficult! But we can take the trouble and the difficulty to the One who rules winds and waves, and he can bring us safely through.

1. What "deep waters" are you being asked to go through now?

2. What assurances do you have that God is with you in this?

## Day 3 • Fiery Trials

Daily Reading: Isaiah 43:14-21
*The fire shall not hurt you. . . . (v. 2b)*

Today we look at the second half of that wonderful verse from Isaiah, and the other stanza of that great hymn we mentioned yesterday. The hymn says this: "When through fiery trials thy pathway shall lie, My grace all-sufficient shall be thy supply; the flame shall not hurt thee, I only design thy dross to consume and thy gold to refine."

Ah! the fire! Trouble like deep water is one thing. This fire touches something else in us all. It may come in the form of rejection by someone we care very much about. It may come in the form of criticism by people whose opinion means much to us. It may come in the form of rejection of some project we have created or some work we have submitted. It may come in the form of a bad grade, a low rating, or failure to be chosen for some coveted position. Whatever form it takes, it brings P A I N !

And what is the pain but hurt pride? What is the pain but bruised self-esteem? What is the pain except our dross being consumed and our gold being refined? For God allows things like those we have mentioned (and others you can supply from your own experience) to come to us in order to wean us away from emotional dependence on praise and success. Jesus did not live by such things. When success came, he went straight forward, following the course the Father had laid out for him. When rejection came, he wasted no time in self-pity or regret. Even as his enemies crucified him, he could pray, "Forgive them, for they do not know what they are doing."

I believe that we Christians often misunderstand and misinterpret what God is doing when we experience this fire. We look at the pain rather than the promise. We look at the feelings rather than the results. God is purging that which is unlike the image he is working in us. But he requires our faith and our cooperation if the operation is going to be successful. The fire can make us bitter and resentful—or it can do its purging work. The result is up to us.

1. What "fiery trials" are you being asked to go through now?

2. How can you cooperate with God in facing these trials?

## DAY 4 • LONESOME VALLEYS

Daily Reading: Psalm 23

*Yea, though I walk through the valley of the shadow of death, I will fear no evil, for thou art with me. (v. 4)*

"But I thought you said that Jesus is always with us. Now you tell me there are lonesome valleys."

True, Jesus is walking with us all the way, as the psalmist said, and as he himself promised in Matthew 28. But we are accustomed to walking with others, and we expect that they are going to be there to share life's experiences. Then comes a time when someone is taken from us. There comes a time when others are not available. The way seems very lonely, and we are in what the old song called, a "Lonesome Valley." Why? Because there are experiences that no other human being can share. In the mystery of life, we have to face certain experiences with Jesus alone.

People do sit by the bedside of loved ones in the long watches, with no one to talk to except God. People face surgery and, in spite of all the help medical science can give, they still must go into the "darkness" alone. But, thanks be to God, there are no experiences in which we are truly alone.

These lonesome valleys are meant to strengthen our dependence on and faith in the One who is entirely to be trusted. Other helpers fail and comforts flee, but then—"Help of the helpless, O abide with me!" And he does.

We do not have to project into the future how we shall deal with the lonesome valleys that *may* await us. We are foolish if we allow ourselves to worry ahead of time about how we will deal with them. What we can do, should do, and must do now is to strengthen our relationship with our divine Companion. He is with us, and no lonesome valley will await us without him.

1. Can you name some "lonesome valleys" you have walked through?

2. What did you learn about Jesus' presence in those valleys?

## DAY 5 • A LIFETIME JOURNEY

Daily Reading: 2 Timothy 4:1-8
*I have finished the course. . . . (v. 7)*

How are you at finishing what you begin?

The Bible is full of admonitions to us to finish the race. Jesus said, "He who endures to the end shall be saved." Halfway is not enough.

There is something wonderful about getting on with the journey, and pressing on towards the goal. Paul must have sensed this when, near the end of his life, he wrote young Timothy, "I have fought the good fight; I have finished the course; I have kept the faith." What a satisfaction that statement must have contained! There is always a just reward in seeing that we have been able to complete what we began. There is a good fulfillment in it, even when it is of small consequence. How much more if we continue on with Jesus in this way!

Jesus has pledged to go with us all the way. Daily we can renew our promise to go with him.

1. How are you at finishing what you begin?

2. Looking back over the past 12 weeks, how do you feel about your perseverance in these disciplines?

## DAY 6 • IS JESUS ENOUGH?

Daily Reading: 2 Timothy 4:9-18
*But the Lord stood by me. (v. 17)*

Our question is not a rhetorical one. It is answered every day in the way we handle our lives. If we insist that our lives be full of people, things, events, successes, rewards of all kinds, are we not saying, in effect, "Lord, I love you, but I must have *all these things too.*" What happens then, if these things are taken from us? Is Jesus enough?

Paul had had his share of successes. He had been the most successful missionary of his time, and had been responsible for carrying the gospel of Jesus far beyond where any of the others had taken it. He had organized and built up Christian congregations all over the Roman empire. He was one of the best known and most widely-loved of the apostles. So he knew the taste of success.

He had also had his share of "failures." His entire ministry was dogged by those who opposed him and tried to belittle what he was doing. They insisted he was making it too easy for Gentiles to come into the Church, and they wanted to insist that even the non-Jewish Christians should be forced to obey the Old Testament laws. It was a lifetime battle for the truth of God's gracious outreach to all peoples against a narrow view which would have restricted the Good News and barred many from knowing Jesus Christ as Lord and Savior.

Now he is an old man, and as he writes about his trial, he tells the sad story of how those he had trusted had forsaken him. "At my first defense, no one took my part; all deserted me. May it not be charged against them" (verse 16). And then he adds: "But the Lord stood by me and gave me strength to proclaim the word fully, that all the Gentiles might hear it." Jesus was enough.

How else can we find out that he is indeed enough, except to have others disappoint us or fail us? When that happens, it is good to remember this word of Paul.

1. When "these other things" were taken away, did you find Jesus was enough?

2. Write a prayer asking Jesus to show you that he is enough for all your needs.

## DAY 7 • UNEXPECTED PRESENCE AND BURNING HEARTS

Daily Reading: Luke 24:13-35

*Did not our hearts burn within us as he talked with us on the road? (v. 32)*

It was a sad journey to Emmaus on which the disciples were embarked that first Easter day. They did not know for sure that Jesus had risen. The stories they had heard seemed much too good to be true. And it is certain that they had no expectation that Jesus himself would join them on their journey.

Their lack of expectation and acceptance of the reports they had already heard kept them from recognizing him once he joined their company.

Obviously they were not of the band of those closest to him, because they did not recognize him even as he talked. As the walk went on, they were increasingly aware that his presence was a blessing, and that his understanding of the Scriptures was a key to opening up their own. Still, they did not know who he was.

How like them we are as we journey! Our own weak faith discounts the valid reports of others. We seek naturalistic explanations for the miracles they report in their own life. And like the people who prayed for Peter's release from prison, when the answer comes, we are so full of "unfaith" that we are surprised to have our prayers answered! Our lack of expectancy fills us with gloom when glory is at hand. No wonder Jesus called them, "O foolish and slow of heart to believe!" And doubtless he has the same word for us.

It is wonderful, though, that our dimness of faith does not diminish his faithfulness to us. His patience and mercy are ever toward our weakness, and he leads us along with the encouragement not to stay bound to the past. Our hearts do indeed burn within us at strange times, and often it is only after the fact that we realize, "Ah! It was you, after all, Lord." That's the way it was with those two disciples. Looking back they could only say, "Did not our hearts burn within us as he talked with us on the road?" Look for those heartwarming times as you continue your journey with Jesus.

1. Relate any experience in which you were keenly aware of the presence of God.

2. When you remember this experience, how does it help you in times when you do not *feel* his presence?

# HEART BEATS
—∽

# THE EXAMINED HEART

*Search me
and try me,
O God, and
know my heart.*

Psalm 139:23

## DAY 1 • THE HEART: WELLSPRING OF LIFE

Daily Reading: Proverbs 4:20-27

*Keep your heart with all vigilance, for from it flow the springs of life. (v. 23)*

Plato said that the unexamined life is not worth living. That thought was very similar to our text from Proverbs. In both cases, we are being asked to examine the wellsprings of our thoughts and actions.

The truth is, however, that most of us, most of the time, live "unexamined" lives. We rush from one event to another, from one decision to another, with little thought as to what is really moving us. In fact, psychologists say that a very large part of our motivation is unconscious—out of reach, as it were, from our conscious thinking.

What can we do then? The psalmist knew the answer, and we can rely on the same help he called for: "Search me and try me, O God, and know my heart." This is our challenge as we enter this period of growth: to be more open to God than we have been heretofore, to allow him to help us as we take seriously the fact that the springs of life come from deep within, often from unconscious motives.

As we grow in our faith and move forward in our Christian pilgrimage, we become aware of two things coming from the heart: there are dark and unwelcome thoughts and feelings that "well up" from within, and there are yearnings and desires that spring up to give us hope. So we begin this journey knowing that we will meet some unwelcome truth about ourselves—perhaps every day! But we will also be aware that deep within the heart there has been planted a new life, a new spirit, a growing spirit that comes from God and is always seeking God. Paul said, "Christ in you, the hope of glory." By the grace and the accomplished work of our Lord Jesus Christ, we can now make choices between the darkness and the light, between what comes from the old nature and what comes from the new nature. What a cheerful thought! Thanks be to God that we can "keep our hearts with all vigilance," because he is answering our prayer to search and try us, revealing any places where he is asking us to change.

1. What is your response to God's invitation to be more open to him?

2. Can you identify what areas of your life you would rather keep *closed* to the Lord?

## Day 2 • Truth in the Inward Part

Daily Reading: Psalm 51

*Behold, thou desirest truth in the inward being; therefore teach me wisdom in my secret heart. (v. 5)*

Psalm 51 is probably one of the most loved of the psalms, because its honesty helps us to be more honest with God. The battle we all fight is spelled out: allowing ourselves to know the full truth about ourselves. Overcoming the tendency to be dishonest with ourselves is one of our greatest challenges.

A good illustration of this can be found in the area of physical health. We are told that denial is one of the major causes of allowing cancer to get too far before doing anything about it. The same is true of symptoms of heart trouble. They can be ignored and denied but eventually they will cause deadly trouble if not recognized and treated.

In the spiritual realm we can see how denial keeps back the miracle of forgiveness and the freedom it offers. If we are denying our need, Jesus cannot be to us what he wants to be. "Those that are whole have no need of a physician."

In another psalm, the writer says that as long as he denied his problem, "thy hand was heavy upon me; my strength was dried up as by the heat of summer" (Ps. 32). In other words, he was miserable. Then he goes on, "Then I acknowledged my sin to thee, and did not hide my iniquity." This is the explanation of his opening words, "Blessed is he whose transgression is forgiven!" God's desire for truth in the inward parts so he can free us to be the new people he created and redeemed us to be. The process is not always pleasant. Indeed it is sometimes very painful, especially if we have been "in denial" for a long time. But it is worth the effort and the prayer.

God honors us by requiring that we be honest with him. He treats us as a people who can respond to his own truthfulness and who can choose light rather than darkness. What a joy it is to know that he loves us enough not to put up with our self-deceptions!

1. Where does denial operate in your life?

2. What are the consequences of keeping iniquity hidden?

## DAY 3 • THE PERIL OF DENIAL

Daily Reading: 1 John 1:1-10

*If we say we have no sin, we deceive ourselves, and the truth is not in us. (v. 8)*

This little book was written to give us joy. "We are writing this that our joy may be complete" (verse 4). So its motive is to remove those things that would keep us from our inheritance as children of God. What a beautiful thought!

Recently, someone was quoted as saying, "I don't like looking at all those things about myself. It's too negative!" What made the remark noticeable was that none of the Christian material she was reading was written to be "heavy." It was written to bring people into a new level of self-understanding, freedom and joy!

As we reflect on today's Scripture, we run into one of those "negative" passages. The apostle is quite definite about this: If we deny our sin, we are in gross self-deception. And that puts us into a perilous situation.

First, to deny our sin is to leave it undealt with, and therefore able to do its mischief in our lives. Have you known someone who is very self-righteous and opinionated, but who sincerely and strongly believes he or she is open-minded and simply "right"? If you do, you know how much trouble such self-deception can cause in human relationships. I would venture to guess that the inability (or refusal) to look at our wrongness is one of the major causes of marital conflict, either open or hidden.

Second, to deny our sin robs us of the joy and miracle of forgiveness. Look through any old hymnal or gospel song book and see how much of the singing of the church has dealt with "the joy of sin forgiven." One of the great Easter hymns of the ancient Church even calls Adam's sin "happy" because it led to the redemption of the world by Jesus Christ. That is a poetic way of expressing the inexpressible joy of knowing that we are accepted by God on the basis of his grace and not of our worthiness.

Third, to deny our sin condemns us to keep working at being right and righteous, and such a task is emotionally exhausting! Once we accept the fact that we are what God calls us—sinners—and that we have been loved and redeemed by his Son, we can enter into a new, closer, more trusting and joyful relationship with him. The peril of denial is that we miss what God's great love has meant to give us. That, it seems to me, makes it worth the pain it costs to face the truth!

1. Have you experienced how dealing with your sin can lead to a heart full of joy? If so, when?

2. What about confession leading to joy? Jot down an instance or two.


## DAY 4 • THE TEMPTATION OF HYPOCRISY

Daily Reading: Matthew 7:1-5
*You hypocrite, first take the log out of your own eye. . . . (v. 5a)*

I suppose Jesus could say that to any one of us. If we are honest with ourselves, would we not have to admit that it is much easier to see our sister's (or brother's) fault than our own? Somehow, we seem to develop 20/20 vision in seeing what is wrong in another, but have great difficulty in really seeing our own.

Several people were talking recently with a friend about a situation in which all of them thought he was wrong. He had made a couple of decisions that disturbed someone else, but instead of admitting that he had been wrong, he kept shaking his head, saying, "I just don't see anything I did wrong." I suspect all of us have been in that situation at one time or another. The important thing, however, is to "stay the course," to keep with the subject under discussion until there is some kind of breakthrough. If we allow our feelings to get hurt, if we feel insulted or put down, we can abort the process and harden in our self-righteousness. It is probably the danger that this will happen that makes Christians so reluctant to speak to one another about a fault. But spiritual progress can be greatly retarded by the wrong kind of silence, and greatly accelerated by a willingness to enter into such an honest relationship with others.

Jesus' warning, however, is to those who take it upon themselves to speak to another person about her or his sin or wrongness. He warns that it is easy to speak from a "hypocritical" position. The dictionary defines "hypocrite" as "one who feigns to be other or better than he is; a false pretender to virtue or piety." I'm afraid we would all have to plead guilty to that description, because I suspect we have all feigned more piety than was really in us. If we know that about ourselves, we can go before the Lord and acknowledge that we need grace and mercy to overcome our desire to look better than we actually are.

Avoiding "practicing hypocrisy" means that we keep current with

God about our inner condition. He is merciful to us and does not reject us because we have some spiritual "log" sticking out of our eye. To be sure, we look ridiculous walking around with such an encumbrance, trying to help our sisters and brothers get the specks out of their eyes! But he is willing to remove the "log" once we acknowledge that it's there and ask him for his help.

1. Where do you think self-righteousness operates in your life?

2. How does our faith in Christ render our self-justification unnecessary?

## DAY 5 • WHAT DEFILES US

Daily Reading: Matthew 5:27-30; 15:10-20

*Out of the heart come evil thoughts, murder, adultery, fornication, theft, false witness, slander. These are what defile a man. . . . (Matt 15:19, 20a)*

The people were accustomed to watching carefully what they ate. This was a part of the Law and a vital part of their tradition. But in observing this they had forgotten some basic truths and this is what the Lord is calling to their attention.

"Out of the heart." We thought earlier this week about the heart as the wellspring of life. We can never say too often that it is our inner attitude that controls what we are. Outward circumstances simply provide the setting. They do not make us what we are nor who we are.

Any of us who have tried dieting or any kind of food discipline—or other kinds of disciplines for that matter—quickly become aware of how easy it is to blame other people or our circumstances for the way we feel. We can easily excuse ourselves for "breaking the rule" by thinking of how someone hurt our feelings or failed to understand what we were trying to say. But then, in spite of all the rationalizations, we have to live with the result of our own decision.

Jesus here mentions some serious things—not just innocent little things. Where do they come from? From that same heart that convinces us that it wants only good for others. Think of your own inner life, and how many unkind and ungracious thoughts have risen unbidden. Our jealousies, envyings, curiosities, resentments and hatreds all come from this inner resource, and when we realize this, we know where we must do battle. This is the positive and encouraging thing that greater understanding of ourselves brings with it. We are no longer doomed to harbor these negative, destructive emotions as though there was nothing to be done about them. As long as they lie in their festering pool of hiddenness, we may even be dismayed at how negative and hopeless we feel. But once they are exposed to the light, and we can say, "My problem is . . ." and locate it as coming from within, then we have something to take before the Lord. He has promised that we will find grace to help in time of need.

It's not what's happening around us that we have to worry about. It's what happens within.

1. Can you identify with Jesus' statement in today's text? If so, note an instance or two where you have observed the truth of this statement.

2. What "antidotes" have you discovered for dealing with this problem?

## DAY 6 • PONDERING IN OUR HEARTS

Daily Reading: Luke 2:15-19 and 41-51
*But Mary kept all these things, pondering them in her heart. (v. 19)*

There must have been many "things" for Mary to ponder in her heart. And that process certainly did not begin there in the Bethlehem stable. She must have had many months to wonder at what God was doing and how things were going to work out. It is encouraging to remember that she knew as little about her future as you and I know about ours. She was only told the essential things to enable her to make a decision to cooperate with God. When she had said "Yes" to God ("Let it be to me according to your word"), the process began and she was apparently left to walk through it without understanding everything.

Mary becomes a kind of "model" for the rest of us. She is given the honor of being the first believer, and all generations since have called her blessed. Hers was a walk of faith, however, from the beginning right up to the time when she beheld her Son hanging on the cross.

"Pondering them in her heart" seems to have been her technique for deeper understanding of what she was given to do or to be. Pondering our own lives "in our hearts" can be a good technique for deeper understanding of who we are and what God is asking of us. It means taking into account the various components of our lives, not evading or ignoring them, but plumbing the depths of what they can mean. We are not called just to behave well, to relate to others pleasantly, to "finesse" our various responsibilities. We are called to be growing, vital souls, persons who are fully alive to God and to those around us. Pondering in our hearts is not a way of escaping from relationships into some kind of introspection. Rather, it means requiring ourselves to feel the full ramifications of our decisions.

A friend came to talk about a situation in which he had hurt someone's feelings. When faced with his responsibility for the problem, he reacted (as most of us do) by feeling hurt and misunderstood. But as he talked about it, he "pondered in his heart" what had been said, and began to see that he had indeed done something that hurt another person. He moved deeper than his accustomed reaction, "I didn't mean it," to see that at some level he did mean it, though he did not realize it at the time. This is simply an example of how pondering things in our hearts (sometimes with the help of others, but always with the light of the Holy Spirit) can be a means of healthful change.

1. What is your response when someone hurts your feelings?

2. How have you dealt with your hurt in the past?


## DAY 7 • RIVERS OF LIVING WATER

Daily Reading: John 7:37-44

*He who believes in me, as the scripture says, "Out of his heart shall flow rivers of living water." (v. 38)*


Aha! So it is not just blackness, sin, and shame that can flow from this wellspring of our heart! There is something better that we can experience. These hearts of ours, so full of trickery and misinformation about what's going on, can also be reservoirs of that "living water" which comes from God.

And this is the thing we must always keep in mind. From that same inner source can come messages of truth and light, and messages of garbled untruth.

As we have been looking this week at the heart as "the wellspring" of life, it is important to hear what the Lord says. Taking his presence and power into our lives, seeking his help with the everyday, down-to-earth decisions we make, assures us, he says, of "living water" flowing out of our hearts. For what does it mean to "believe in him" if it does not mean this daily walk of faith, this daily fellowship in the practical issues we face?

Too much of our religious language and religious faith tends to be "up in the air." What we need is a solid connection with One who can help us in the daily struggle. It will not always be clear just what we should do. We have to make decisions without knowing absolutely that these are the right decisions, absolutely in line with God's perfect and holy will. But make them we must, and life moves on. The great thing about this "living water" picture is that life—flowing, free, abundant, life-giving life—is ours. So it doesn't matter what the struggle is, or how hard the task that is facing us, Jesus Christ in our hearts can make all the difference. Instead of dead, stale, death-dealing attitudes, he puts into us a different spirit, and that's what he means by "living water" flowing out of our hearts.

You cannot read the words of this text without associating them with the words of the psalmist: "He is like a tree planted by streams of water, that yields its fruit in its season, and its leaf does not wither. In all that he does, he prospers" (Psalm 1:3). The stream of water brings life-giving nourishment and refreshment to the favored tree. The "rivers of living water" which flow from the depths of our hearts bring renewal and hope. It is not a super-spiritual fantasy to recognize the truth of this text. Rather, it is an invitation to move on with the knowledge that something new has happened in us and will keep happening. It is life, and the One who says, "I am the life," abides in us, to give us continually new life.

1. Are you daily asking Jesus to change your heart? If you are, what have been some changes you have experienced as a result?

2. How are you responding to Jesus' invitation to move on with him? What does this mean to you?

# THE TROUBLED HEART

*Let not your
heart be
troubled, neither
let it be afraid.*

*John 14:27b*

## DAY 1 • LIFE IS DIFFICULT

Daily Reading: John 16:25-33

*In the world you have tribulation; but be of good cheer, I have overcome the world.*
*(v. 33b)*

A book by a well-known writer begins with these words: "'Life is difficult." At first this may sound like a trite and well-worn truism. But just think for a moment. Do we really expect life to be difficult, or are we constantly surprised and perhaps often discouraged when we run into its inevitable difficulties?

A friend said that just reading that sentence helped him, because it enabled him to begin to look at life from a different perspective. He could choose to give up his fantasy world in which he expected only blue skies, good sales reports, happy, trouble-free children, and a wife who did his every bidding. Instead, he could expect that in all these areas there would be difficulties.

Jesus was certainly in a position to be concerned for himself when these words were spoken. It was the very night of his arrest, and the day before his final agony that ended on the cross. It was a time of supreme crisis for him. Yet as we read these words, his real concern seems to be to prepare his disciples for what lay ahead of them. If they expected to go "from victory to victory" they were going to be disappointed. Some severe shocks and troubles lay ahead for every one of them. And so he is mindful of their need to face reality.

Our hearts are often troubled by these "tribulations." We take them wrongly. We take the tribulation or trial as a negative thing, instead of accepting it as a part of life. In choosing to be unrealistic about what to expect from life, we set ourselves up for much unnecessary inner conflict.

Since life involves suffering for us all, the question is, how shall we use the difficulties we confront? What shall we do with them? Shall we waste them in self-pity, self-indulgence, resentment and anger? Or shall we let them turn us to the real purpose and point of living? We have a choice.

Marcus Dods says, "Worldliness is the spirit which uses the present world without reference to the lasting and spiritual purposes for the sake of which men are in the world. It ignores what is eternal and what is spiritual; it is satisfied with present comfort, with what brings present pleasure, with what ministers to the beauty of this present life. . . . To each of us the question which determines all else is, Am I to live for ends which find their accomplishment in this present life, or for ends which are eternal? . . . We are, every one of us, living either with the world as our end or for God."

Jesus says we will have troubles. Life is difficult. But to what end are we using the difficulties? That is the question.

1. Have you learned more about God's provision and love from your successes or from your failures? Give an example.

2. Paul writes, "We glory in our tribulations." What is your experience of this concept?


## DAY 2 • THE OVERBURDENED HEART

Daily Reading: Luke 21:29-36

*But take heed to yourselves lest your hearts be weighed down with dissipation and drunkenness and cares of this life. . . . (v. 34)*

"And as for what fell among thorns, they are those who hear, but as they go on their way, they are choked by the cares and riches and pleasures of life, and their fruit does not mature" (Luke 8:14).

In both these texts from the Gospel of Luke, Jesus is talking about overburdened hearts. He sees them, not as an inevitable result of the pressures of life, but as a condition which we must "take heed" lest it happen to us.

Most of us would not view ourselves as greatly threatened by "dissipation and drunkenness"—not at least at this stage in our lives, when we have committed ourselves to Jesus Christ and are seeking to walk with him. But Jesus does not seem greatly to separate these deplorable conditions from the third category: the "cares of this life." These, we will have to admit, do a good bit of choking and weighing down of our hearts.

We are all more "cholesterol conscious" today than ever before. We may even have seen pictures on TV of heart operations, showing in graphic color what a heart "overburdened" with too much fat looks like. It is not a pretty sight. So we are warned, if we want to do what we can to maintain healthy hearts, to cooperate with "nature" in giving our hearts and circulatory systems what they need—and not more than they need. But that is not an easy order, if we have long-established habits of overburdening our hearts.

These are the "cares of this life"—the burdens we put on ourselves, on our souls and spirits, by carrying what only God can carry successfully. Since he is God, and since he is a loving God, he has said, "Come to me . . . all who labor and are heavy-laden," and he means to lift the too-heavy load from our hearts. If we refuse to hear and heed, our overburdened hearts will simply go on overworking—to their hurt and ours. Surely we can make better choices!

1. What burdens would you like to give to the Lord?

2. How might you start today to do that? Be as specific as you can.

## DAY 3 • UNHEALTHY RESENTMENTS

Daily Reading: Ecclesiastes 5:13-17

*What gain has he that toiled for the wind, and spent all his days in darkness and grief, in much vexation and sickness and resentment? (vv. 16b, 17)*

This little book of Ecclesiastes is something of a mystery. Most of us don't read it often, and may shake our heads at what we read. The author seems full of discouragement, and at times even sounds cynical. That is why when I ran across this little verse, I was so fascinated by it. For with all the wisdom the writer has gained in his many experiences he has come up with some profound insights into human nature and the folly of seeking wrong things. That seems to be the theme of the whole book.

Here in these verses he is talking about seeking riches and keeping them to one's own hurt. Remembering that "we brought nothing into the world, and can take nothing out of the world," he muses that it is the height of folly to strive after wind, the emptiness of false choices.

The heart of the matter for us is that "vexation, sickness, and resentment" seem to be clustered together, resulting from bad attitudes of the heart. Certainly we know enough about the psychosomatic make-up of our bodies to know that attitudes affect our health. And here is a hint—just a hint, I think, that the Preacher of this book saw those relationships quite clearly. The person described in these verses "had everything," so to speak. It was not the lack of blessing that caused him to live in such misery. It was the burden he was laying on himself with these bad attitudes. The person described here lived primarily for his own sake.

What we are learning in these weeks is that there are positive choices to fight against these negative impulses we all have. God in his great mercy has come to our aid, so that we are not left to "live in darkness with much vexation and sickness and resentment." We are called to a different level of life. We are meant to see the folly of thinking only of the pleasure of the moment. Yet we are also meant to appreciate and savor the joy of each new day. "This is the day the Lord has made; we will rejoice and be glad in it." We are meant to see the folly of striving to "leave something" for the children, who may even be harmed by our "good intentions" rather than helped by them. We are meant to deal with the hurts and wrongs of the past, learning to forgive others—and even ourselves—and learning our need to be forgiven. Erasing the "bill of resentments" we carry can be a way of lightening the heart. Surely we are meant to be a "light-hearted" people, a people who carry the Light in our hearts.

1. Have you experienced how a negative frame of mind can frustrate our appreciation of God's activity in our life?

2. While many freely accept Jesus' forgiveness, they find it difficult to forgive themselves. Has this been true of you? If so, why do you suppose it is so hard to forgive yourself?


## DAY 4 • TROUBLED ABOUT MANY THINGS

Daily Reading: Luke 10:38-42

*Jesus said, "Martha, Martha, you are anxious and troubled about many things. . . ."* (v. 41)

Martha's trouble was a lack of focus in her life. She loved Jesus, loved having him stop at her house, and wanted his visit to be a good experience for him. Yet in her lack of ability to distinguish between the important and the trivial, she lost her temper and complained to her Guest about her sister's failure to help her.

It is good to note that Jesus was very tender and compassionate with Martha. We know that he loved this family very much. In John 11:5, we read, "Now Jesus loved Martha and her sister and Lazarus." So when Martha came with her complaint, instead of supporting her, he pointed out a better choice. "Mary has chosen the good portion." He was saying, in effect, "Martha, you, too, could choose the good portion and save yourself a lot of worry."

Is that what he is saying to you and me in our busy, fractured lives? There are so many demands on most of us that we may find ourselves furiously running and never catching up. The image that comes to mind is that of a chase in a cartoon in which the character finally runs so fast he meets himself.

There is only one answer to this frantic, unfocused life. It is to learn and choose "the good portion." Are we living our lives willy-nilly, trying to survive "the rat race," and hardly knowing why—or are we living our lives for Jesus Christ, learning when to say yes and when to say no? The answer to that question can make all the difference.

Stress is a big worry today. It is especially deadly in the Western countries like the United States. Somehow the tranquillity that we read about (and sometimes sing about) escapes us, and the toll is sometimes very heavy indeed. Today's thought is intended to remind us that we have choices. We can choose a focused life, or drift into an unfocused one. Which will it be?

1. Is there a time of day when you feel particularly flustered? How might you embrace "the better part" of Mary's choice?

2. Distractions take our eyes off Jesus. What is it about distractions that make us concentrate on them rather than on the Lord?

## DAY 5 • A PROMISE TO ALL

Daily Reading: Matthew 5:1-12

*Blessed are those who mourn, for they shall be comforted. (v. 4)*

This is a great and positive word to everyone called to undergo grief and loss. Certainly on its most obvious "face value," it is a promise like one we read in other parts of the New Testament: that we do not have to grieve as those who have no hope. So the promise that we shall be comforted is reassuring to everyone who believes in Jesus Christ.

There is another, perhaps less obvious, meaning hidden here. We need to remember that the message of Jesus was the same as that of John the Baptist: "Repent, for the kingdom of heaven is at hand." His call to repentance meant that his hearers needed to change. In order to change, one must *want* to change, and in order to want to change, one must see where one is wrong. It is that simple and that logical. But when we begin to see (I mean *really* see) where we are wrong, we do not experience instant joy. Instead we feel grief. We cannot see and take responsibility for wrongness in ourselves without some feeling of pain and grief.

Here is where this verse seems to come alive with a helpful word. "Blessed" are they who feel such pain and grief, for comfort will be theirs! This is a word of cheer even when we are in the throes of woe. Who wants to look at how out of line we are with God's will? Who enjoys being told that her attitude is not right, or that he is making life difficult for his wife and children. Our first impulse is to get angry at the speaker. But if we allow the Holy Spirit, the Spirit of Truth, to get past our defenses, we will find a wonderful thing happens. It doesn't even matter whether our "truth teller" has all the facts correctly sorted out. The Holy Spirit can and will show us where we have been inwardly wrong, and will point us to Jesus, our Savior, who forgives "wrong ones," (also called "sinners").

When we read "Blessed are those who mourn" we can include the genuine grief and mourning we feel when we are convicted of our sin. "We are truly sorry and we humbly repent," we say in the prayer of General Confession. Rightly mourning who we are apart from God is a good and healthy thing for a Christian. And thanks be to God, "They shall be comforted." There is no shortage of grace and healing as over and over again we turn to the Healing One. He is our peace, and his comfort is balm for every wound. Yes, truly blessed are those who mourn for their sins, "for they shall be comforted!"

1. Have you ever felt *really* wrong? What did you do about it?

2. In what ways is it possible for an inner realization of our wrongness to lead us quickly to the Cross and God's forgiveness?

## DAY 6 • A GOAL TO BE SOUGHT: HEART-REST

Daily Reading: Hebrews 4:1-13

*So then, there remains a sabbath rest for the people of God. . . .(v. 9) Let us therefore strive to enter that rest . . . .(v. 11a)*

As we read this portion of Scripture, it seems at first glance that what is being talked about is a future rest that awaits all the faithful as the consummation of their journey. And certainly that is one legitimate meaning of these words. Just as God had led Israel out of Egyptian bondage in order to bring them into the Promised Land, so he leads us out of our old lives in order to lead us into that blessed future he has prepared for those who love him.

But there is a more immediate meaning here we ought not miss. That is the "heart-rest" which comes when we are at peace with God, with ourselves and with others. Conflicts are inevitable, because we are fallen creatures in a fallen world. The world is not in harmony with its Creator, and in truth we ourselves are not always in harmony with him. If we know ourselves at all, we know that at times we are not even in harmony with ourselves. So the image and attraction of "heart-rest" that awaits God's people spurs us on.

How do we experience heart-rest in a practical way? I believe it comes about as we become increasingly willing to look at the places we are out of harmony with God and with ourselves, and discover that genuine peace replaces conflict when we are in a state of repentance and grace. God's "Sabbath rest" is meant to be a renewal of our souls as we go on with our journey towards him.

Yet we are told that we should "strive" to enter that rest. For many of us, this is the striving: to see and accept our wrongness before God in place of our habitual self-justification. When we become convicted that our demands, feelings, and attitudes have not been holy, that is the time when the striving must begin. We must strive to let these things go, to abandon whatever God is asking us to abandon, and to accept his "heart-rest." This is not an even exchange, for we receive far more than we give up.

Our human condition is so bent on self-justification that it may take many, many experiences before we have a prolonged "sabbath rest." But that doesn't matter! As long as we know we're on the right road, headed in the right direction, it makes no difference how long the journey takes, does it?

1. Can you relate to the statement in today's meditation that we are often out of harmony with God and with ourselves? Note a few instances.

2. Today's text promises "a sabbath rest for the people of God." How might you "strive to enter that rest," beginning today? Be as specific as you can.

## DAY 7 • LET NOT YOUR HEARTS BE TROUBLED

Daily Reading: John 14:18-27

*Peace I leave with you, my peace I give unto you, not as the world gives, give I to you. Let not your hearts be troubled; neither let them be afraid. (v. 27)*

Yes, Jesus says that in the world we will have tribulation. Life is difficult. There are thorns on the rose, rocks in the road, and enemies who fight against our best interests. Some of those enemies (the very most dangerous of them) lurk within our own breasts.

The ingrained attitudes we take for granted, our instinctive impulse to be "right" in any conflict, our insatiable desire to have others think well of us, and our striving to prove that there is good reason for them to—these can bring burdens to the heart that are heavy indeed. Who has not felt them? Learning to "unburden" is one of life's most difficult tasks and one of its most exciting challenges. We have taken on the "discipline" of learning to lighten the burdens of the heart. If we succeed, our hearts will be lighter; we will find more abundant joy, and peace that passes understanding.

Is this peace worth the price? The price is sprinting forward with God—or walking courageously forward with him, or plodding if need be—through the sloughs of despond and discouragement, until we break out into some new clearing. But always, the price is facing forward with Jesus by faith.

There is no reason to enlist in such a program as this unless we believe that God has something good in store for us. There is no reason to deprive the flesh and the emotions of their demands unless by such deprivation we are seeking and finding a higher good. So Jesus gives us his assurance that, even in the midst of our difficulties and uncertainties, he is our peace. "Not as the world gives do I give you," he says. The world gives and takes away. The "peace" of the world is a sometime thing. Just when it looks as if there is a moment of peace, some new conflict arises. That's the world's way. The world has no lasting peace to offer, either to us personally or the nations of the earth. We may seek peace, long for it, and wonder why it doesn't come about. But the world cannot give lasting peace.

Jesus' peace does not exclude conflict. But in the conflict, beneath it and beyond it, there is a Presence and a Power which does not depend on circumstance. That is the peace the world cannot take away. When Jesus bids us, "Let not your hearts be troubled," he provides the means of unburdening our hearts and entering into his peace.

1. Where have you sacrificed for a higher good?

2. Have you experienced Jesus as your peace, as today's meditation states?

# THE BEST OF ROOMS

*In my Father's
house are many
rooms. . . .*

*John 14:2a*

## DAY 1 • OUR DIVINE GUEST

Daily Reading: Revelation 3:14-22

*Behold, I stand at the door and knock; if anyone hears my voice and opens the door, I will come in to him and eat with him, and he with me. (v. 20)*

The church in Laodicea was in trouble. Its problem was that it thought things were going well. So it had fallen into that dangerous state of *lukewarmness*, a state always threatening to undermine our commitments. There is only a step from lukewarmness to indifference.

In the midst of his message to that dying church, the Lord issues the timeless invitation that has been an inspiration to artists and poets over the centuries: "Behold, I stand at the door and knock."

We who bear Jesus' name and sign often keep him outside. We do not allow him full access to the seat of our affection and motivations. We keep back much of ourselves from him.

This week, as we look at the heart as a house of many rooms, let us be open to all the places where we are tempted to hold back on God. The searchlight of truth will help us, and we can make new beginnings.

In the great cathedral of St. Paul in London, Holman Hunt's famous "Light of the World" hangs in the south aisle of the nave. It is the picture of Jesus, wearing a kingly crown, with a brightly glowing lantern in his hand, knocking at a wooden door representing the human heart. It is shut tight with nails; its hinges are rusty; ivy grows freely over it.

> O shame, thrice shame upon us,
> To keep him standing there!

1. Is there a place in your life where you have not yet admitted the Lord?

2. What would happen if you opened the door today?

## DAY 2 • THE LIVING ROOM

Daily Reading: Ephesians 4:25-32

*Be kind to one another, tenderhearted, forgiving one another, as God in Christ forgave you. (v. 32)*

Thinking of the heart as a house of many rooms, we start at the front— the living room. This is the room most carefully cleaned up and readied for company, a room where we entertain our friends. Did you ever see one of those old-fashioned Victorian parlors? They were often kept closed, sometimes with the shades drawn. They were kept strictly for important visitors, and were not very comfortable rooms for anyone. Yet they were making a statement: Guests are important, and we want to offer you our best.

Nowadays we are more casual in our entertaining. The living room is furnished with more comfortable seats, and often contains the television set—meaning it is for everyday use as well as for guests. Yet it remains a center of our social life, where we receive and give support and where we enjoy the encouragement and fellowship of people we love.

Is Christ the center of our living room? By that I mean, is he pleased with what goes on there? Are we careful not to speak critically of others behind their backs? Gossip is a very appealing and temporarily enjoyable "sport" but it exacts a heavy price. This is why we are cautioned in the Scriptures, "Be kind to one another, tenderhearted, forgiving one another. . . ."

A friend recently told me of a very hurtful remark another friend had made to her several years ago. She was deeply offended, but thought she had forgiven the person. However, something happened to bring up some buried feelings, and she quoted to me what the other friend had said to her which had hurt her so deeply. I was offended for her, and joined her in her feeling of offendedness. A day or two later she came to me to say how wrong she had been to share that incident with me. She was convicted that she had "led me into sin," so to speak, by sharing her old hurt. I realized I was wrong, too, to listen and to agree against the third (absent) person. This is not an uncommon thing with Christians, but it is something we need to watch more carefully. We cannot have the love of Jesus for one another while we brood upon past wrongs and wounds. Jesus offers a better way.

"As God has forgiven you." That was Paul's measure of the degree of forgiveness we owe to others. And as we learn the secret of forgiving where we have been wronged, we welcome with open arms the Forgiver, who not only shows the way, but with his living Spirit makes forgiveness a present possibility.

1. What in your life do you hold more dear than the Lord?

2. Can you think of people you have not yet forgiven?

## DAY 3 • THE STUDY

Daily Reading: Proverbs 4:1-9

*The beginning of wisdom is this: Get wisdom, and whatever you get, get insight. (v. 7)*

There is an intriguing description of a certain mind set in the second letter to Timothy. Here are described people "who will listen to anybody and can never arrive at a knowledge of the truth" (2 Tim. 3:7).

In his book, *The Closing of the American Mind,* Alan Bloom says that every student arriving at a university today believes (or says he believes) that truth is relative. Recent polls indicate that a majority of us feels the same way.

All of this brings us to the place in the heart we might call "the study." Most homes are not equipped with a room with such a fancy title, but the name nonetheless indicates the part of us that learns, yearns for more knowledge, and seeks understanding and wisdom.

We are flooded on every side with information, misinformation, propaganda, and subtle seductive lessons that are directly contrary to what we believe as Christians. We are encouraged to believe that all truth is relative—true for me, but not for you! We are encouraged to believe the words, "after all, you're worth it"; "indulge yourself"; and so on. We are bombarded with thinly veiled pressure to begin accepting as normal behavior that which only a few decades ago was not even talked about in "polite society."

What are we doing to counteract this pressure? The world, coming into our "studies," the places we get our ideas, seeks to force us into its mold. While proclaiming "diversity" of this or that, it really seeks to press us into conformity with a single idea: nothing is absolutely right, and nothing is absolutely wrong. It's all a matter of taste and personal choice.

If we go into our study with Jesus as our teacher, we will get a different idea of life. He talked about the narrow gate, and the narrow road that leads to life. He warned that the broad way leads to destruction, and surely we see the fruit of that broad way all around us—some of it very close indeed.

Yet Wisdom is still available to those who seek it. Truth has not been destroyed. The Light still shines in the darkness. And the choice is ours. Will we seek God's truth, or be pressed into the world's mold?

1. In the face of today's prevailing relativity, what do you hold as absolute?

2. How can you nurture and maintain your knowledge of the truth, of what is right and wrong?

## DAY 4 • THE KITCHEN/DINING ROOM

Daily Reading: Matthew 5:1-11

*Blessed are those who hunger and thirst for righteousness, for they shall be filled. (v. 6)*

Is it true that the kitchen is the "heart of the house?" I suspect that most of us spend more hours there than in the living room. The kitchen is dedicated to the satisfying of the appetite. Together with the "dining area," it is where the appetite reigns.

What has this to do with the heart? In this "area" of the heart we find many appetites waiting to be satisfied. We find in the heart even those appetites we try to satisfy through eating. Emotions not only cause us to lose our appetites; they also cause us to gain appetites for what we do not physically need. Learning to identify and deal with these emotions can be a great challenge, if this is a problem for us.

And what has Jesus to do with such problems? Years ago someone wrote the question, "Does God care about what you eat?" I for one had never thought much about eating. It was an area where my will and my wishes had free reign, if possible! The story of the people of Israel in their forty-year trek through the desert shows God's fatherly care in feeding them manna. When they complained about having to eat the same thing all the time, he sent them quails, but they became sick when they glutted themselves, and many of them died. Food for Passover was carefully regulated in the Old Testament, and in the New Testament, it was food that Jesus used when he instituted the Lord's Supper. So if our problem is in the area of appetite for food, we can be sure that God does care, because he cares for us in every aspect of our lives.

Learning to be honest about our emotions rather than hiding or denying them is an important step toward maturity. This is not always an easy thing to do, especially if we have spent years convincing ourselves that we are "not angry," "not jealous," "not vindictive." It can come as a very freeing revelation to find that we are indeed what we had tried to deny. But that is only the beginning. Working through such emotions in a healthy way can mean talking about them and confessing them, asking the Lord to change our hearts. This is not a "once for all" thing, but something that we must do whenever the need arises, if we would be free of destructive appetites.

Other appetites demand fulfillment and have to be dealt with. There are appetites for place, for money, for "things," that will snuff out the life of the inner spirit if allowed to rule over us. Jesus stands ready to help us, assuring us all the while that his love is great enough to satisfy the deepest longings we have.

Yes, the kitchen/dining area of the heart is a busy place, and an important one. There used to be a motto found in many homes hanging over or near the dining room table. It read: "Christ is the head of this house, the unseen guest at every meal." May he always be so.

1. What do you hunger for that would make your life complete?

2. How can the Lord satisfy your desire?


## Day 5 • The Playroom/Den

Daily Reading: Philippians 4:4-9

*Whatever is true, honorable, just, pure, lovely, gracious—think on these things. (v. 8)*

"I want what I want." Yesterday we thought about the kitchen and dining areas of the heart. But today we look at another area where another demand may reign: the room where we expect to be entertained.

Some of the things we want do not fit the description Paul uses as models of thought. Our thoughts may be filled with jealousy or envy. The psalmist was aware that this was his condition. "I was envious when I saw the prosperity of the wicked" (Psalm 73:3). At other times we may lose ourselves in fantasy, identifying with some hero or heroine in such a way that we escape from the realities of our more humdrum life. The story of Walter Mitty showed a man who lived in total fantasy instead of reality. When we nurse hurt feelings, and secretly want to get even with another person, we are not thinking "gracious" thoughts.

And what of our "free time"? Some couples get into their most heated arguments over this very thing. If "he" feels that his time is free to do as he wishes, and "she" has the idea that it should be devoted to some undone chores, World War III may not be far behind!

It boils down to this: are we willing to allow Jesus Christ access to this room of our heart? Is our free time under his divine lordship? Are we seeking those things that edify, or are we too much given to things that give a temporary thrill or pleasure? These are not idle questions. Paul cautions us, "Shun youthful passions and aim at righteousness, faith, love, and peace, along with those who call upon the Lord from a pure heart" (2 Tim. 2:22).

1. Who determines what you do with your free time?

2. How would your spare hours be different if Jesus were in charge of them?

## DAY 6 • THE BEDROOM

Daily Reading: Matthew 11:25-30

*Come unto me, all who labor and are heavy laden, and I will give you rest. (v. 28)*

What a comforting word this is! When we are weary, tired, hurting, is there anything more inviting than our bed? There we can rest the weary body and refresh the weary mind—if we have admitted the Lord to this part of the heart

Much of our life is spent in toil of one kind or another. To be sure we do not have to work physically as hard as our ancestors. Modern life has taken much of the drudgery out of our existence, especially in the United States and other Western countries. It is harder for us to realize how merciful was the gift of the Sabbath to God's people of old. Their strenuous work was to be laid aside for this one day. Even the animals were given the day of rest. And the Sabbath gave to the whole week, and to all of life, a beneficial rhythm and tone. God gave his people rest.

What is there to disturb this gift of rest from the Lord? If we are cut off from fellowship with him, if we are at enmity with ourselves or with others, we may not experience the rest he wants to give us. Bad feelings are not conducive to peaceful nights. That is probably behind the counsel in Scripture, "Do not let the sun go down on your anger." Like so much of the Bible, the counsel is, above all, practical.

Are we tempted to use the bedroom as an escape from the place we should be? If so, we can depend on being stirred up, roused from our lethargy by the divine Spirit. He will not leave us to use his gifts as a way of avoiding the realities of life. A wise spiritual counselor used to say,

"True spirituality is *reality*." So we must never be lulled into using our faith as a way of escaping life. God will deal with whatever we have to face, and will give us the grace to face it in him. We can be absolutely sure of that because he has given us his word.

1. "God gives his people rest." What disturbs this gift for you?

2. "Do not let the sun go down on your anger." How might you follow this more closely in your life?


## DAY 7 • THE WHOLE HEART

Daily Reading: Psalm 119:1-16

*Blessed are those . . . who seek him with their whole heart. . . . (v. 2) With my whole heart I seek thee; let me not wander from thy commandments! (v. 10)*

We speak of people being "half-hearted" about certain things. We talk about having "a divided heart" on this or that subject. And what we are called to as children of God is to seek God with our whole heart.

Why do we hold back from this wholeheartedness? What is it that keeps us from throwing ourselves without reserve into our commitment to Jesus Christ? Is it not a lurking fear that if we give over "control" of our lives completely that we will miss something? Is it not a subtle doubt that we entertain that makes us want to keep our options open in case our faith turns out to be less than true? We think of Thomas, absent on that first Easter evening when Jesus came and stood among the disciples and showed them proofs that he was alive. They had been "half-hearted" in their commitment—witness Peter's denial. They were behind shut doors "for fear of the Jews." And why was Thomas absent? No explanation is given, but when they told him what had happened, he said, "Unless I see in his hands the print of the nails, and place my finger in the mark of the nails, and place my hand in his side, I will not believe" (John 20:25). We call him Doubting Thomas, and somehow take comfort that even one of the twelve who had been with Jesus in his earthly ministry doubted. When at last Thomas' faith was confirmed, and he cried out "My Lord and my God!" Jesus reminded him that the truly blessed are those who have not seen but have believed.

That little band of frightened, hidden disciples found their hearts transformed and filled with the boldness that led Peter and John to fearlessly proclaim Jesus' resurrection right in the Temple. Whatever halfheartedness they had had been there was gone. They now followed with their whole heart.

We need to ask the Lord what we need to make our hearts whole. Half obedience is no obedience. Half commitment is no commitment. We need to rid ourselves of the delusion that we can get by on half. Jesus gave us his whole heart, and he has the right to expect nothing less from us. It's a worthwhile goal to seek, and we should give neither God nor ourselves any peace until our hearts, like the psalmist's, are united, solid, whole in seeking him and his will for us.

1. Ask God to show you where you are not wholeheartedly given to him. Write down what he shows you.

2. What fear keeps you from being wholly committed?

# THE UNCOMMITTED HEART

*How long
will you halt
between two
options?*

*1 Kings 18:21*

WEEK FOUR

## DAY 1 • FALSE STARTS

Daily Reading: Matthew 13:1-9

*Other seeds fell on rocky ground, where they had not much soil, and immediately they sprang up, since they had no depth of soil. . . . (v. 5)*

Lack of commitment is nothing new. It has been around a long time. Our week's theme comes from Elijah's question to Israel when they could not make up their minds whether to be servants of the Lord or of Baal.

Jesus refers here to the same problem. How easy the gospel sounded! It was good news to the poor. It was a promise of everlasting life. It was the news of sin forgiven. Who wouldn't want to "sign on"?

But there was more to the contract. This was not a promise that we would be "carried through the skies on flowery beds of ease." This was a call to something far more serious. There are tough decisions to be made and real problems to deal with. God does not come as a fairy godmother with a magic wand to make everything wonderful. Rather, he calls us to walk a new way, a way that often brings struggle, even pain.

But the Good News of the gospel is still there, still unfolding, still more wonderful than we could have realized when we first heard it.

Why then, this lack of commitment? The Gospel says "they had no depth of soil"; "they had no root." This has to do with the inner decision that only we can make. Even God will not make it for us. He gives us that awesome privilege. We can either commit ourselves to "go the distance, or we can slack off and finally leave the struggle.

All this week we will be thinking about this double-mindedness in different ways. But we should be clear about one thing. We are not talking just about other people. We are talking about ourselves. We are thinking about those contradictory feelings, the uncertainties and doubts, and above all, the strong self-love that plagues everyone who dares to make a start with Jesus. This means, of course, a battle with our adversary, the devil. But most of all, it means a battle with our old nature, the nature that so wants everything to be easy!

What we can do, and what we *must* do if we are to be winners, is to say over and over again, "In spite of my weakness and failures, I believe. Lord, help my unbelief. I want to be faithful. Lord, help my unfaithfulness!"

1. Can you identify where you are double-minded about your commitment to the Lord?

2. How can he help you?

## Day 2 • A Tragic Choice

Daily Reading: Mark 10:17-27

*He went away sorrowful, for he had great possessions. (v. 22)*

We refer to this story as that of the Rich Young Ruler. The Gospel doesn't tell us what his age was, but, whoever he was, he had accumulated "great possessions."

We're talking about "uncommitted hearts" this week, and here is a story that clearly exposes this man's inner condition. He had tried very hard to "be good." He had "observed" all the commandments from his youth. But something still haunted him, because he had come to Jesus with the right question: "What must I do to inherit eternal life?" Jesus knew exactly where his problem lay, and it was his job to lay bare the condition to the man himself. So much of our trouble can stem from a lack of understanding our own hidden agendas and unrecognized motives. And so the answer to the man's question was put in terms he could understand. There was no theological discussion, no introducing of new concepts. Since the man was conscientious in observing the commandments, all that was needed was to get at the place where his heart was divided. "Sell what you have and give to the poor, and you will have treasure in heaven; and come, follow me."

That did it. This command touched the level of "uncommitment," and there was nothing for the young man to do but to decide to make the commitment (represented by giving away what he had), or go on his way, still anxious and still sorrowful. He chose the latter course.

We can be sure that as life goes on, Jesus will touch those areas where we still hold out. We cannot live on both sides of the bridge. We must choose, and then walk through the consequences of our choices. But every day we have the opportunity to make that choice. There is no easy, once-for-all commitment (although that is a good start). We still have to put one foot in front of the other to make the journey. Commitment. That's the word our heart needs to hear from the Lord. Today.

1. "He had great possessions." What do you hold on to that takes God's place?

2. What difference would relinquishing that thing you hold on to make to you in the next few days?

## DAY 3 • SOLOMON'S FOLLY

Daily Reading: 1 Kings 11:1-13

*And the Lord was angry with Solomon, because his heart had turned away from the Lord, the God of Israel, who had appeared to him twice. . . . (v. 9)*

Solomon is known as "the wisest man who ever lived." And there is no question that his wisdom was remarkable. In his day the Kingdom of Israel spread farther than it ever had before and Solomon's fame spread over the world.

It is touching to see how needy Solomon was before God when he first became king. His prayer on that occasion is a model for anyone who is undertaking a high office: "'I am but a little child; I do not know how to go out or come in. . . . Give thy servant therefore an understanding mind to govern thy people, that I may discern between good and evil. . . .'" God blessed that prayer, and gave Solomon the promise of great wisdom and a long life.

What happened then? The same thing that happens to us in our relationship with God. Solomon got his eyes on desirable goals—to build and enlarge his kingdom. He wanted peace, and one way that was accepted as normal was to marry daughters of neighboring rulers, thus uniting the interests of both kingdoms. And so the "diplomacy of marriage" began, and continued until he had 300 wives. He had chosen his own course to protect and enlarge his interests. In the process, his devotion to God had declined and diminished. The very God who had met him in his need, had given him greater wisdom than one could imagine, and had promised to be with him— this God was forgotten and neglected. Other altars were raised for one or another of his wives. Other gods were being served and worshipped.

Alas! Do we not always run the danger of doing the same thing? How easy it is, when we get caught up in our short-range goals, to substitute them for what we should be offering to God alone. We quickly serve other masters and put them between us and the true God, if we do not constantly watch our hearts.

Solomon's folly is not a pretty one to see, and he left a legacy that soon resulted in the splitting of the kingdom. But his story is a cautionary tale for every one of us as we walk the road with Jesus.

1. "You shall have no other gods before me" is the first commandment (Ex. 20:3). Can you identify people or desires you have put before God?

2. What choice have you made that is not God's choice for you? What would it cost you to give it up and choose what the Lord desires?

## DAY 4 • JUDAS' BETRAYAL

Daily Reading: John 13:21-30

*The disciples looked at one another, uncertain of whom he spoke. (v. 22)*

The betrayer was in their midst, but they did not know who he was. Judas has always been something of a mystery. People have tried to figure out what motivated him, and various theories have been advanced. But there is a lesson in Judas for us all.

First, it would seem clear that Judas did not join the band of disciples with the intention of betraying Jesus to his enemies. Whatever his motives were for joining himself to the group, there is no indication that betrayal was his goal. That is confirmed, also, by Judas' behavior after the crucifixion. He is quoted as saying, "I have betrayed innocent blood," and the fruit of his remorse is well known.

So what transpired between his enrollment as a disciple and this terrible hour when he went out into the darkness to lead the enemy to the One whom Judas called "Master"? Was it a step by step process by which his commitment to what Jesus was teaching and what Jesus' call demanded of him grew weaker and weaker, and his love of the world and what it might have to offer grew stronger? I think so.

In this we can see where we and Judas are not that different. Our motives certainly are not 100% pure (not even 99 and 44/100 per cent). Our expectations as Christians are often unrealistic, and we hear the "good" part of the message with all God promises. It is harder to hear the "hard" part—which means we have to engage in some basic and sometimes painful changes of attitude and behavior.

It is good to know that the disciples were so much in the dark about what might be in them that they sat at table and asked, "Lord, is it I?" We would do well to ask the same Lord to show us what is in us that could lead us to an unplanned and unwelcome betrayal of the One we love and wish to follow.

1. Can you imagine yourself in Judas' place?

2. Ask God to show you any places hwere you are divided, where you prefer a way that is not his. Jot them down.

## DAY 5 • WEAKNESS AND WAFFLING

Daily Readings: Romans 14:1 and 15:1-6

*As for the man who is weak in faith, welcome him, but not for disputes over opinions. (Romans 14:1) We who are strong ought to bear with the failings of the weak, and not to please ourselves. (Romans 15:1)*

Paul is dealing with a touchy situation in the young congregation in Rome. Some of the Christians there were still tied to their old patterns of observing certain days as holy, while others felt strongly that every day was the Lord's day, and was to be lived to him. You can see some of that divergence of opinion still existing in the churches, where some observe many "holy days" and others do not. Our Puritan forebears would not observe Christmas or Easter, but they did put heavy emphasis on the Sabbath observance (Sunday).

But the principle here is an important one. Many things come up to cause us to waver or waffle in our Christian walk. Differences of opinion are among those, and people have been badly hurt by fellow Christians who insisted that "unless you believe as I believe, you are less than 100% Christian!"

Someone came to my desk yesterday to check on a decision she and I had agreed on over a week ago. She had not changed her mind about it, but she had become "uncertain" as to whether things were sealed. It was obvious that it was very difficult for her to make up her mind and stick to her decision. So it is for many of us. Circumstances change, and we begin to wonder, "Was I right in that decision I made?" The mind can play strong tricks in getting us to waver in our commitment.

Paul's advice here is aimed at those who felt their way was right. They were the strong ones. And the temptation of the strong ones is to judge the wafflers, the weak ones. One way of dealing with that temptation is to remember the times we have failed, the times we have not lived up to our own resolves and best intentions, and to remember, as Paul says elsewhere, "Therefore let anyone who thinks that he stands take heed lest he fall" (1 Cor. 10:12).

1. Is there someone whose weaknesses and failings really bother you? What can you do to help rather than judge that person?

2. What is your attitude toward yourself when you fail?

## DAY 6 • A HEART APPEAL

Daily Reading: Romans 12:1-21
*I appeal to you therefore, brethren, by the mercies of God. . . . (v. 1a)*

I am impressed more and more by the "tone of voice" we sense as we read the Bible's call to us. This text today is a case in point. And those who set out on any path of discipline, with any kind of emphasis on obedience and faithfulness, need to be reminded of the ground on which discipline and obedience are based: the love and mercies of God. Much more than a command based on fear is the appeal from love. That, after all, is what we see at Calvary: "God so loved that he gave his only Son, that whoever believes in him should not perish but have everlasting life" (John 3:16).

Day follows day, and blessings come and go. How quickly we forget them or take them for granted! The prophet says, "I will mention the loving kindnesses of the Lord, according to all that the Lord hath bestowed on us, and the great goodness toward the house of Israel, which he hath bestowed on them according to his mercies, and according to the multitude of his lovingkindnesses" (Isa. 63:7 KJV). The psalmist joins him saying, "The Lord is gracious and full of compassion, slow to anger and of great mercy. The Lord is good to all, and his tender mercies are over all his works" (Psalm 145:8, 9).

Paul makes his appeal to the church at Rome on this firm basis. They are living in an unfriendly, even hostile world. The church had not been around 2,000 years, and had not yet spread itself across cultures and continents, so it had to be founded on something sure enough to stand Christians in good stead in their struggle against sin, self, and Satan. What was that sure foundation? God's infinite mercy, God's tender mercies shown in Jesus Christ. Knowing that they had been loved and favored to hear the gospel, those early Christians went out to face all kinds of hardship. Compared with them, our lives are embarrassingly easy—even with the problems we all have to face. But if our faith stands on that sure foundation, and we hear and heed the appeal "by the mercies of God" to present our bodies a living sacrifice, we are going to be able to "go the distance," and finish our race with gladness of heart.

1. Make a list of all the blessings you have received this week.

2. Find a psalm that expresses your gratitude and read it as a prayer.

## Day 7 • Commitment is Possible

Daily Reading: 2 Thessalonians 2:13-17

*But we are bound to give thanks for you, beloved by the Lord, because God chose you from the beginning to be saved. . . . (v. 13)*

We don't have to get into the question of who is chosen and who isn't. That is for people who have nothing better to do. We *do* have something better to do: to rejoice that God has chosen us from the beginning to be saved! The wonder of that should be enough to occupy us for several eternities. I love the lines from the great sixteenth-century English poet and priest George Herbert:

> Seven whole days, not one in seven,
> I will praise thee;
> In my heart, though not in heaven,
> I can raise thee.
> Small it is in this poor sort to enroll thee,
> E'en eternity's too short to extol thee.

The positive and hopeful thing here is to begin to realize that God is on our side, that he is for us and not against us. So many of us spend too much time bewailing and bemoaning what we are not that we forget to express our thankfulness for what we are. It is not to our credit or merit that we are beloved. It is because God is God; it is because God is merciful; it is because God is loving. He has set his heart on you, and does not want to see you "go to waste" so to speak. Whatever your problems in the past have been, he comes with a word of hope and cheer.

I remember the words of an elderly English minister years ago who was asked if he could sum up the Gospel in 25 words. With only a little hesitation he replied, "Yes. I think I can. It is this: You don't have to stay the way you are."

That was why Paul could rejoice over the Christians in Thessalonica. They had already begun to change, and would change even more. Commitment was possible. And still is.

1. When have you felt that God was against you?

2. Paul asks rhetorically, "Who shall separate us from the love of Christ?" (Rom. 8:35a). How do you respond to this?

# THE HUNGRY HEART

*Blessed are*
*they that hunger*
*and thirst after*
*righteousness,*
*for they shall*
*be filled.*

*Matthew 5:6*

## DAY 1 • THIRSTING FOR GOD

Daily Reading: Psalm 42

*My soul thirsts for God, for the living God. (v. 2)*

Yes, our hearts are hungry. It seems they are perpetually hungry. The psalmist expressed it in terms of thirst. He compared his soul with a "dry and thirsty land where no water is." So, whether we speak of it as a hungry longing or a dryness, we know what it is to feel unsatisfied inside, and that is a condition all too common with most of us.

Do we need to be reminded yet again that we have in us what has been termed a "God-shaped blank"? That we are made for God and that anything less than God will not ultimately "fill the bill"? Do we need to be reminded that we waste a lot of our lives seeking what cannot satisfy and what will leave us empty, even when we are physically full or overfull? Do we not yet know that?

Thank God for that hunger and thirst! Thank God that he will not let us be satisfied with anything less than himself. So we endure the pain, the ache, the emptiness, until it gets so strong that we cannot endure it. Then we begin to turn. It's the old, old story of the stubbornness of human nature, our headstrong insistence on trying everything but the one thing that works.

This week we're going to be exploring this strange mystery in a little more depth. The Bible gives us plenty of material for thinking about it, and the Holy Spirit will continue to stir up that hunger to make us more willing to make those decisions that have to be made, if we are to find the blessed fulfillment we seek.

Our souls do thirst for God. If it were not for that thirst, where would we be? Where indeed? We need only to think of the potential within every one of us, not only to stray, but to get completely lost. So it is with joy as well as with repentant sorrow that we come to this awareness a little more deeply than ever before.

1. "As a hart longs for flowing streams, so longs my soul for thee, O God" (Psalm 42:1). Have you experienced this in the past? Write a brief description of the situation.

2. What substitutes have you tried to use to satisfy this thirst?

## Day 2 • Ho, Everyone Who Thirsts

Daily Reading: Isaiah 55:1-13

*Why do you spend money for that which is not bread? and your labor for that which does not satisfy? (v. 2)*

The perennial question most of us ask ourselves (and the Lord) is this: Why don't we learn from our experience not to concentrate on "that which is not bread." What the Lord is asking is this: Why continue with these inverted priorities when we know the truth? Chasing rainbows is an empty, vain thing. And so is our preoccupation with pride, position, place, and the good opinion of others.

A discipline is intended to help free us from such pointless bondage. It is intended to help us get a clearer look at ourselves, at life—what it's all about—and at the loving, caring Savior who broods over us in his infinite mercy. He has so much more to offer us than any of us has experienced to this time. He said to us, "I am the bread of life. He who comes to me will never hunger." And what that says to me is that once we have tasted and seen that the Lord is gracious, our hearts can begin to find their satisfaction in him instead of in the gaudy toys life offers us.

Those of us who are parents can certainly agree that we would be grieved to see a child of ours wasting his or her life on pointless, self-defeating pursuits. We would probably do what we could to steer and guide the child into a better course. But the time comes when each child must make his or her own decision. The parent can no longer be "in charge." God in his infinite respect for his creation has refused to control us into making right decisions. He allows us to make wrong ones and learn from them. Yet you can hear the heart cry of the loving Creator when he says through the prophet, "Why? Why? Why?"

Reading this makes me want to make better choices. It stirs me to want to discern what my heart really needs, and to reach out for the food that satisfies.

1. What is there about lesser satisfactions than Jesus that makes them so attractive?

2. What is there about him that should make him the sole object of our desires?

245

## Day 3 • Thou Givest Them Their Food...

Daily Reading: Psalm 145

*The eyes of all wait upon thee; and thou givest them their food in due season.*
*(v. 15)*

Today's text is a testimony to the faithfulness of a faithful God. The psalmist looks over the world and sees the dependent neediness of all creation. "The eyes of all wait upon thee." We are dependent on so many things over which we have no control, and not only are we dependent, but all living creatures, too, "wait upon thee."

This is being written at a time when the United States is experiencing one of the most devastating floods in memory. Constant rains have dumped water into the midsection of our country, and the great Mississippi cannot contain and handle it all. People's homes, farms, and even whole towns are "at risk." "The eyes of all wait upon thee." We can be quite sure that in addition to trying to control the water levels behind the great dams with their computerized flood gates, those affected are sending up many prayers to the Lord to spare the land.

A testimony of the faithfulness of a faithful God! Even in times of emergencies which we cannot explain, we can go back to a verse like this: "Thou givest them their food in due season." This was what the psalmist observed, and his words brought a thankful response in his heart. "My mouth shall speak the praise of the Lord, and let all flesh bless his holy name for ever" (v. 21).

We would not be asked to trust and follow an unfaithful God. He has shown you and me in unforgettable ways that he has not forgotten us. He has come to our aid in trouble. He has placed in our hearts a hunger and thirst which only he can satisfy. He has revealed himself in Jesus as our caring, faithful Good Shepherd who lays down his life for his sheep. And so when the floods come and the waters of trouble rise, we can say, "He is my Rock! I shall not be moved." In other words, circumstances can strengthen and deepen our faith, even through the struggles and doubts that arise in our hearts. It is no "Pollyanna" faith that we are called to exercise, but one that will carry us through the darkest hours.

And so today, as we pause to meditate and contemplate, let us remember his many mercies and his great goodness. "I will extol thee, my God and King, and I will bless thy name for ever" (v. 1). Let us rehearse in our hearts some of the things that come to mind, and bless his name, thanking him for mercies past, and renewing our trust for all that is to come.

1. Where have you experienced the Lord's faithfulness?

2. Where do you still need to trust him?


## DAY 4 • WHAT THE PRODIGAL LEARNED

Daily Reading: Luke 15:11-24

*How many hired servants of my father have bread enough and to spare, and I perish with hunger! (v. 17)*

It wasn't until the prodigal "came to himself" that he was able to make this statement. Before that he was first eagerly, then desperately, trying to satisfy himself with food other than his father's bread.

It seemed to work at first. Have you known young people who decided to "throw over the traces" and live life as they wanted to live it, and watched as things seemed to go pretty well? You may have even tried that course yourself. That seems to be what Jesus was saying in this little parable. But after a time, things changed. For one thing the prodigal foolishly ran through his inheritance. He spent everything. "And he began to be in want." We've all heard the details of this story dramatized and told again and again. But we can say, knowing what we know, "Thank God for that want." That was the beginning of blessing.

The heart is a peculiar thing. It is fussy about what satisfies it. And you can keep feeding it all kinds of husks—entertainment, trips, shopping, social events, achievements—[you can fill in what comes to you]—and that fussy heart will still refuse to be satisfied! You can even stoop as low as the prodigal did, and begin to drink from the swill of swine—the perverse and shameful paths the world offers those who have been deluded by it. Still the heart refuses to be satisfied!

Has the revelation dawned for us? Is it dawning day by day? Have we allowed our souls to stray so far from the Father's house that we need to rise up and repeat the prodigal's words? Going to the Father is a daily thing. It requires a continuous decision or chain of decisions on our part to keep ourselves where we can enjoy the Father's hospitality. Straying like lost sheep or lost children only means that we will have to find our way back—with his help, of course. The difference between the Lost Sheep and the Lost Son is that the Father waited, respecting the decisions the son had made—the decisions we have made. He will help us see them in the light of truth and reality, but he will not force us to return. He wants us to come back because we *want* to return home.

Home is where we belong. In our Father's house. In his presence. Eating at his table, and finding joy in doing what he wants us to do. That is our created purpose. He will do his part and he waits for us to do ours. It's a wonderful plan that allows us to grow and mature as children of God.

1. Have you experienced life in "the far country"? What were the results?

2. What caused you to return to the Father?

## DAY 5 • NOTHING BUT THIS MANNA

Daily Reading: Numbers 11:4-15

*But now our soul is dried away: there is nothing at all beside this manna before our eyes. (v. 6)*

It would be easier to judge the Israelites for their ingratitude and forgetfulness if we did not realize how much like them we are! Think of their situation. They have been delivered from intolerable bondage in Egypt, slavery which had grown increasingly severe and unmerciful. Their cries for deliverance had been answered. They had seen the Egyptians suffer God's just punishment through the plagues that had come upon them. Then they had marched "dry foot" through the Red Sea toward the land God had promised to their forefathers. The land through which they had to go was desert-like, and they had to protect their cattle and carry seed for the planting of crops when they arrived at their destination. So their food supply was severely limited. Then God showed them the "manna" which he had provided for their sustenance. They would not starve, for God would give them bread from heaven. Day by day they could gather enough for the day, and that would keep them going.

Human nature is a strange thing, isn't it? We so quickly forget past blessings and hanker for things better or different. The sad thing is that we often despise the very gifts God is giving us day by day to sustain our life.

How is your gratitude quotient this week? Do you remember to thank God for the privilege of prayer, for the gift of praise? Or do you find that you get a little bored with the whole thing? Are you keeping alive the sense of wonder that God loves you, cares for you personally, and allowing that knowledge to flood your soul—or are you hankering for a little more praise, a little more attention from [you supply the name here]? These are ways we turn our backs on the blessing and long again for the bondage of the past.

It would not have taken the Israelites many days or hours, had they returned to Egypt, to become aware again of what God was doing for them. And if we, in our perversity, turn away from the path in which God is leading us toward freedom, we will fall back into the old destructive patterns and relationships of the past.

Today, we can choose not to complain about the "manna," but be grateful for our "daily bread" which our loving Father supplies on our journey.

1. Where have your blessings grown commonplace? Which of God's gifts do you take for granted?

2. Write a prayer of gratitude for the favors he has bestowed upon you.


## DAY 6 • LEARNING TO BE CONTENT

Daily Reading: Philippians 4:10-20
*I have learned. . . . (v. 11) But I have all, and abound; I am full. . . . (v. 18)*

Here is a great example and a strong encouragement for every one of us! Paul is writing from prison. His very life is at risk, and according to Christian tradition, he was eventually martyred in Rome. Every glimpse we have of his life indicates sacrifice, conflict and suffering. Yet from his words we glean some of our greatest comfort and solace in grief and some of the strongest words of encouragement ever written. Here are three little clauses that sum up the secret of his life:

"I have learned. . . ." You can go through life and fail to learn from it. I have known people who reached well into middle age (even into old age) who had never learned that God is good, that his mercy endures for ever. And so they lived in unease and fear of the future. Life is a great teacher. It brings us many things we don't like, things we'd rather avoid. We may do everything we can to avoid them, and still they come. Do we use them or waste them? Paul says, "I have learned in whatever state I am to be content." That's a goal worth seeking. Most of us could not say we have arrived at that point yet, but by God's grace, we're still learning.

"I have all, and abound." The secret of contentment is not in having more, but in learning to enjoy what we have. Years ago I had a friend who had composed a number of anthems (mostly for children's choirs), which had been published by a well-known music publisher. She was speaking to a small group one day about her compositions, and said, "I have enjoyed a modest talent, and it has given me much satisfaction." She did not over-rate her talent as a composer, but neither did she despise it. I have known other people who hid their talents under a bushel, because they feared they would not be acceptable. Paul says, "I have all, and abound." He had learned to make the best of what he had. And with God's help, we can all emulate his example. Most of us will live on modest incomes the rest of our lives. At times, they may seem less than modest! But if there is a spirit of contentment in our hearts, our life will "abound." The key lies inside, not in outward things. Some of the most "frazzled" and uneasy people I have ever known were people who had much wealth.

"I am full." He was often "empty" in a physical sense. In other places he is quite frank in describing his life. "In weariness and painfulness, in watchings often, in hunger and thirst, in fastings often, in cold and naked-ness" (2 Cor. 11:27). But now he says, "I am full." Why? Because his inner satisfaction did not depend solely on outward circumstances. I'm sure he didn't enjoy being hungry and cold. But God gave him grace to endure it and come out the better for it.

Whatever deprivation you or I are asked to face in this life, God intends it for good. Jesus said, "I have come that they may have life and have it in abundance." There's nothing measly or stingy about the way he deals with us.

1. Describe a difficult time you benefited from and another you did not profit by.

2. What made the difference?

## DAY 7 • THEY SHALL BE SATISFIED

Daily Reading: Jeremiah 31:7-14

*My people shall be satisfied with my goodness, says the Lord. (v. 14)*

We have been thinking this week about the former condition of God's people, when they were not satisfied with his goodness. And we have been thinking, not only of the way things were in these Old Testament times with those people long ago, but of our own tendency to make little of the things of God and much of the things of this world.

Now we come to this remarkable vision of the prophet Jeremiah, in which he sees God's people "coming back." "Behold, I will bring them from the north country, and gather them from the farthest parts of the earth . . . a great company they will return here" (verse 8). On one level of inspiration this can be read as a prediction made ahead of time about when God would bring Israel back from its captivity. That, we know, took place about 70 years after Jeremiah had spoken these words.

There is another level, however, in which we can see the truth being spoken here. Our "return" is much like that of the prodigal in the parable of Jesus. Our captivities have been to the seductions of the world, the flesh and the devil. We have been in bondage to the unresolved conflicts and rebellions of our own natures, and at some point, we begin that painful, difficult, but joyful return.

It is remarkable to me how many times the New Testament speaks of the spiritual satisfaction and peace which God offers us through Jesus. It is no wonder that gospel song writers, in the blush and excitement of God's goodness, have written words that do not fit easily in the mouths of most Christian congregations and have become almost embarrassing to sing. In my own quiet time recently, I found the words of that old song, "In the Garden," come to mind, and smiled when I realized how many times I had sung the words with no real appreciation or understanding of what the author was trying to describe. But these words of the Bible are not meant to be a short-cut to some "happy" but unreal state of mind. They are not meant to lead us out of facing ourselves and our situations honestly. Spirituality is not an escape from reality. But they are meant to encourage us. God intends us to be satisfied with his goodness. He is leading us toward that goal. We shall be satisfied with his goodness—if we persevere!

1. Our bondages to "the world, the flesh and the devil" are usually specific actions or attitudes we can identify. Can you identify any? Jot them down.

2. The way to freedom from such captivity needs to be just as specific. How can you free yourself from each of these entanglements?

# A WANDERING HEART

*The righteous
man is like a tree
planted by
streams of water.*

Psalm 1:3a

## DAY 1 • THE PERENNIAL HEART PROBLEM

Daily Reading: Romans 7:14-25

*I do not understand my own actions. For I do not do what I want, but I do the very thing I hate. (v. 15)*

I have a heart problem. You have a heart problem. Would that it were not so, but it is. That is reality! And part of my problem and yours is that often we do not understand our own hearts. We are in conflict between what we know we should want and what we actually want. We are in conflict between what we know to be right and what we do. That is the universal condition of the human heart.

"Now, if I were God. . . ." I can almost hear someone saying, "I would change all that and give people different hearts, new hearts." To which two things can be said:

First, God respects what he has created—a race of people with an awesome amount of freedom. It is not total freedom, but it is real. That means we can choose a course of action that is in keeping with God's loving will and purpose, or we can choose against it. He did not create us to be automatons or robots, capable only of doing what the Creator willed. It would reduce our humanity to a sham if he took away the gift of freedom.

Second, all choices have consequences, and we are living with the fruit of the "forbidden fruit" we read about in Genesis 3. The "forbidden fruit" was disobedience, going against the loving will of God for his creation. But once the choice was made, it led to a condition with which the race has lived ever since. God had told his children, "You will surely die." And when Adam and Eve made that fatal choice, something died; the situation altered, and confusion came into the picture. "I do not understand my own actions," could be the universal complaint ever since.

But there is a third thing to be said here: God is giving us "new hearts." He is enlightening our darkness. He is encouraging us to make right choices and giving us grace to do so, even when we do not understand how it all works. Paul says, "I thank God through Jesus Christ." That, he had found, delivered him from the despair his own heart problem caused. And the same Jesus is working in and with you and me today. He is at work on our heart problem.

1. Paul writes, "I do not understand my own actions. For I do not do what I want but I do the very thing I hate" (Romans 7:15). Can you identify with Paul's experience? Give an example.

2. Note also the part you played in the turnabout from good to ill.


## DAY 2 • PRONE TO WANDER, LORD I FEEL IT

Daily Reading: 1 Cor. 10:1-13

*Therefore let anyone who thinks that he stands take heed lest he fall. No temptation has overtaken you that is not common to man. (vv. 12, 13a)*

We saw yesterday how Paul recognized that there were motivations and drives in himself that he did not fully understand, just as there are in all of us. Here he warns the Corinthians and warns us not to get too confident in our spiritual self-appraisal. The Corinthians were notoriously apt to overrate themselves, and some of them fell into the grossest sins.

A healthy self-doubt seems to be an important element in our spiritual walk. Too much self-confidence leads to an obnoxious self-righteousness. A little skepticism about what lurks in the murky depths of one's soul can be a useful antidote to that spiritual pride which is the first of the Deadly Sins.

What to do about all this? God has provided the remedy—the way of escape from these tugs and pulls which plague us all. Anyone who has attempted a discipline of any kind knows how subtle but powerful these temptations can be to give in and give up. Knowing the trickiness of the heart, its proneness to be enticed, is a healthy and useful bit of self-knowledge that can make us more ready to call on the Lord for what he alone can give.

1. What differences do you see between the "healthy self-doubt" mentioned in the meditation today and a habitual putting down of oneself?

2. What are the benefits of maintaining a distrust of one's own motives and drives?

## Day 3 • A Delight to the Eyes

Daily Reading: Genesis 3:1-13

*When the woman saw that the tree. . . was a delight to the eyes. . . . (v. 6)*

Let's talk about the heart problem of temptation. What is it that makes temptation so temptable?

First: Temptation has to be geared into its potential market. Whenever people want to sell something, it is the style nowadays to test the market—find out who may be willing to buy and use the product or service they have to offer. So temptation had its "market test" right there in the garden of Eden. The garden of Eden was a perfect place. It sounds like the place we'd all like to retire to or live in. Everything needful was provided. It was beautiful, and all that one could wish for was offered freely.

But wait—there were some restrictions. There was one tree which was "off limits," and strictly forbidden. And so the marketer (if we can call the tempter by that name) decided to point out the desirable qualities of that forbidden tree. Among other things, "it was delightful to the eyes." Human nature, even before the Fall, was temptable. And here the "delight" obscured the dark warning that "in the day you eat of it you shall die" (chapter 2:17).

The tempter still operates on the same principle: make sure the temptation is "a delight to the eyes." That means not only the physical eyes, but even more important, the inward imagination. Who can say how many enticements begin in the imagination with no outward, physical image at all! But the dazzling delight which appears, the immediate satisfaction which is promised, obscures the price to be exacted. Alas! since this Eden scene, it has been all the easier for us children of Eve to buy the enticement of the marketer. He has studied his potential customers well, and has had all too much success.

There is, however, an answer to this contemptible strategy of temptation. Knowing ourselves better, knowing something of the power of Jesus Christ in helping us resist the blandishments of Satan and the pull of our lower nature, we can flee to him for help. We can resist him in the strength of the truth that sets us free. Not every encounter will be victorious, but we can count on God's most certain aid, and we can overcome.

1. Can you discern areas where you are easily tempted?

2. How might you successfully *resist* the tempter in each instance?

## DAY 4 • BUT WHEN HE CAME TO HIMSELF

Daily Reading: Luke 15:11-24

*But when he came to himself he said, "How many of my father's hired servants have bread enough and to spare, but I perish here with hunger! I will arise and go to my father. . . ." (vv. 17, 18a)*

There is always a "coming to oneself." After we choose to wander into the far country of disobedience, after we listen, spellbound, to the tempter's blandishments, after we buy his lies and his suggestions and follow them, we always, *always* find that we have been cheated. Rather, we might say, we find that we have cheated ourselves! We "come to ourselves" and remember who we are. We remember that we had set out on a different course, that we had planned to live our life a different way. And now we are back, like the prodigal—can we say, feeding on pig's food? What does that mean but that we have stepped into a path of self-hate and defeat, that we are living at a level below that which we were meant to live, and able to live?

Yes, there is that awful moment of guilt—perhaps more than a moment, when we realize what we have done. Peter had such a moment when the cock crowed and he remembered Jesus' prediction about his denial. Peter went out and wept bitterly. Sometimes that is a good step: to look squarely at where we are and let tears flow! Judas also had that moment, but did not let it turn him to good. He said, "I have betrayed innocent blood," but instead of repenting, he chose another way to try to get rid of the pain. The burden of our sins, as the prayer book says, "is intolerable."

In truth, the burden of them is a gift of God. If we could go on without these awakenings and depressing feelings about our disobediences, we could find ourselves in irreparable ruin. But in God's mercy, as we become sad, afraid, and anxious, we are more ready to return and find God's answer to our needs. And so, even the burden is a gift! If we can begin to look at it in this way, we are, as they say, "more than halfway there." Remember that the Father in Jesus' parable, while the son was yet a great way off, went out to meet him. He is no less willing to meet us as soon as our hearts turn back in genuine desire to return to our true home.

1. Jesus said, "Come unto me, all who labor and are heavy laden, and I will give you rest" (Matt. 11:28). Can you recall a time when you laid down an intolerable weight of disobedience by accepting his yoke?

2. Is there any area of your life today where you need to give up the burden of your own way and find again the rest that comes in doing the Lord's will?

## DAY 5 • FINDING OUR WAY BACK

Daily Reading: Jeremiah 3:21-25

*Return, O faithless sons, I will heal your faithlessness. Behold we come to thee; for thou art the Lord our God. (v. 22)*

It would be wonderful if such a verse as this did not need to be written to God's people. It would be wonderful if we did not need such an invitation. As a matter of fact, it is such a wonderful idea that some people have convinced themselves that they are exempt from any such invitation. Spiritual delusion is always a temptation for those who want to love God with all their heart mind, soul and strength. The only problem is that when we think we are there, it is (certainly for most of us, if not all of us) a delusion. One thinks of the emperor's new clothes, in which he convinced himself (with the aid of the tricky tailors) that he was clothed in the finest garments human beings could imagine. It took the honesty of a little boy to cry out, "The emperor has no clothes on!" before the people were brave enough to begin laughing at the foolish emperor.

If the testimony of the saints of the ages means anything, it is that the closer we draw to God, the more we are aware of our own backsliding and the distance we still have to go in our spiritual journey. It is not the saint but the Pharisee who is convinced that he has few if any flaws that need correcting.

Having said that, it is doubly important that we hear the gracious word the Father speaks to us. "Return." Ask yourself, "What does it mean to me, today, to hear that word? From what 'far country' do I need to turn and make my way back? Is it from some long-held grudge against someone? Is it some hurt that I have not been willing to give up? Am I perhaps even blaming God for something in my life that doesn't change?" Whatever it is in your life, the invitation is coupled with a promise: "I will heal your faithlessness."

If we allow that part of our heart to be "healed," the part that pulls away into a kind of self-imposed prison, we can look at the negative aspects of our lives without fear of condemnation. God is in the business of helping, healing, and welcoming us into further growth and closer communion with him. He is not interested in condemning us or turning us away.

1. Are you in the "far country" in any sense today?

2. If so, what would be the first step home?

## DAY 6 • GUARDED AND GUIDED

Daily Reading: Exodus 14:19-29

*Then the angel of God who went before the host of Israel moved and went behind them; and the pillar of cloud moved from before them and stood behind them, coming between the host of Egypt and the host of Israel. (vv. 19, 20a)*

There is no greater picture of God's majestic and trustworthy care of his people than this. The Israelites were fleeing from their overlords, and one can only imagine what would have happened to them if their flight had not been successful! It is important to think of this, not in terms of our knowing the end of the story and all that, but in terms of how it must have felt for them. They were moving out in faith on the basis of what Moses had told them and because their life was so intolerable.

And that is what makes this picture so relevant to our lives. We are, alas, a people of puny faith! Our loyalty wavers, and our resolve weakens. This is the common lot of most of us. Now and then a Moses arises who can give a crystal clear call for us to move forward in greater faith, but most of us find that we are easily discouraged and tempted to turn back from time to time.

There is a good lesson to be learned here. Turning back was more dangerous than moving on! The known enemy behind was more dangerous than the unknown enemy that awaited them. And is that not true of us, as we move forward in our spiritual walk? No matter what may lie ahead, if we really think about what it was like before we were apprehended by the grace and love of God, do we want to go back? God uses not only the attraction of the promised life to which we are moving. He also uses the whips and pain of our old slave condition to motivate us to leave our Egypts behind and venture toward his promised land. In terms of this earthly pilgrimage, it is a call to move to maturity, to a more consistent and faithful discipleship. Jesus calls us out of our self-motivated prisons into the wider freedom of his plan for us.

How are we guarded and guided in this? The Israelites saw the cloud and pillar leading them forward, and then standing between them and their enemies when it was time to pause. In both cases it was the divine presence, the protecting power of God that stood between them and any danger. And we have the assurance that if we follow Jesus according to the light and truth we have, we shall be kept safe from harm. That does not mean that we will be protected from all pain, trouble or care. Those things are a part of life, and he will use them. But we will be kept from harm, because he is faithful who promised. We are his, and even with our unsteady, prone-to-stray hearts, that faithfulness is sure.

1. Where have you experienced the faithfulness of God in seemingly impossible situations?

2. Do those recollections give you any hope about his ability to handle the difficulties you see looming in the future?

## DAY 7 • THE ETERNAL PROMISE

Daily Reading: Isaiah 55:6-13

*Let the wicked forsake this ways, and the unrighteous man his thoughts; let him return to the Lord that he may have mercy on him, and to our God, for he will abundantly pardon. (v. 7)*

What a comfort it is to know that in spite of our wandering hearts, the Lord does not waver or wander in his care for us! Here the prophet is addressing a whole nation that has gone astray, seeking pleasure and profit, letting self-interest lead them into spiritual dead ends. The word of the Lord came to the prophet to warn that their ways could only lead to further suffering. In the earlier verses of this chapter he says, "Why do you spend your money for that which is not bread, and your labor for that which does not satisfy?" That is a question that can be put to us, over and over again, because it is so easy to be led astray by our own desires!

The first place to "return" to the Lord is in our thoughts. When we allow our minds and feelings to harbor ill feelings of hurt or resentment, it is "the easiest thing in the world" to decide to make up to ourselves. So the place to begin our return (when we find we have gotten off course) is in our thoughts. "Let the unrighteous man forsake his thoughts," is another way of looking at this verse. Are we "right" in our thoughts and feelings? Of course, we feel we are right, especially when someone confronts us with the possibility that we are wrong. But if we take this invitation of the prophet seriously, we will soon find that we are harboring unhealthy, wrong, "unrighteous" thoughts and feelings. Then—*then*—we can move on to the next phrase in this wonderful verse.

The eternal invitation is this: "Let him return to the Lord, that he may have mercy on him." It sounds as though our willingness to return is all that it takes to invoke and "activate" the mercy God has in store for us. There is no indication of any unwillingness on his part—just a waiting for our willingness, so that '"he may have mercy" on us.

"O Jesus, thou art standing outside the fast-closed door, In lowly patience waiting to pass the threshold o'er." Can you see how this invitation applies to your life and mine, and how wonderful it is that, in spite of our wayward hearts, he still waits to be gracious to us?

1. Which thoughts do you need to forsake? Jot them down.

2. Paul says we need to "take every thought captive to obey Christ" (2 Cor. 10:5b). How might you do this?

# THE BROKEN HEART

*Out of the
depths I cry to
thee, O Lord!
Lord, hear my
voice!*

Psalm 130:1

## DAY 1 • WHY HEARTS BREAK

Daily Reading: Psalm 42

*All thy waves and billows have gone over me. (v. 7)*

It is clear that the psalmist who composed Psalm 42 knew what it is to have a broken heart. We catch the spirit of his lament very early when he says, "My tears have been my food day and night" (v. 3a). We do not know exactly what the occasion was, but there are references here to voices taunting the believer, "Where is your God?" and taking pleasure in the difficult time he was facing. In verse 9 he says, "Why go I mourning because of the oppression of the enemy?"

Why do hearts break? Sometimes our hearts are broken by things people do to us or say to us. They may intend to hurt us, or their action may not be intentional. But in either case, something comes from others that deeply wounds our spirits. Unkind words, slights, insults—all these can contribute to the broken heart. The broken heart may come from someone very close, a relationship that has been severed with much pain. Our "love songs" are full of such feelings, and many people find a kind of solace in hearing them sung.

Why do hearts break? Because our plans and dreams and wishes sometimes come crashing to the ground, and we feel helpless to do anything about it. Because people we love are in distress and we can do nothing to relieve them. There are many, many things that can break a heart.

As we look this week at this aspect of our feelings and our inner life, it may be something of an encouragement for you to remember that we are not alone in experiencing these heartbreaking times.

The lesson to be learned over and over again—possibly the most important and hardest lesson of our lives—is to find what God is saying and doing in these circumstances. If he has allowed them, he intends them for good. If our hearts break over circumstances we cannot control, we know that he has not lost control and can use everything for good. This is not to make light of the pain, but an invitation to us not to let the pain drive and control us. God is still God. That is what the psalmist was saying. "Hope in God . . ." beyond the heartbreak, beyond the pain. We can hold on to what we already know of his love and mercy, so that when all his waves and billows go over us, we shall not be drowned. So we can look up, even through our tears, and see the sunlight of his love.

1. Recollect when your heart has been broken in the past.

2. What did you discover God doing in and through these painful experiences?

## Day 2 • Why Hearts Break II

Daily Reading: Psalm 32

*When I declared not my sin, my body wasted away through my groaning all day long. For day and night thy hand was heavy upon me. (v. 3, 4a)*

Yesterday we thought about the many outward things that can happen to us that break our hearts. Today we are invited to think about the inward things that can cause heartbreak.

In this 32nd Psalm the psalmist describes, as nothing else in the Bible does, what happens when we do not deal with our sin. Holding it in, not dealing with it, allowing the conscious or unconscious guilt to harden inside, results in the condition described here: "day and night thy hand was heavy upon me." That sounds like a low-level depression that refuses to go away. There is a phrase in the General Confession of the old Book of Common Prayer which reflects the same thought. Referring to our sins, the prayer says, "The remembrance of them is grievous unto us; the burden of them is intolerable."

It is this intolerable quality that breaks our hearts. When we have run out of excuses for what we have said or done, run out of excuses for who we are, it is "heartbreaking." Pride and honor "crack open" from the strain. This is not a bad thing, however, for it is the process by which God seeks entry. We must remember that he heals the broken in heart. And when hearts break from the burden of their own faults and failures, he is just as ready to heal them as when they break from outward pressures and sorrows.

As we meditate on this, think of the times when you have experienced what the psalmist is talking about. As painful as those times may have been, did he not compass you with deliverance as he did to the psalmist? (verse 7). After all, our psalm begins with the affirmation, "Blessed is the man [or woman] whose transgression is forgiven, whose sin is covered." So from the beginning, we are talking about a God who blesses, who deals with us in mercy and love, who is mindful of our needs, and is prepared to meet them. We are indeed a blessed people!

The alternative to allowing this heartbreak to occur is to become increasingly hard, bitter, and full of self-justification. I have known enough people who took that route to make me want to avoid it if at all possible! As one grows older, what has been hidden under various forms of disguise often become more visible, and it is not always a pretty picture. An oversensitive, cranky, argumentative old person is hardly a model we want to copy! And so God offers us this painful but healing process: facing up to what we need to face, letting the searchlight of truth penetrate whatever darkness or delusion lurks in our hearts and thoughts, and allowing the heartbreaking truth to confront us that we need forgiveness in some specific place. That is the healing process that the psalmist, who was none other than David himself, referred to.

1. When have you experienced the intolerable pressure of sin not dealt with?

2. Are you currently in such a state of mind? If so, how might you open your heart to allow the Lord to forgive and change you?

## Day 3 • Help is Near

Daily Reading: Psalm 34
*The Lord is near to the broken-hearted, and saves the crushed in spirit. (v. 18)*

We thought about why hearts break. The good news is that it doesn't really matter why or how they are broken—help is still near! Whether our crushed spirit is from the outside or the inside is not the issue. The great point here in this psalm is that God is near and that the Lord is ready to deliver us out of our afflictions.

Why go over such familiar ground as this? Don't we all, after all, know that God loves and cares for us—in our unacceptability as well as our victories? The answer is, no, we do not know that! We have heard it, have partially believed it, and may have found real joy in it. After all, every time we feel the miracle of sin forgiven, we know that God's love and grace are greater than our faults. Yet, being who we are, we need to be reminded over and over again that God truly cares, and that his help is near.

Help is near when we need it. We do not have to wait to prove we are worthy of it, because as a matter of fact, we are not. We do not have to wait until the situation becomes so desperate that we cannot think of anywhere else to turn. Afflictions are meant to turn us to the source of life, not into ourselves. Discouragement should be only for a brief moment, to remind us that only in God can we find the way out.

The key to finding God's help is our willingness to accept it. Here is where our big battles are fought, because it does not always come like a "Christmas-wrapped package." Sometimes his help requires that we face things about ourselves we would rather not look at. Sometimes his help requires us to make efforts against our habits and against our nature that we would just as soon not make. But he never fails to help us when we really want and need it. "When the righteous cry for help, the Lord hears. . . " (v. 17).

1. This meditation declares we may actually not want the Lord's intervention in our lives. Have you had that experience?

2. If you feel that way today, what changes would be required of you if you admitted him?

## DAY 4 • NEW LIFE AND NEW HOPE

Daily Reading: Isaiah 57:14-21

*I dwell in the high and holy place, and also with him who is of a contrite and humble spirit, to revive the Spirit of the humble and to revive the heart of the contrite. (v. 15b)*

Let's make no mistake about it. God's interest in us is "new life and new hope." The entire Bible is a record of his loving concern for his creation, and his saving plan to reach those who will respond to his love.

It is not only for heaven and the world to come that God's concern reaches. Heaven is important, and not to be overlooked as our desired goal. A book written by a Christian philosophy teacher several years ago summed it up in its title: *Heaven, the Heart's Deepest Longing*. So looking at the way God's concern is involved with our daily life, we must not forget that this life is a preparation for the true fulfillment God plans for his children. It is also true that everything we achieve in this life is, in a sense, temporary and incomplete. No matter how hard we try, there will always be flaws, since perfection exists only in God. Even in our best efforts, we know that there are places where we let down or miss the mark in some way, little or great. So we have to be prepared to deal with this reality.

Nevertheless, we are called to "new life and new hope." We are called to know what it is to embrace "newness" as a gift from God. Since we believe that God is offering us new life and new hope, the only thing that could prevent our experiencing it would be our refusal to embrace it. I use the term "embrace" deliberately, because it carries the meaning of drawing something or someone close, and it even has an element of daring in it. We become vulnerable to what we embrace. We expose our weakness, our unprotectedness, to whatever we embrace. And that is the very thing that could keep us guarded against the newness of God's concern. He comes to "revive" the spirit and the heart. He comes to waken us to new possibilities and new opportunities to accept what he has for us. He comes to bring new life, for that is what the verb "revive" involves: to awaken to new life.

Will we embrace new life today? Will we look for signs of it in the things that happen to us? Will we listen for the still, small voice within, suggesting what it is, identifying it as it comes? If so, we will join a very happy group of people who through the ages have found courage to embrace "new life and new hope" in the midst of ordinary life. In the ordinary chores and choices he comes with his offer to "revive the heart of the contrite." Embrace it!

1. What would you like most in your life right now? Is it something God wants you to have?

2. What would be the cost for you of obtaining it?

## Day 5 • When Troubles Return

Daily Reading: Psalm 30

*As for me, I said in my prosperity, "I shall never be moved." By thy favor, O Lord, thou hadst established me as a strong mountain; thou didst hide thy face, I was dismayed. (vv. 6, 7)*

Have we painted too rosy a picture of the life of a disciplined Christian, a "would-be disciple" of Jesus? Have we made it look as though a few prayers will "turn the trick" and things will go beautifully thereafter? If so, it is time to correct such an impression. On the one hand, we must always uphold the fact that God is God, and we are his creatures.

His grace is greater than our need, and we can always, always depend on his love. Those truths are so important, so foundational that they must be repeated again and again.

On the other hand, we must avoid a kind of flight into spiritual unreality. This is not a "mind game" we are called to play. It is life in the real world, with real problems, real struggles, real pain, successes, and failures.

That is why this psalm is so helpful and so important for us. The psalmist had experienced a time of prosperity—material and emotional, I think. Perhaps we have all been there and know how wonderful it feels when, as the song from "Oklahoma" put it, "I've got a wonderful feeling everything's going my way." If we had our "druthers," that's the way it would always be. But have you ever noticed that when everything was going their way for others, that they were sometimes (perhaps often) obnoxious? When we're having this wonderful spate of prosperity, we can become insensitive to others who are not having that kind of experience at the moment. We can even become proud and think we deserve all the good fortune that seems to be coming our way.

Then the light fades—gradually or suddenly. We no longer feel the comforting presence or we find problems that do not respond to the prayers we are offering. Our techniques don't seem to be working any more. Areas where we had tremendous spiritual victories may turn into areas of disheartening defeat. And so, like the psalmist, we have to say, "I am dismayed."

Here we enter into suffering in a different dimension: a suffering out of our own despair and inability to manipulate life as we would like. Here we come into a deeper understanding of our human "creature-hood" and our dependence on God. We thought we depended on God, but find that much of our faith was in ourselves and our techniques. So the darkness brings forth new light. The shadows produce substance we never found in the sunlight. Suffering produces patience, and patience produces character. These things are not given in a moment. They are grown in the experiences of disappointment and defeat.

Do not think that such a return of the problem is a sign that nothing has happened! Think rather that it is a new occasion to send the roots of faith deeper into the soil of God's goodness.

1. Identify a time when your prayers went unanswered, or a time when you lost control of your life. How did you handle that experience?

2 What did you learn by having to go through it?

## Day 6 • From a Broken Heart to a Tender Heart

Daily Reading: Ezekiel 36:22-32

*A new heart I will give you, and a new spirit I will put within you; and I will take out of your flesh the heart of stone and give you a heart of flesh. (v. 26)*

Yes, into every life circumstances come which "break the heart." Not once, but sometimes repeatedly things happen that cause "heart-pain." Yet who would want a heart that could not feel pain as well as joy? There was a popular song back in the 60s that said something like, "I am a rock! I am an island!" Who would want hardness to so encrust us that we could not be moved by another's sorrow? Such a condition would be death, not life.

And so comes this great promise through the prophet. God says he will give us new hearts and will take the stony ones away. To allow this process to happen means that we must become vulnerable. We must give up the techniques by which we have shielded ourselves and allow God to become our protector. A friend of mine, many years ago, began to realize that all his life he had used anger to protect himself. When anything came close to hurting him, he let go a terrible barrage of angry words and looks, and usually the other person would back away. Then he became convicted that he was not only driving other people away, but was actually holding God off, too. So he knew what he must do. He had to lay down his anger and threat of anger, that other people might find it safe to confront him when he needed it. It was an important milestone in his spiritual walk.

Indifference, escape into books, TV games, fantasies of all kinds—these are just some of the ways we keep our "hardness" intact. Then, in spite of all, something happens to break the heart. It may be sickness or death, or some family or work crisis. Whatever it is, God intends to use it for good. If we look to the places where our hearts are encrusted with these false protectors, we can see how good and loving he is not to allow them to remain.

I suppose the most important thing one should consider in this matter is this: If something has happened to you to break your heart, or if something should happen that breaks it, don't waste the situation. Don't let the opportunity pass, and don't let it harden your heart further. Either is a possibility, but it is not what the Lord intends. He looks for a people whose hearts are like his.

1. In what ways do you fend off others or wrap your heart in protection?

2. One reason for such defenses is fear. Is this true for you? How might God help you to be more open to others?

## DAY 7 • THE LONGED-FOR HEART

Daily Reading: Ephesians 4:17-32

*You were taught . . . to put off your old self, which is being corrupted by its deceitful desire, to be made new in the attitude of your minds; and to put on the new self, created to be like God in true righteousness and holiness. (vv. 22-24, NIV)*

A recent conversation with a friend concerned "feelings." She is confused about the angry and dark emotions that well up in her. She is going through a period of grief, and, not unusual, finds herself questioning, doubting, hurt, lonely, and angry. But in the midst of it all, she voices a desire to have a different attitude. As yet she doesn't know how to achieve it, but, like Pilgrim in the Slough of Despond, she has not turned back.

Putting off the old self takes some effort! Not only is it corrupted, but as our text says, it "is being corrupted by its deceitful desires." We might think it would be nice if God had taken away all those desires when we committed ourselves to Jesus Christ in faith. We fantasize that life could be beautiful if our hearts were pure. But the testimony of the saints through the ages is that this is not the way life works. For whatever inscrutable reasons, God has chosen to let us fight the good fight of faith, and leaves the goal to be sought: a pure and good heart.

When you stop to think of it, God is actually honoring us in this way. He is not making us infants who must be spoon-fed. He is giving us the elements by which we can cooperate with him in his work of completing what he began. Our salvation is a gift—a free gift of grace. It was accomplished by Jesus Christ in his earthly life and death, and we became new persons. Paul says in Philippians 2:12, "Work out your own salvation with fear and trembling, for it is God at work in you, both to will and to do." In other words, what God has provided for us is a goal to be sought, the means to pursue it, and the invitation to allow our hearts to be continually changed toward that longed-for state.

Where would we be if it were not for "the hope set before us"? It would be easy to grow lax and presume on God's grace. It would be easy to allow that old self which is not only corrupted, but is "being corrupted by its deceitful desires" to dominate. And so, in his great love and wisdom, God has provided what is best, that we might grow and mature as beloved children, until we reach the full measure of our humanity in Christ.

1. How does the promise of God's blessing and presence help you to "fight the good fight" against your old nature that is easily hurt, prone to doubt, and subject to anger?

271

2. Are you facing a situation today where renewing your grasp of such truth would be helpful?

# THE HEART HAS ITS REASONS

*The heart
has its reasons
which reason
knows
nothing of.*

Blaise Pascal

WEEK EIGHT

## DAY 1 • LIVING BEYOND REASON

Daily Reading: Hebrews 11:8-12

*And he [Abraham] set out, not knowing where he was going. (v. 8)*

The moment we begin to talk about faith, we are talking about something that goes beyond reason. It is not that faith is unreasonable, but that reason can only carry us so far. There may have been perfectly good reasons why Abraham should leave his kindred at Haran. But beyond any good reasons that may have been present, he was called to go out, "not knowing where he was going."

One of the things that holds many of us back in our Christian walk is that we think it is safer to live "in the head" instead of "by the heart." We do not trust the intuitive thoughts that come to us, and often dismiss them out of hand. Yet they may carry the seed of something extraordinary, if we choose to take them seriously. Not that we should obey every impulse or whim! God forbid! We are told to "test the spirits and hold fast to what is good."

Rational reasonableness keeps our faith walk tame and predictable. it allows us to keep intact those little areas of self-will which we ought to surrender to God. Reason is very good at justifying what we want to keep, and can give us many reasons why we should not venture very far from the predictable in this walk.

As we look at the way our life is going, we can ask ourselves two questions: Am I letting faith and the Spirit of God go in front, or am I living by logic and reason? Do I find each day a new experience of God's surprises, full of challenge and hope, or is it just a round of everyday concerns, one very much like the other? Somehow, without becoming romantic or idealistic, I think our experience is supposed to be more of the former rather than the latter. These devotions are meant to stir up our minds and hearts—to get us to think beyond a cold, proper image of what a Christian is or should be—and to challenge us to let God begin to remold and make us anew. We, too, are called to go out, not knowing where we are going. John says, "Beloved, it does not yet appear what we shall be." That's a call to faith. I don't know who I will be when God gets through with me. (I'm sure there are people who hope it won't be the same as now!) You don't know who you will be when God is through with you. Of course you will still be you—but he sees us as we were meant to be— and we are called to go out, "not knowing where we are going."

1. We cannot trust every whim as heaven-sent. John warns us to "test the spirits to see whether they are of God" (1 John 4:1b). How do you do this?

2. How might you live more by the spirit and less by the mind?

## DAY 2 • A DARING, FOOLISH ACT

Daily Reading: Luke 19:1-10

*So he [Zaccheus] ran ahead and climbed a sycamore tree to see him, because he was going to pass that way. (v. 4)*

Talk about letting the heart lead! If Zaccheus had any dignity about him, he threw it away at that moment when he climbed up that tree like a young boy: Here was a Roman tax gatherer, apparently quite rich. Although we know tax gatherers were despised by the people, nonetheless, we can believe that Zaccheus had his circle of friends and his own self-respect. He had already ordered his life by "reason." It was "reasonable" to collect taxes for Rome, since they were going to collect them anyway. His quick word later on, "if I have defrauded any man, I will restore it fourfold," would indicate that here was an honest tax collector. So his life, successful and prosperous, had been ruled by reason.

But the heart was not satisfied. No amount of success could fill the blank, empty space that still remained. And when he heard about Jesus, something quickened in his heart that brought a new intensity of desire. He wanted to meet this Man, to talk with him, to listen to him, and for that privilege he would be happy to sacrifice his dignity.

I remember sharing the worship service in the Moscow Baptist Church the week after Easter, about two years before the Soviet Union broke up. The church was full of people, young and old. Every seat was taken, and some were standing. We were in the choir loft, so I had a good view of it all, and noticed here and there Soviet soldiers in their characteristic uniform. At the end of the service, an invitation was given, and to my amazement, I saw a uniformed soldier go down to the altar rail, kneel and weep. It was one of the most impressive sights of my entire stay in Russia—someone who was letting his heart prevail over his reason. I have often thought of that young man, and pray that he, like Zaccheus, found the answer he was seeking.

1. Where have your heart and head been in conflict in the recent past?

2. How did you determine God's will?

## DAY 3 • BREAKING THE ALABASTER BOX

Daily Reading Matthew 26:6-13

*Jesus said, "Why do you trouble this woman? She has performed a good service for me." (v. 10)*

Again we are faced with a situation where a person followed her heart instead of her head. She had nothing to gain, from a worldly standpoint, by taking this "very costly ointment" and pouring it on Jesus' feet. It was a sacrifice and everyone there reacted to it. One of them remarked that it could have been sold for "a large sum, and the money given to the poor."

Love is a spendthrift, someone has remarked. Love does not take into account the "waste" involved in presenting something to the beloved that will bring joy. O. Henry tells a poignant story of a young struggling couple facing their first Christmas together. Each one chooses to give something to the other intended to bring happiness. The young husband pawns his watch to buy combs for his wife's beautiful long hair, while the wife has her hair cut off and sells it to buy a beautiful fob for his watch. Ironic, but it makes the point: Love is not afraid to sacrifice.

As we look at this woman who performed "a good service" to the Lord, it is good to ask ourselves whether we move by calculated reason in our giving to him, or if we allow our heart to lead. Isaac Watts holds up the image of "the wondrous cross on which the Prince of Glory died." At the end of that hymn, he says, "Love so amazing, so divine, demands my life, my soul, my all." Those are beautiful words, but do they grip us as they are meant to do? After all, God has led with his heart in his approach to us: "God so loved the world that he gave his only begotten Son, that whoever believes in him should not perish, but have everlasting life" (John 3:16). When we begin to deal with God, we are face to face with a love that defies reason and insists on giving us the best God has to offer.

It would be well to ask ourselves today, Where is my alabaster box of costly ointment? What of myself, my inward life, my thoughts, dreams, aims, and desires can I offer the Lord today? He will show us, we can be sure, and then we have a choice: the same choice the woman had when she chose that beautiful sacrifice, and made the heart of Jesus glad.

1. What is the treasure you will not give to the Lord?

2. What would giving it to him mean to you in the next few weeks?

## DAY 4 • JOSEPH'S RESOLVE

Daily Reading: Matthew 1:18-25

*[Mary's] husband Joseph, being a righteous man and unwilling to expose her to public disgrace, planned to dismiss her quietly. But just when he had resolved to do this. . . . (v. 19, 20a)*

We have tantalizingly few glimpses of this remarkable man. He had to be remarkable to be chosen for this special role of providing protection for the mother of our Lord and for our Lord himself in those difficult and dangerous days. What we see is a quiet and good man who was not afraid to listen to his heart.

We do not need to go into detail about the dilemma Joseph faced when he found out that Mary was to bear a son. In those days, not only was Mary disgraced in such a situation (and possibly even in physical danger) but Joseph himself would be a laughingstock. Whatever he may have thought about the whole affair, "he was unwilling to expose her to public disgrace," and thought the best way was to end the matter quietly. "He had resolved to do this." That resolve was a heart decision. And there is something else here worth noting: Whatever personal hurt he felt in this situation, it did not lead him to vindictiveness and a desire to add to Mary's suffering. His love was greater than his hurt.

As those words confront us, we might do well to ponder them. Is our love greater than our hurt, or do we live and move by the little slights and insults we feel? So often it is our feeling of being slighted, or left out, or neglected that looms large. And it is very easy in such a situation to punish. We punish directly, and we punish indirectly. In our anger, we may even hurt ourselves in order to make others sorry. Did you ever hear of "eating worms and dying" when you were younger? There was none of that in Joseph's heart. He tried to make the best of a difficult and painful situation.

Logic and reason can always be called in to justify a lack of mercy. The heart, on the other hand, can feel the pain of another, even identify with it in some way, and seek to find God's answer to the problem. That's what Joseph did. What a model for us! May our hearts be more like Joseph's heart when we are faced with difficult decisions.

1. Jesus forgave his tormentors from the cross. Can you identify what keeps you from following his example?

2. Is there anyone today whom you need to forgive?

## DAY 5 • HEART COURAGE

Daily Reading: Exodus 2:1-10

*By faith Moses was hidden by his parents for three months after his birth, because they saw that the child was beautiful; and they were not afraid of the king's edict.* (Hebrews 11:23)

They had every right to be afraid. Pharaoh was determined to bring the Hebrew population into some kind of controllable size, and the way he had decided to go about this was to destroy the male infants. Infanticide was not uncommon in those days.

It is a particularly touching thought in this Hebrews text, that the writer says they did this "because they saw the child was beautiful." What parent has not looked at his or her child and wondered at the beauty there? There is a great deal to cause wonder when we look at what God has done in creating and bringing to life a human person in a newborn child!

It is our faith in a God who loves us that enables us to attempt new and "risky" deeds for him. Abraham left home for an unknown country. Zaccheus climbed up a sycamore tree. The unnamed woman in the house of Simon broke her alabaster box of costly ointment and poured the contents on the feet of Jesus—preparing him, as he is quoted in one of the Gospels, "for the day of my burial." And now Moses' mother and father follow their hearts and defy the king's edict. History turns on such quiet decisions, and this is but one dramatic example of it.

We are not talking this week about doing foolish things. There is a difference between following the heart and following foolish impulses. Jesus was tempted to do several dramatic and "unreasonable" things, but countered them all with his unswerving loyalty to his heavenly Father. True faith is always consistent with God's own nature. He does not lead us to do harmful things, even though what he asks is, as we have been emphasizing, beyond reason. When all is added up, it will be seen that faith is eminently reasonable. I am reminded of a well-known puzzle. Four dots are placed within a box, and the player is asked to join all four dots without crossing a line over another. The answer is that in order to do it, one has to draw the lines outside the box, but most people do not think of it in that way. That is the difference between following the heart rather than the head. In order to achieve what God intends to accomplish in us, we have to "go outside the box" of our tame, dull Christian walk, and seek an inner renewal that may seem quite risky and upsetting until we realize that it is eminently reasonable, because God is dependable and faithful.

1. Do you face any decisions today where heart and mind lead in different directions?

2. [to be completed after the day is over] Which way did you go? What have you learned through this experience?

## DAY 6 • HEAD WORK VS. HEART WORK

Daily Reading: Romans 10:1-13

*For one believes with the heart and so is justified and one confesses with the mouth and so is saved. (v. 10 NRSV)*

Henry Foster was a dedicated physician who lived in the middle of the nineteenth century. He founded a hospital in Western New York and from his little talks in chapel someone compiled a book entitled *Life Secrets*. Here is what he said about "Head vs. Heart":

It is necessary for us to understand what the Scriptural idea of believing is. It is quite different from what we have in our ordinary demands in society; when any subject comes to us, it appeals to our intellect. We conclude that such and such are the facts; we say we believe them and we settle the matter. It is simply an intellectual process. But it is not an intellectual belief that answers God's purpose; that never brings a soul from death into life; for one to take this blessed Book and read it and say, "I believe it," and think because he believes it, he must be good; or to take up the plan of redemption through our Lord Jesus Christ, and say: "I believe it," and think that is going to give him a passport into heaven, such a belief is not worth a last year's bird's nest, so far as salvation is concerned. All it does is simply to let the intellect accept some phase of undisputed truth. But when the heart takes hold of Christ, so as to receive him as a Savior, and obeys him as King: then, the heart believes with a faith which works righteousness; which brings man from death into life, and receives him forever as one of the Lord's own. It is the faith of the heart.

It is this "heart faith" that produces the motivation and the strength to venture on with Jesus Christ. Our Christian walk will have many difficult moments and the head may even tell us at times that the cost is too great. But the heart remembers, if we have allowed it to open to the love of God. It remembers that it was empty and unfulfilled without him. It remembers that there was no peace without him. And so we renew our commitment and continue on. It's the faith walk that has been walked by millions before us, and they rise up to greet us with the assurance that we shall yet receive the fullness of his promises.

1. A muscle atrophies from disuse—so also the heart as a receptor of the Spirit's guidance. In what ways can you exercise your heart to hear God more clearly?

2. "Faith is . . . the conviction of things not seen" (Heb. 11:1). Where have you experienced the truth of this statement?

## DAY 7 • THE HEART HAS ITS REASONS

Daily Reading: Hebrews 10:19-25

*Let us approach with a true heart in full assurance of faith, with our hearts sprinkled clean from an evil conscience and our bodies washed with pure water. (v. 22)*

We have talked a great deal about following the heart instead of the head this week. Yet we know that the heart is not always a dependable guide! It, too, is capable of making foolish choices. One can only think of the foolish things men and women have done out of "love," destroying home and marriage for the sake of some infatuation. "Bigger than both of us," is the old saying.

Our text gives us a clue as to how to avoid such calamities. It is not by retreating back into the head and living without feeling. It is rather that we are to seek to have a true heart, an examined heart "made clean from an evil conscience." In other words, by self-understanding, the conviction of the Spirit of Truth, repentance for what we find in our hearts that needs to come out, and finding the forgiveness and cleansing we need that our hearts can then approach God "in full assurance of faith." There really is no shortcut. Much as we might like an easier approach, one that spared us of all this messy "clean up" process, it won't work. Our kitchens and bathrooms may not be pleasant to clean, but cleaning is necessary, and the rewards are plentiful. And the same is true of our lives.

Over the years this writer has known several elderly men who had violated the physical cleanup process I mentioned. So in their latter years they sat dirty, smelly, unkempt. Getting them to change became a challenge to all who cared about them, and it was a difficult challenge indeed. Could that be a picture of us, if we neglect the process by which our hearts become dependable receivers of good guidance? If they are full of jealousy, resentment, greed, lust, hurts, and unconfessed wrongs we have done to others and have forgotten—how can they receive the good and gentle guidance we need from our good and gentle Lord? If they have become encrusted with the neglect of years, it may take a bit of effort to get them sensitized again to the things of God. No matter! The important thing is this: The heart can be prepared for this "full assurance of faith" if we desire it, seek it, wait for it, and believe that Jesus will do what he promised.

1. What process might you follow for maintaining an '"examined heart," such as is mentioned in today's reading?

2. Having others to hold us accountable is an invaluable aid in this process? Can you identify one or two others who might help you in this regard?

# THE STEADFAST HEART

*My heart is
steadfast,
O Lord, my
heart is
steadfast!*

*Psalm 53:7a*

## Day 1 • The Uses of Adversity

Daily Reading: James 1:2-8

*My brothers and sisters, whenever you face trials of any kind, consider it nothing but joy, because you know that the testing of your faith produces endurance . . . so that you may be mature and complete, lacking in nothing. (vv. 2-4b)*

"Whenever you face trials of any kind. . . ." That is a blanket statement that covers just about everything that "happens" to us. "Trials of any kind" include those which are so trivial that we hardly call them trials at all, and those that are so severe that we term them tragedies. In each case, our text tells us, our faith is being tested. Adversity is a hard school, but a useful one.

In every generation, there have been those who repeated this truth for us. They have faced tests harder than most of us can imagine, and let their faith produce heroic endurance. Yet they considered themselves weak, needy souls. Think of the martyrs facing the stake or the lions; think of the missionaries venturing out to unknown and sometimes hostile parts of the earth, impelled by their desire to share the gospel with those who sat in darkness. Think of the soldiers who face enemy bullets, sometimes for a cause they could not understand. Looking over the long history of faith heroes, the book of Hebrews says, "Of whom the world was not worthy!"

We come back from reading about these trials that others have lived through, and look at our own lives. Our problems may be small, but they are still problems, and they are *our* problems. The trials may seem trivial to others, but when we are going through them, our faith is being tested. Will we have steadfastness? Will we continue to believe that God is for us and that it is well to go on with him? Will we believe that although today the sky is dark and foreboding, there will be an answer to this trial? Can we "count it all joy" when these trials come?

Henry Foster says, "Our Lord and Master demands that our spirits be so anchored in Christ; our natures so wholly committed to God, that we shall not be moved from the one right line of action, no matter how the flesh may shrink from the trials that come, the crosses given."

As I think about "the steadfast heart," I am reminded of how often my own heart shrinks from pain and conflict, and wants to run away and hide. Yet, by the grace of God, I can come back to the "line of scrimmage," the place of decision, and decide: No turning back!

1. Cite a time of suffering in your life and write down what you learned through it—about God, about human nature, or about yourself.

2. Locate a psalm that you can use as your prayer of thanksgiving for God's faithfulness.


## DAY 2 • BUILDING ON THE ROCK

Daily Reading: Matthew 7:24-27

*Everyone then who hears these words of mine and acts on them will be like a wise man who built his house on rock. The rain fell, the floods came, and the winds blew and beat on that house, but it did not fall, because it had been founded on rock. (vv. 24, 25 NRSV)*

All of us are building a life of one kind or another. And Jesus is particularly emphasizing here that what we build on will have a lot to do with what happens in the hard seasons.

The first church where this writer was pastor had two towers flanking the front entrance. They were not tall, and they were built of wood, shingled in the topmost part. But one of them was leaning (somewhat reminiscent of the tower of Pisa) away from the church. Its foundation had rotted away, and the people had not gotten around to straightening it up. The new pastor was "horrified" and immediately began a campaign to get the tower straight again. Before many months it was accomplished. A new foundation had to be laid, and old beams had to be replaced with new, and with much effort the whole structure made perpendicular. It was a much harder task than building it new, and would never have been necessary if the tower had been set on a proper foundation.

That tower is a kind of metaphor of our lives. Unless we are solidly planted in our faith in Jesus Christ, we "lean" away on our own. We may even become a danger to ourselves and others in our instability. Jesus is telling his hearers that life is too difficult to settle for anything else but "solid rocks" on which to base our lives.

There is so much "sand" today that parades as acceptable spiritual truths that we have to be quite severe in "testing the spirits." The devil has always been a clever counterfeiter, and he knows how to make a product look like something desirable. Our first parents were "fooled" by his clever misrepresentations, and suffering and sorrow are the sad consequences of their disobedience. God's Word has not changed, and he calls us still to be a holy people, a people consecrated to him and his purposes. That call is grounded in his wisdom and his love. If we are to become truly free and happy, we must become like him. So he bids us to be careful about the foundation. We know, do we not, who is the Rock on which we must build?

1. What people or possessions do you think are indispensable?

2 How can you determine when they become substitutes for the Lord?


## Day 3 • Steady Hearts—Living Stones

Daily Reading: Matthew 16:13-20

*And Jesus answered him, "Blessed are you, Simon son of Jonah! For flesh and blood has not revealed this to you, but my Father in heaven. And I tell you, you are Peter, and on this rock I will build my church." (vv. 16:17,18a)*

As we talk about steadfast hearts, certainly Simon Peter comes to mind. As we first meet him, with his brusque impulsiveness, he seems anything but "rock-like." His feelings go up and down, and even to the end of our view of him in the New Testament, there is something wonderfully human and emotional about him.

What we have here is what the church calls "The Confession of Peter," and a special day is set aside to honor it in some traditions. Peter seems to have been the first to grasp the full scope of who Jesus is and what his divine mission was on earth. Jesus had been teaching and training these men with the message of the Kingdom of God and its nearness. But he seems to have waited for them to discover his identity rather than dwelling on it. It is a particular cause of rejoicing for him when Peter bursts forth with his great confession.

We know that not only was Peter called "a rock" (Petros in Greek) but in Peter's first letter we read, "Come to him, a living stone, though rejected by mortals yet chosen and precious in God's sight, and like living stones, let yourselves be built into a spiritual house to be a holy priesthood, to offer spiritual sacrifices acceptable to God through Jesus Christ" (1 Peter 2:4,5). So there needs to be something "rock-like" in our commitment to God.

During the Civil War, one of the Confederate generals won the nickname "Stonewall" because he stood so steadfast in the face of fire from the Union side. To this day "Stonewall Jackson" is an honored figure in many parts of the nation, for his steadfastness under testing.

Where do we find temptation not to be steadfast? Is it when duty seems dull, chores seem irksome, gossip seems good, and truth seems unimportant? Is it when we seek an easier way that will give short-term satisfaction instead of braving a longer-term path that will yield better results in the end? Whatever it is for us, the heart, the steadfast or the fickle one, will be the deciding factor. Not by feeling, but by the will does the heart maintain its steadiness.

1. Where do you waver in your steadfastness to follow the Lord?

2. Compose a short prayer asking him for help and grace in such situations.

## DAY 4 • STRENGTH FOR WEAK HEARTS

Daily Reading: Hebrews 3:12-19

*Take care, brothers and sisters, that none of you may have an evil, unbelieving heart that turns away from the living God. (v. 12)*

We want steadfast hearts, but we know that our hearts are often weak. We are strong in our resolutions, weak in carrying through with them. That is our lot, because we are all still "in process."

Our text today sets our weakness in a slightly different light. Instead of decrying the weakness and helplessness of the heart, our writer warns against an "evil, unbelieving" heart. That's a bit more negative, but it also gives us something to fight against. What can we do with that weak, helpless heart that wants to slink away and hide, except to feel sorry for it? And what good does that do? Can you ever remember when your self-pity did you any good? I can't. So our text, setting the whole matter in a different context, warns, "Look out!" The testings will come. The thoughts of how hard it is to be faithful to Jesus Christ and our commitment to him will rise up. The old flesh will cry out for its wanted satisfactions. But all this may be preceded by an "evil, unbelieving" heart.

How does the heart go from being a believing one to this sorry state? Not suddenly, I'm sure. But little by little, thought by thought, decision by decision, it moves from a state of fellowship, worship and prayer to a state of estrangement, doubt, and alienation. We may have seen this happen in people we loved, and found ourselves unable to stop the process.

Although we cannot stop the process in others, we can do something about it in ourselves. Hence this warning.

We want steadfast hearts, and if that is our goal and desire we can surely expect God's help. He does not lay claim on our lives to abandon and confound us when things get tough. He "signs on" for the duration, and has promised that he will never leave nor forsake us. So we can tackle this temptation to cave in with the assurance that we have the best help imaginable—the help of God Almighty himself. He will not, however, act against our will. That is a given. He so loves us, and so respects what he has created in us, that he will allow us to make foolish choices, without forcing us to make wise ones. We may think we would like him to intervene, but I think that is a fantasy. Our freedom to make choices is tied up with our essential humanity, and we must take it as a valuable treasure to be used wisely. Wise choices, though sometimes painful and made only with difficulty, lead to good ends. The steadfast heart is made steadfast by such choices. The old spiritual says, "Sometimes I feel like I'm almost gone." And even in such a time, we can still make the choice to stand by what we know to be true. "Stand, therefore," says Paul, "and having done all, stand." That is what it means to have a steadfast heart!

1. A daily time with the Lord—Scripture, prayers, silence—is essential if we are to keep our hearts filled with Life. Jot down what you do in your time with him, and how often you do it.

2. What seems to intervene in your "best laid plans" of a daily private time with him?

## DAY 5 • LIKE HIND'S FEET

Daily Reading: Psalm 18:31-42

*He made my feet like hind's feet, and set me secure on the heights. (v. 33)*

On my first visit to Yellowstone National Park, I learned of the mountain goats that range high above the valleys. You can look through binoculars, and if you are lucky, you can see these magnificent creatures going about their business in their chosen environment. Television has also introduced us to many wonders of animals cavorting among the rocks in slippery, dangerous areas with seemingly little or no thought of danger.

We humans were not made for such cavorting. These words are written a week after news came of a young man who froze to death climbing in the White Mountains of New Hampshire in the dead of winter. Whatever impulse sent him and his friend (who survived with severe frostbite) to that dangerous place, it was clearly foolish to give into it.

Not so with things of the spirit. Here we are made to climb to the heights. Here we are invited to breathe the cool air of God's mercy and goodness. An old gospel hymn says, "Far above the noise and strife . . . I'm dwelling in Beulah land." Beulah land in Christian symbolism denotes a state in which things have become settled, firm, at peace with God.

Our text (and two others in the Old Testament which convey the same phrase), express the psalmist's gratitude for God's protection and provision. He says, God "made my way safe." And again, "You gave me a wide place for my steps under me, and my feet did not slip" (v. 36). Think of that in terms of your daily life, the struggles and hopes you entertain as you go about your ordinary affairs. Sometimes you may feel hemmed in. You may face something that seems to have no way out, just a blank wall before you. Then you see God move, and a door is there, an answer to your prayer. It may be dramatic, or it may be just a small "tight place" that turns out not to be so tight after all. "You gave me a wide place." If we are looking for God in the ordinary course of our life, we will find ourselves praying prayers of thanksgiving not unlike that of our text. "You made my feet like the feet of a deer!"

What we are talking about is not some kind of unusual, "kooky" spiritual experience for special people. What we are talking about is getting a different view of ordinary life. Each day should be "shot through" with the reality of God. God is not simply to be visited on Sundays and then obeyed remotely through the week. If we are learning to walk with God in a steady fashion, we will be treading on new, uncharted ground each day. Our hearts will be inspired with a new vision of what life is meant to be, and we will find an inner impulse to venture on with the Lord who has loved us, called us, forgiven us, and waited for us to catch on to what a wonderful life he had in mind for us.

1. When have you experienced a narrow space that was miraculously widened by God?

2. What challenge do you face today where there appears no way out?

## DAY 6 • FAITH OR FEAR: WHICH?

Daily Reading: Joshua 1:1-18

*This is my command: be strong, be resolute; do not be fearful or dismayed, for the Lord your God is with you wherever you go. (v. 9)*

It seems increasingly clear to me that one of our greatest sins against God is our unbelief. No matter how determinedly we may try to go on our pilgrimage, if we are carrying the baggage of unbelief in our hearts, we are sinning against the faithfulness and mercy of God.

Some of us are very, very fearful people. We may have denied that through our younger years, and tried to appear "noble, brave, and true." But inside we knew that we were scared, afraid of—the dark? our own shadow? what other people might say? what terrible things might be awaiting us in the future? Any or all of these can make a heavy weight for a child of God to drag through life. And we can justify some of these fears under the pretext that we are being "responsible." The result? Too often there is a stress level that belies our songs about the "peace of God that passes all understanding."

Joshua had a big job before him. "My servant Moses is dead; now it is for you to cross the Jordan, you and this whole people of Israel, to the land which I am giving them." Notice the situation there, and how similar it is to some of the situations we face in life, when those we have depended on are no longer available to lead us as before. Joshua had been with Moses a long time, and no doubt had been very grateful for his anointed leadership. But that was no longer available. Now it was Joshua's turn. I suppose that every adult, as we come into maturity, gets some of that feeling when we see parents no longer in their accustomed roles. We know, somehow, that it is up to us. We are the "cutting edge" of God's purpose.

But Joshua did not have to face that job alone. God's command, "Do not be fearful or dismayed," gives him something to work on, because he would sometimes feel fearful. Then he would have to choose to put his trust in the Lord who had called him to this task. But the command is joined with the most incredible and wonderful promise: "The Lord your God is with you wherever you go." Joshua could not simply sit down passively and wait for God to work some kind of miracle. He would have to lead his army and do his job. But he has the promise ahead of time, an inner secret, that God will prevail. All that is required of him is faithfulness, and faithfulness is always full of faith, belief in God, trust in God, reliance upon God. Joshua's hand might even tremble as it held the sword, but if he has done his "homework," and if he is learning the daily lessons God is teaching him, he will be resolute in his heart, knowing that God's promise is sure: "I will never fail you nor forsake you" (v. 5).

1. What are your fears for today, or for the future?

2. "Let not your hearts be troubled; believe in God, believe also in me," said Jesus (John 14:1). How can this promise help you?

## DAY 7 • THE STEADY "YES"

Daily Reading: Luke 5:1-11

*Simon said, "Master, we have worked all night long but have caught nothing. Yet if you say so, I will let down the nets." (v. 5)*

In this encounter with Simon on the Lake of Gennesaret, we find the "simple fishermen" going about their trade, "minding their own business," as it were. Jesus enters their life and invites himself into one of the boats. From then on, though the fishermen did not realize it, life would never be the same for them. It is the same for us—wherever we were or whatever we were engaged in when Jesus came into our lives, life could never be the same again. It might be more difficult, more challenging, even more scary than before—but it would not be the same. And there would be something so very grand about the whole experience that we would never want to go back to the way things were before he came.

I suppose that fishing all night with no success was not an unusual experience for these men. Sometimes you found the fish; sometimes you didn't. That's just the way it was, and there is no indication that they were particularly discouraged by their lack of success. Of course, if that kind of thing happened too often, they would be in trouble. It's the same with us. We can take an occasional setback, even a small disaster from time to time. Most of us will try to take such things "in our stride." But when troubles come too often, or when they are too severe, we find ourselves in need of more than lies within us. Simon would certainly find that true later on. Right now, in this story, there is a clue to Simon's faith and Simon's character that made it possible for Jesus to give him a new name: Peter, A Rock. "We have worked all night long and caught nothing. *Yet if* you say so. . . ." That's the turning word. That's the key to unlock the marvels and mysteries of our walk with Jesus Christ. No matter what we may think; no matter what we may have experienced, if we can just say, "Yet if you say so . . .," I will do it. So much of our life has to be lived out beyond simple reason and logic. We are called to be a people of faith, and we are called to a "faith walk." That means that there will be times when, in spite of all our logic, we say, "Yet. . . ."

Here, in the early days of their discipleship, Peter learned that by obeying beyond where his eye or his experience could take him, Jesus had a blessing in store. That is as true for us as it was for him. Jesus Christ, the same, yesterday, today, and forever. He still asks for a deeper level of trust than most of us have dared give him. He knows "where the fish are," and he knows what lies ahead in our future. Since we know neither, does it not make sense to add our little, "Yet if you say so . . .," and do it?

1. What is your habitual reaction when things get too difficult, or too much is required of you?

2. What "impossible" situation do you face now, where saying "Yes, I will" to Jesus would provide a way out of your dilemma?

# A HEART FILLED WITH GRATITUDE

*I will give*
*thanks, O Lord,*
*with my*
*whole heart.*

Psalm 138:1a

## Day 1 • It Is a Good Thing

Daily Reading: Psalm 92:1-15

*It is a good thing to give thanks to the Lord, to sing praises to your name, O Most High. (v. 1)*

Is there anything more unattractive than a selfish, ungrateful heart? The picture that comes to mind as this is written is a story many of us read in our childhood about two beautiful girls, Snow White and Rose Red, and their encounter with an unspeakably ugly dwarf who had the habit of getting himself into trouble and was rescued by the girls over and over. Each time, however, he stormed and screamed at them for doing something wrong.

Perhaps the reason this story made an impression on me is that it manifests something of my own critical nature. I have been corrected many times for making little critical remarks about some dish or meal that has been lovingly prepared. It is embarrassing to realize that when someone gives one something nice or does something nice, that one's heart finds fault.

Our text says it is a "good thing" to give thanks to the Lord. That means that each day—yes, each hour—we are being given good things. We are the recipients of his love, his care, and his tender mercies. If we are critical, ungrateful, we can run carelessly over all such blessings without even being aware of them.

Ingratitude breeds discontent, and discontent breeds a sickly frame of life. Out of the heart proceed the emotions and energy that bring wellness or un-wellness. An ungrateful heart is bad medicine!

And so the psalmist bids and encourages us to give thanks because it is good for us. Praising God for his goodness and his manifold gifts is an antidote to that selfish dwarf that lives within many of us. It "puts him in its place," as it were. And we all need that.

It is typical of God's great goodness and love that even when we render him his due, we receive back more than we give! He deserves our thanks and praise. He is the Giver of every good and every perfect gift. He is the Creator and owner of all that there is. We are creatures—created ones—and we do not have even the power to keep ourselves alive apart from his will. So without expecting anything "in return," we owe him thanks and praise. But his generosity is too great to allow that. So, built in to the whole process is this truth: It is a good thing—a good thing for us—to give thanks to the Lord.

1. Glance through the Book of Psalms—Psalms 116, 117, 139, 145-150, especially—and choose one or two verses that best express your thankfulness to God. Jot them down.

2. Where have you had the experience that praise leads to a joyful heart?


## Day 2 • Learning to Give Thanks

Daily Reading: Psalm 100
*Give thanks to him. Bless his name. (v. 4b)*

God never asks us to do anything without giving us the grace to do it. That would be cruel, and it would be totally unlike God. So when he says, "Give thanks to him," (as a command), that means we can do it.

This does not mean that we can make ourselves feel thankful. Feelings don't work that way. We cannot command feelings. Feelings are or are not. But giving thanks and feeling thankful may not come simultaneously. If we are ruled by our feelings, we will be erratic, sporadic and unstable in all our ways. Being led by our feelings has already gotten many of us into difficult situations, and even now we may be trying to work our way out of some of the conditions that resulted from living by the feelings of the moment!

But we can give thanks. We can take the circumstances of our life, piece by piece, and give thanks verbally, consciously, for the various elements in them. If we make a list of the things, good and bad, which figure in our lives we will find some elements on both sides of the ledger. There will be things that are undeniably good. There will be other elements that seem almost indescribably bad—things that bring pain, suffering, heartache, even fear. Can we give thanks for them all? Yes, by an act of will, trusting that somehow God's hand is over them all and in them all, we can say, "Thank you, Father, even for this. I do not know how it will work for good, I do not know how it can be a blessing, but I believe that you intend good, not evil in it." These words are intended to be a "prayer-starter," and you can make them specific for yourself.

In taking such a step of faith, we are in the process of learning to be grateful. We first learn to give thanks, and then we learn to be thankful. Since most of us are quite unpracticed in this area, we have plenty of room to learn and grow.

1. What elements of your life do you find it difficult to be grateful for?

2. Would you accept an assignment this week to find one positive aspect in each of these and to jot them down here at the end of the week?

## DAY 3 • WHERE ARE THE NINE?

Daily Reading: Luke 17:11-19

*Then said Jesus, "Were not ten cleansed? Where are the nine?" (v. 17)*

I suppose this is the classic example of the ungrateful heart. There could be no more dread disease in Jesus' day than that of leprosy. Unlike other ailments, this disease carried a social stigma and meant isolation from one's family and community. So when you had leprosy, you were, in a sense, thrice cursed. There was no cure, so it meant a slow, creeping death.

Here were ten lepers, sharing their misery, and having heard of Jesus, they "stood at a distance" (it was unlawful to come close), and they cried out, "Jesus, Master, have mercy on us." He was the only hope they had ever heard of. Nor was their hope in vain. "When he saw them, he said to them, 'Go and show yourselves to the priests.'" In those rare instances when the leprosy disappeared, the law provided certain ritual inspections to certify that it was safe to readmit the person into society. And it was this provision that Jesus was bidding them to use. Then we read of the miracle: "As they went they were cleansed." The Gospel has such a wonderful way of understating these great events! "As they went they were cleansed." But did they turn back then to thank the Healer? Only one of them thought to do that.

Where are the nine? Is that the percentage of those who recognize the mercies of God which are new every morning, the incredible gifts of love and grace which pour into our lives? Is it a one to nine ratio of those whose heart overflows with gratitude and thanksgiving? Or, stating it another way, do we return to give thanks for only one of every ten blessings God pours on us? It's worth thinking about.

The old "Adamic" heart is not a thankful one. Because of that innate selfishness within us all, it is possible to "use up" a thousand gifts without having the gratitude we should for them. That is why it is so vitally important to desire and cultivate the spirit of gratitude within. One could believe that the disease of ingratitude which the nine carried away that day was worse than the leprosy of which they had been cured!

1. What elements of your life are, on reflection, gifts from God that you have taken for granted?

2. What might you do to cultivate a more grateful heart?

## DAY 4 • MARY'S SONG OF JOY

Daily Reading: Luke 1:39-56

*My soul magnifies the Lord, and my spirit rejoices in God my Savior. (vv. 46-47)*

If the lepers we read about yesterday were classic cases of ingratitude, we could posit this beautiful song of Mary as the classic case of gratitude. The announcement of the angel to Mary that she was to become the mother of the Son of God, the Messiah of Israel, certainly had its difficulties. She was unmarried, and being pregnant could be not only disgraceful but actually dangerous for her. She had much to lose through what God had chosen to carry out his plan. But such was Mary's faith, and such was her relationship with God, that she was able to rise immediately beyond preoccupation with her own concern. "Be it to me according to your word," she had replied to the angel.

Some time later when Elizabeth greeted her with the recognition that she, Mary, carried a wonderful secret within, Mary could express her thankfulness. "All generations will call me blessed."

Does our soul magnify the Lord and do we rejoice in God our Savior? Or do we allow our eyes to be focused on the gifts? Mary's focus had already been fixed on God—his interests and his concerns. This whole song expresses that focus—and praises the largeness and sureness of God's divine plan. As long as we allow ourselves to be consumed with our petty concerns, as long as our gaze is downward and inward, we cannot join Mary in her song of joy. But like her, we can choose to remember that "he who is mighty has done great things for me." We can strengthen the small movements of thankfulness that stir within our hearts. We can be changed from the "nine ungrateful lepers" syndrome to the "Mary's song of joy" syndrome, for the same God whom Mary praised is ours. "His mercy is on those who fear him from generation to generation."

We cannot truly enter into Mary's thoughts and feelings except by imagination. We can wonder at her courage, her willingness to brave this new situation, and her obedient spirit. We can not only wonder at them but be encouraged by them and seek to emulate them. She, after all, is one of us. She became the first to know and to have faith in Jesus. But because of her faithfulness and the faithfulness of the others who came after her, we, too, can learn to sing with her the song of joy. We can say with the psalmist, "O magnify the Lord with me, and let us exalt his name together!" (Psalm 34:3).

Today is a good day to start. In fact there is no better day to start than today! Perhaps all heaven waits to hear us join in this song of joy!

1. Mary's song of joy grew from her acquaintance with God her Savior. Are there any specific ways you can grow to know him better?

2. "O magnify the Lord with me" (Ps 34:3), invites the psalmist. List several aspects of the Lord that best express who he is for you.

## DAY 5 • PAUL'S THANKSGIVING

Daily Reading; Philippians 1:3-18

*I thank my God in all my remembrance of you, always in every prayer of mine for you all making my prayer with joy, thankful for your partnership in the gospel from the first day until now. (vv. 3-5)*

As we read through the letters of Paul to those early Christians, we find many references to thanksgiving—his own thanksgiving and his call to others to be thankful. It is important to remember that many of these words were written from prison.

Again, we are confronted with a choice. We can take the circumstances of our life as they are and do either of two things with them: we can inwardly complain about their negative aspects, or we can give thanks for the positive ones. We may even get to the place where we can, by faith, give thanks for the negative ones, having become convinced that God uses all things to work out his good will, and that all things do work together for good.

We know that Paul had a physical affliction of some kind that did not respond to prayer. God said instead, "My grace is enough for you. My strength is perfected in [your] weakness" (paraphrase of 2 Cor. 12:9). If he had been of a different stripe, he could have spent his latter years feeling that he had been wronged or, at best, neglected by God. After all, he had risked his whole career and his standing with his own family and countrymen in order to be faithful to the heavenly vision he had seen on the road to Damascus. I have known people who said quite bluntly that, after all they had given to God, he owed them. They felt he owed them some kind of reward for having tried to be faith-filled people.

Not so with Paul. At least that is not the impression we glean from reading these letters. This man has been deserted by his trusted friends, he has been beaten, stoned, shipwrecked—attacked by his enemies everywhere he went. But he says to the Philippians, "Have no anxiety about anything, but in everything by prayer and supplication, with thanksgiving, let your requests be made known to God" (Phil. 4:6). Thanksgiving seems to be the keynote in his prayers.

So can it be with ours. Are we facing difficult times? Do we have uncertainties which we can do nothing about? Then there's no better time to give thanks for what we have already received, and to lay our needs before the same loving God for the future. Do we find some delay in our prayers? We can even thank God for the delay, and ask him to show us why the answer is long in coming, or if we are praying the right kind of prayer. "Give thanks in all circumstances," Paul tells the Thessalonians (1 Thess. 5:18). So we can.

1. How have you responded in the past when God's answers to your prayers were delayed?

2. What have you learned that might help you the next time this happens?

## DAY 6 • THE SACRIFICE OF PRAISE

Daily Reading: Psalm 50, Hebrews 13:15, 16

*He who brings thanksgiving as his sacrifice honors me; to him who orders his way aright I will show the salvation of God! (Psalm 50:23)*

In this passage thanksgiving is called sacrifice. What is a sacrifice, anyway? Do we not understand it as something we offer up, give up, at some cost to ourselves? When Araunah offered to give David his threshing floor on which to build an altar, David replied, "No, but I will buy it for a price. I will not offer burnt offerings to the Lord my God which cost me nothing" (2 Samuel 24:24).

In what sense, then, could we call "thanksgiving" and "praise" a sacrifice? There are several levels, and it would be good to look at them.

The first level would be to thank and praise God for the small and large blessings we recognize. We saw in the ten lepers that we do not always even rise to this level, to make this small "sacrifice of praise." So it may take a little effort, a little determination on our part to remember to remember—and to give thanks.

The second level, I think, would be to thank and praise God when we are weary and don't feel particularly thankful. Most of us are driven more than we realize by the feelings of the moment. If we feel joyful, we look at life in a certain way. If we feel "down," that feeling can color the way we perceive everything. We've all seen children display this quality, where nothing pleases because the child does not wish to be pleased. Making the "sacrifice of praise" is a step in overcoming this kind of bondage.

The final level, I think, is to thank and praise God when we cannot see the good in a situation, but rather see it as an evil. There have been a number of situations in my life where I would have moved heaven and earth to prevent something from happening. And it happened anyway. Only later could I look back and see how God had used that "evil" to bring forth greater good. I suspect we all have these situations, and will have them in the future. Why not begin today to prepare for this level: to thank and praise God when we cannot see the good. That is the sacrifice of praise to which we should aspire.

1. In what circumstances do you find it the most difficult to praise God?

2. What adverse circumstsance are you now facing, for which you can start to thank God even though you do not "feel" like it?

## Day 7 • A Continual Thanksgiving

Daily Reading: Luke 22:14-23

*He took a loaf of bread, and when he had given thanks. . . . He took a cup and when he had given thanks. . . . (vv. 17, 19)*

When Jesus asked his disciples to "do this in remembrance of me," he was instructing us in a perpetual act of thanksgiving. Very, very early the Church began to call this meal the Eucharist, which in Greek meant "the thanksgiving."

As we read the Gospel accounts of Jesus' earthly life, it is remarkable how many times he is recorded as giving thanks. There is the feeding of the 5,000, where the giving of thanks is associated with the divine increase of the five loaves and two fish. There is the time, recorded in Matthew 11, after John the Baptist had sent messengers to ask "Are you the one who is to come, or do we look for another?" In reply, Jesus rehearsed the signs of the kingdom which were accompanying his ministry: "The blind receive their sight, the lame walk, the lepers are cleansed, the deaf hear, the dead are raised, and the poor have good news brought to them." And a little later on, he says, "I thank you, Father, Lord of heaven and earth, because you have hidden these things from the wise and the intelligent and have revealed them to infants; yes, Father, for such was your gracious will." Not only was our Lord a man of prayer; he was preeminently a man of thanksgiving.

So it is not surprising that in this wonderful Sacrament, he calls us to a perpetual thanksgiving. Now the Church has spread around the globe, and as one evening hymn puts it, "the voice of prayer is never silent, nor dies the strain of praise away." It is the obvious intent of the Lord that the world become a universe of thankful hearts, and one of the helps he has given along the way is the Eucharist, the Lord's Supper, the Holy Communion. There we are reminded graphically, with words and physical food, action and sound, that God has come to us and that he is indeed our Savior. We come to him because he first comes to us. So praise and thanksgiving naturally arise in that case. No matter how difficult life may become, we are not to allow ourselves to wander far from this central truth: we are bought with a price; we are not our own. Love has claimed us for love.

I close this week's thoughts with these words from the great Apostle Paul, writing to the church in Rome:

"O the depth of the riches and wisdom and knowledge of God! How unsearchable are his judgments and how inscrutable his ways! . . . For from him and through him and to him are all things. To him be the glory forever. Amen" (Romans 11:33, 36).

1. What things for which we can be thankful are brought to mind through Holy Communion?

2. Is there one paramount gift for which you are grateful to the Lord this day?

# THE AWAKENED HEART

*I will sing*
*and make*
*melody!*
*Awake, my*
*soul! Awake,*
*O harp and lyre!*
*I will awake*
*the dawn!*

*Psalm 57:7b-8*

## DAY 1 • A WARNING AND A PROMISE

Daily Reading: Ephesians 5:11-20

*Awake, O sleeper, and arise from the dead, and Christ shall give you light. (v. 14)*

We are going to think this week about "the awakened heart." And it will become clearer, I think, as the days go on, just what are some of the implications of the heart's being awakened.

At the outset, however, we have this word from the apostle, which includes a strong warning and a wonderful promise. The warning is this: we do not have unlimited time to rouse ourselves out of the death of spiritual drowsiness. In verses 15 and 16, we read: "Be very careful, then, how you live—not as unwise but as wise, making the most of the time, because the days are evil." If that was true in Paul's day, how much more in our own!

There is something about the spiritual torpor that is beguiling and appealing. Shakespeare called sleep "death's counterfeit." In other words, we may choose the pleasant state of being only half-awake over having to deal with unpleasant realities. The only problem with this is that sooner or later, reality catches up with us, and we have to "face the music." So Paul urges his readers to "arise from the dead."

But he does not leave us with only this sharp warning. He couples it with a great promise: "Christ shall give you light." If you have ever struggled through a dim, shadowy night when your body would not cooperate with sleep, and in which you found mental fantasies and fears too plentiful to be entirely erased, you know how welcome the signs of morning were.

God's call to us to awake is the call to be fully alive, not to miss life as we "use it up." Only those who respond can fully know what is being offered here.

1. Has there been an incident in your life where you preferred to bury your head in the sand like the ostrich, rather than face and deal with reality?

2. What results of that denial are you living with today?

## DAY 2 • THE HOUR HAS COME

Daily Reading: Romans 13:8-14

*Do this, understanding the present time. The hour has come for you to wake up from your slumber, because our salvation is nearer now than when we first believed. (v. 11 NIV)*

"To everything there is a season," says the Preacher. And we know that life has moments when it is "time" to do something. Someone has said, "There is nothing stronger than an idea whose time has come." Paul speaks of Christ as coming "in the fullness of time."

How does this relate to our common, everyday life? It means that there are times, moments, when "the hour has come." We sense that we are being given an opportunity to change. We sense that there is grace to make some decision that perhaps we have long neglected to make. And Paul here is telling the Romans that the hour is now. They have lived careless, pagan lives. They have lived for themselves, and have been far away from God. (Their general condition is graphically described in the first Chapter of Romans.) But God has "invaded" their lives, as it were. He has found a way to reach their souls, and has acquainted them with his love and mercy. He has called them out of darkness into the light, out of death into life.

Every one of us who reads these words has felt some touch of God on our hearts. It may not have been dramatic (there is no indication that the Roman Christians had been "dramatically" converted). But if we are at all aware of God's presence in the things that have happened to us, we can say, "Surely God was in this place and I knew it not"—even before we became conscious disciples of Jesus.

"Understanding the present time," Paul says. It was a crucial time. Some of the people to whom he was writing would be severely tested, even martyred, for their faith. It was a very hard time to be a Christian. But God was at work in them and in the world. Things were being changed. "Our salvation is nearer than when we first believed."

What about your life at this moment? Is God "putting his finger" on some area "whose time has come?" He seems to do that. He doesn't work with everything all at once, for we couldn't quite take it! But lovingly, he lets something in our life come to its time, and then it is up to us to cooperate with him in moving forward.

1. Can you identify an area of your life where God is asking some response from you?

2. What do you think he is requiring you to do? What would happen if you did it?


## DAY 3 • AWAKE, MY SOUL, AND SING

Daily Reading: Colossians 3:15-17

*Let the word of Christ dwelt in you richly, as you teach and admonish one another in all wisdom, and as you sing psalms and hymns and spiritual songs with thankfulness in your hearts to God. (v. 16)*

Let's talk about singing! Over and over in the New Testament, we find reference to these first Christians singing their joy in their newfound faith. Nor does the singing die away, century upon century, as the Church moves on. Whenever there has been a renewal of faith, when hearts have been awakened to God, singing results.

There has to be something significant and important in this, and we do well not to ignore it. For, as someone has said, "The devil hates to hear a Christian sing." I knew a man once who had a long-term problem of mental depression and paranoia. He had to be treated medically, but even that at times was not enough. One of the things that seemed to calm him down and help him back into reality was singing. And when the heart is sad, when things look glum, it is not an escapism to resort to this tried and proven method of getting back into the light of hope and faith.

One thinks of the centuries of slaves who rose above their condition with the use of spirituals and hymns. Their heritage still lives on to bless new generations.

Why sing? Because there is something to sing about! Words alone sometimes fail to express what the heart feels. Singing penetrates the small openings in the walls we build up to protect our emotions, and through singing, need and reality join in a deeper way in our hearts. The awakened heart has to be a singing heart if we are awake to the greatness of the love which has claimed us.

1. What memories and associations have you with hymn-singing in church, or in more casual settings?

2. Note here a hymn or song you particularly like, and what it helps you express.

## Day 4 • Out of Our Haunted Sleep

Daily Reading: 1 Thessalonians 5:1-11

*So then, let us not be like others, who are asleep, but let us be alert and self-controlled. (v. 6)*

For many years the words of that hymn have intrigued me: "Would man but wake from out his haunted sleep!" The poet seems to look at the world and sees it deluded, almost as if under an evil spell. And can we not sympathize with that view when we look at the violence on our television screens, people against people, creating new ruins and new tragedies in pursuit of some deluded "good."

Paul must have had some of the same feelings when he traveled across the Roman world with the new message of the gospel. People were asleep. They were asleep to the things that would bring real life, real hope, real joy. They were going frantically about pursuing wrong goals. So his counsel to the young Christians at Thessalonica was, "Let us not be like others, who are asleep."

Here we are, 2,000 years later. We are inheritors of a long line of testimonies of people who have trusted Jesus Christ and found him sufficient for their needs. They have told us how they met temptation, trial, and trouble, and how he brought them through. They did not consider themselves heroes, even though some of them undoubtedly were deserving of that name. But they were needy folk, ordinary "human clay" who had found the inner secret of life. That secret is ours for the taking. It doesn't always come easily. We may have to struggle with illusions, choosing to embrace the hard truth at times instead of the easy delusions and answers the world offers. The awakened heart has heard something—a call to life. Let us embrace it anew today in every dimension. We do not have to stay in the "haunted sleep" of those who still run after false goals. We "have heard the joyful sound," and it calls us to press on toward the goal.

1. Is there any aspect of your life today that you would prefer to "sleep" through?

2. Can you be specific about what aspects of life you prefer not to face?

## DAY 5 • KEEP YOUR SPIRITUAL FERVOR

Daily Reading: Romans 12:1-13

*Never be lacking in zeal, but keep your spiritual fervor, serving the Lord. (v. 11)*

I suppose that one of the hardest things we Christians face in our walk with Jesus is keeping our spiritual zeal or fervor. It's like those marathons we see on television. You can see the enthusiasm and zeal in the faces of the runners as they move bravely out on their many-mile run. But as the hours go on, it becomes obvious that for some, zeal flags. And we know there are many, many more whose zeal ran out during training time, before the marathon even began.

There is an interesting passage in the prophet Malachi in which the Lord is taking his people to task about their attitude toward him. "'What a weariness this is,' you say, and you sniff at me, says the Lord of hosts" (Mal. 1:13). They have obviously flagged in their zeal for the Lord.

What has God provided for us to keep our spiritual fervor? One of the things that regular worship with God's people in God's house is meant to supply, is to fulfill our need to keep renewed in spirit. If we neglect regular worship, it will be only a matter of time before we begin to slip in other ways. Another provision is a regular, private time with the Lord. These meditations are meant to be little helps along that line. Establishing the pattern of going apart and being with Jesus is one of the ways we can maintain a sense of lively fervor.

We humans are good at taking things for granted. No matter how beautiful our surroundings, natural or otherwise, they easily become "ordinary" to our eyes. We can lose our ability to "see" them, whereas once we looked on them with pleasure and thanks. And that is true not only of our surroundings but of the circumstances and the people God has put in our lives. Are we giving thanks for them? Are we lifting them up with the simple trust that difficult things are also part of his plan and that he is working through them?

Finally, sharing our faith and our trials with others can also be a means of protecting our spiritual fervor. When we are weak, they may be strong. When they are struggling, we may be able to say an encouraging word. How wonderful that God has provided all these ways in which we can "keep our spiritual fervor"!

1. Referring to yesterday's problem, can you see how, as today's meditation mentions, these "difficult times are part of his plan, and that he is working through them"?

2. From the viewpoint of faith (not necessarily of feelings!) note here what good might emerge from your current difficulty.

## DAY 6 • OPEN EYES AND OPEN HEART

Daily Reading: 2 Kings 6:8-23

*And Elisha prayed, "O Lord, open his eyes so that he may see." Then the Lord opened the servant's eyes, and he looked and saw the hills full of horses and chariots of fire all around Elisha. (v. 17, NIV)*

Elisha was "in trouble." The king of Aram was eager to find him, because he had been told that it was Elisha's gift to warn the king of Israel where he, the king of Aram, was planning to attack. Elisha was a military threat, and would have to be dealt with accordingly. So troops were sent to carry out the task of capturing Elisha.

Elisha's attendant went out early in the morning and surveyed the scene. Enemy troops were all around the place where Elisha was staying. The situation looked grave indeed.

Before going on with the story, let's see how it parallels some of the circumstances we face in life. We see the outward "skin" of the circumstances, and sometimes they seem hopeless. Like the servant in our story, we look out and think that it's "as plain as the nose on your face" that things are very serious. What is reality? How do we separate reality from illusion? We think often that "illusion" is a pleasant substitute for hard reality. And it can be that. Some people simply escape into a kind of dream world because things get too difficult for them.

But that is only one kind of illusion. This other can be even more dangerous: the illusion that we are defeated before we start! This was the young man's problem in the story. He saw only the negative, the enemy, the danger. He did not take into account what every child of God has a right to take into account: the power of God! "He that is in you is greater than he who is in the world." If our eyes and our hearts are open, truly open, we are going to see and take into account the fact that we are not alone in our struggle. We are a cared-for people.

Elisha didn't say much when he saw the condition of his servant-attendant. He just prayed for reality to replace illusion. "O Lord, please open his eyes that he may see." And what follows can bring a thrill through your heart and tears into your eyes as you read it. "So the Lord opened the eyes of the servant, and he saw; the mountain was full of horses and chariots of fire all around Elisha."

I don't know about you, but I know that I often need to have that prayer answered for me. I need to have my eyes opened to the great realities of God's all-sufficient provision. When the fire of faith burns low, when I feel lonely or isolated, I need to have the eyes of my heart turn from the illusion of this broken world to the reality of God's goodness and sufficiency. How else can we come to know how great he is unless we see the chariots of fire surrounding us in our need? And he never fails!

1. In what aspects of the situation you have been discussing these past few days is the power of God operating?

2. What are some areas of need in your life in which you can begin to be aware of God's provision?


## DAY 7 • ARISE, MY BELOVED

Daily Reading: Song of Solomon 2:10-17

*Arise, my beloved, and come away. See, the winter is past, the rains are over and gone. Flowers appear on the earth; the season of singing has come. (v. 10, 11)*

We have been thinking this week of the awakened heart. The heart must be awakened to the dangers it faces. And we thought about some of those dangers earlier in the week. The heart must be prepared to face reality, not the fantasy of its own self-constructed dreams or the illusion that the enemy troops are too strong for it. It must be awake to the "times," the moments when we are called on to make significant decisions or to allow significant changes to take place in us. All these are part of having a heart awakened anew to its own interests and to God's purposes.

This little book which we call "The Song of Solomon" is in many ways a hard book to understand. I frankly admit there are parts of it that are locked to my understanding, and I have simply to offer them back to the Lord until he shows me what is hidden in the words. But there are places, places like our text, where the beauty and love of God break forth in a very special way. Here the soul is addressed by the divine Lover. "Arise, my beloved, and come away." Does the Lord not address each of us in those tender terms? Whether he is calling us to leave our fears, our sadnesses, our defeats, our shame and guilt—whatever it is that we are lingering in, his voice says, "Arise, my beloved, and come away." "Day by day," says the hymn writer, "his sweet voice soundeth, saying, 'Christian, follow Me.'"

When the heart awakens to this voice, the winter indeed is over, and the season of singing has come! Why? Because there will be no problems to face? No. Because life from here on will be "a bowl of cherries"? No. The cross is still part of our life. The battles and struggles will still have to be faced. But, ah! Before all that, the word is addressed to that awakened heart, "Arise, my beloved, and come away!" We have been called into a relationship so gracious, so tender, so full of mercy, that it requires words like this to describe it.

Each trysting place with the Lord, each time we pause for a word of prayer or a word of praise; each time we say "Thank you" because we have caught a glimpse of some little kindness he has bestowed on us, we answer this call. And as we journey on, light rises in the darkness. Help comes from unexpected sources. Encouragement is given for what we have to face. And all this because there is One who loves us and calls us to be his.

"Arise, my beloved, and come away. For lo! the winter is past; the rains are over and gone. Flowers appear on the earth; and the season for singing has come."

1. How might you respond to the Lord's invitation today—"Arise, my beloved, and come away"?

2. Write here a prayer of commitment that puts into words your intentions.

# THE SATISFIED HEART

*Thou satisfiest*
*the desire of*
*every living thing.*

Psalm 145:16b

## DAY 1 • THE UNENDING SEARCH

Daily Reading: John 6:22-40
*They said to him, "Give us this bread always." (v. 34)*

We cannot blame these people too much for seeking Jesus in hope of being fed. Physical hunger is not a welcome guest—then or now. And those of us who have never known real hunger have a hard time realizing how desperate the search for food may become when there is no food available.

Jesus never despised people's need for physical food nor their need for physical healing. He knew that we must be carried beyond that, to seek for "the food that endures to eternal life," but he was moved with compassion by their physical hunger. He had said to Philip, "How are we to buy food, so that these people may eat?" (v. 5). Acquainted as he was with what is in us, he is compassionate toward our needs and desires.

But the hunger we feel for God is an unending hunger. We have looked in the weeks past at some of the many ways we get misdirected and substitute poor counterfeits for the one thing we hunger for most. And what is that? The love of God. Our hearts are empty, no matter how full we fill them with other things, until they are filled with the love of God.

This week we are looking at "the satisfied heart." "Why," asks Isaiah, "'do you spend your money for that which does not satisfy?" (Isa. 55:2). And that is the question we have to ask ourselves, because we have available to us that which can satisfy our hearts.

Finding, receiving, and accepting this love which satisfies the heart is a lifetime challenge. Other answers may seem temporarily to be adequate, but they always betray us in the end. One after another, human relationships (no matter how good they may be), material goods, success, money, position—all fail in this crucial area: to satisfy the heart. It is not that these things are evil in themselves; they are evil only if they are put in the wrong place. But in that wrong place they are deadly. They choke off the spiritual wellsprings that are meant to feed the soul and prepare us for eternity. They cannot do what they were not created to do, and we do them great injustice in putting them in the wrong place.

"I am the bread of life," says Jesus. "He who comes to me shall not hunger, and he who believes in me shall never thirst." He's talking about the satisfied heart.

1. Jesus said, "I am the bread of life." What substitute do you find yourself using to satisfy life's hungers?

2. What can you do to accept God's personal love for you?


## Day 2 • Don't Settle for Less

Daily Reading: Luke 15:11-24
*But when he came to himself. . . . (v. 17)*

The story of the prodigal son is the story of a young man who settled for less. Of course he didn't think of it that way. He thought that he was getting the better part. So, not waiting for his father to die, he asked for his share of the inheritance, so that he could sow his wild oats while he was still young. It must have come as a great surprise to him that things didn't work out as he had expected. Jesus' story covers this part with a discreet phrase: "He squandered his property in dissolute living."

It seems that human nature is slow to learn the most basic of all life's lessons: to turn our back on our true identity means settling for less. The prodigal son was not created to throw his life away in riotous or dissolute living. He was created for higher and nobler purposes. And even if our choices do not take the same expression as his, we, too, settle for less when we try to live to satisfy ourselves. It's a strange paradox: try to satisfy yourself and you guarantee that you will be unsatisfied! Jesus said that if we try to save our life, we will lose it.

I love the phrase we're using as a text for this meditation: "When he came to himself." Up to this time, the prodigal was so bent on trying to extract everything possible from life that he had put his identity behind him. Thoughts of his father were annoyances rather than helps, because they brought pangs of guilt. And he wanted none of that. But now his friends had deserted him, and his plans had betrayed him. He was reduced to feeding pigs—probably the most detestable occupation imaginable for a Jew.

It was in that state of helplessness that "he came to himself." He remembered that he was his father's son. Unworthy, yes. But still his father's son. And on that basis he decided to go back home.

Do we "come to ourselves" in the midst of our sometimes frantic effort to squeeze everything possible out of life? Do we remember who we are and whose we are? Coming to ourselves is the first step towards home—and toward finding that which truly satisfies our deepest longings.

1. Where have you '"come to yourself" in the past? What did you learn that might be helpful for you today?

2. How can your helplessness today work good for you?


## DAY 3 • MINE EYES HAVE SEEN!

Daily Reading: Luke 2:22-32

*Lord, now let your servant depart in peace, according to your word; for my eyes have seen your salvation. (vv. 29, 30)*

Old Simeon was one of a small group who had faithfully waited for the fulfillment of God's promise to send his Messiah. He was "looking forward to the consolation of Israel" and had been assured by an inner word that he would live to see the Messiah.

All his life had been spent in expectancy. It was not that he avoided the present with thoughts of a glorious future. That would be a form of escapism, and one we have to avoid if we would claim our inheritance in the present, in the Now. But, in spite of the fact that the promise seemed to be delayed, Simeon did not give up hope. He "looked forward" to the fulfillment of God's promise.

Part of a satisfied heart is this "looking forward." Not everything has come to pass yet. We may have prayers that seem long delayed in being answered. There may be people we love, for whom we are praying day by day, waiting to see them turn from darkness to light, from death to life. In the meantime, can we, like Simeon, look forward to the sure fulfillment of God's promises?

For the infant Jesus, life was just beginning. A long and difficult road lay ahead of him. But for Simeon, life was nearing its end, and this little child brought the assurance that all would be as God had said. Mary, too, listening to his words, had a challenging and difficult task ahead of her. But she, too, "looked forward" to the completion of what God had spoken to her by the angel.

Here we are, blessed people, living 2,000 years later, with generations of faithful witnesses assuring us of the truth of what we read here. Our eyes, too, have seen God's salvation, if by faith we have looked at Jesus Christ as our Savior. He not only lived in Palestine, but lives today to bring to fruition all that God has promised us.

Today his grace abounds for us. There is strength for our weakness, balm for our wounds, and strong comfort for our tears. Who could ask for more? Who could demand more of God than he has given? Wherever we are in our journey of faith, we can go on in peace, for our eyes, too, have seen his salvation.

1. Simeon's hope of seeing the Messiah was based on what the Holy Spirit had revealed to him (Luke 2:26). When have you had a similar experience of Spirit-given faith?

2. How might you live today in that expectation?

## DAY 4 • I HAVE LEARNED

Daily Reading: Philippians 4:10-13

*I have learned, in whatever state I am, to be content. (v. 11b)*

This was Paul's answer to the need for a satisfied heart, and it can be ours as well. Outwardly, he had plenty of reasons to be dissatisfied with his lot. This letter to the Philippian church was written from prison, and we know that conditions there were, to say the least, grim.

The question that comes to my mind is this: How did Paul learn this vital lesson? He confesses in Romans 7 the same kind of nature we all have. He found himself doing what he hated and not carrying through on what he loved. So we know that his was no "angelic" nature. He struggled with the same kinds of feelings we all do. How had he learned that important lesson to be content "in whatever state" he found himself.

The first answer, I think, would be that he profoundly knew that God had claimed him. That experience, that "heavenly vision" on the road to Damascus never really left him. It changed his direction, but from then on, he knew that he was not his own. He was God's man. Now, most of us do not have any "heavenly vision" to compare with that. We may not even be aware of a moment when we knew that we were being radically changed. Yet if we have come to faith in Jesus Christ, if we have pinned our hope for time and for eternity upon him, then we are, as assuredly as Paul, God's own. He has laid his hand upon us and claimed us for himself.

That being the case, we can see our life as flowing from God's goodness. Whether the day brings happiness or sorrow, successes or trials, since we are God's, they are from him. He is not the author of evil, but he allows only those things to come upon us which he intends to use for good. Some of those things will be difficult. Paul prayed three times to have the "thorn" removed from his flesh, but was told, "My grace is sufficient for you." And that brings us to the second answer to the question, how did he learn to be content? He took seriously that word from God that "my grace is enough for you; my strength is perfected in your weakness."

Every reader of these pages has some weakness, some need that you would rather be rid of. All of us think we would like to be strong, brave, noble, and true, and instead, find ourselves to be weak and needy, sometimes frightened, and not very true at all! Is God's strength perfected in our weakness? I think so, because if we were strong in ourselves, we would not need him, and we would be quickly led into dark and deadly paths by our own natures. And so, like Paul, we learn—we choose to learn—to be content with our own imperfections. It is not that we do not want to change, and certainly in many ways we need to change. But there is a great difference between the changes that God is working in us with our cooperation and the demand that everything in us and about us be made perfect. God is at work with us where we are and as we are, and we can find a kind of contentment in that. After all, he has promised to complete the good work begun.

Paul's contentment was not a passive one. It was not the contentment of the cat curled up, purring in front of the warm fire. It is the contentment of one who knows that he is loved of God and that God is at work in his present situation—at work for good.

1. What progress are you making in accepting God's love? What can you ask him to change in you that would enable you more to receive his acceptance of you?

2. Find three promises in God's Word that will enlarge your ability to be open to him. [try these for starters—Ex. 33:14; Deut. 7:9; Ps. 95:7; 97:11; 126:6; Mt. 28:20b; Acts 16:31; Phil. 1:6, 2:10-11]

## DAY 5 • SPRINGS IN THE VALLEY

Daily Reading: Psalm 84

*As they pass through the Valley of Baca, they make it a place of springs. (v. 6)*

This is a somewhat strange-sounding but intriguing verse. So intriguing, in fact, that I looked it up in several commentaries to see if my interpretation of it accorded with those who had pondered it in the past.

The Valley of Baca, we are told, was the valley of tears. We could go into how the commentaries arrive at such a conclusion, and what that had to do with the image of pilgrimage to the Holy City, but for our thought, that is enough. Our pilgrimage, too, is to the Holy City—toward what God has prepared for those who love him. Our earthly life goes up hill and down, and sometimes we are called on to go through some very dark valleys. Jesus said, "Blessed are they who mourn, for they shall be comforted."

Many of our tears are tears of self-pity and anger. I remember a friend who cried readily when being spoken to about some problem. I was very impressed with the tenderness of heart until I realized that the tears were really an outpouring of deep anger. No longer did they look like they were from a "tender heart." Another person I know has often told people not to try to use tears as a weapon to keep people from being honest with them. Tears can be very intimidating when used as fighting weapons.

Yet the tears are important. They are not to be despised, and even if they come from the wrong motivation, they are better than the hardened mien, the "stiff upper lip" men so much admire and try to emulate. The wonderful thing about these tears is that they can soften the heart and undermine the defenses—if we let them. They can soften the ground of our soul and enable the seed of truth to penetrate and take root.

"They make it a place of springs." That image calls up a place of refreshment and renewal. When I have to go through a dark time, a time of grief or sorrow, of disappointment or frustration—I can make it a time of renewal. Tears can release the inner tension, and I can listen to the still, small voice which tells me that I am a beloved child of God, that he will not fail me, and that he is with me—in the Valley of Tears.

1. How has the Lord made a "Valley of Baca" you have come through into "a place of springs"?

2. Did you learn anything that would be of help in the situations you face today?

## DAY 6 • WHEN I AWAKE

Daily Reading: Psalm 17

*As for me, I shall behold thy face in righteousness; when I awake I shall be satisfied with beholding thy likeness. (v. 15)*

How to be satisfied without being fully satisfied. That is the challenge. Perhaps it will help to look again at a hymn verse by Adelaide Procter. The hymn is a series of thanksgivings for life's blessings. Then in the third stanza she writes,

> I thank Thee more that all earth's joys
> Are touched with pain;
> That shadows fall on brightest hours,
> That thorns remain.
> So that earth's bliss may be our guide,
> And not our chain.

This is the important lesson to learn, so that life can move onward and not be staked down to the present situation or circumstance. It is sad indeed to see people who have so wedded themselves to what they thought was the absolute necessity for a full and abundant life that when death or a major change came in their lives, they were devastated and embittered. Anything that we put as absolutely essential to our lives is a form of idolatry. God is still a jealous God, and will not allow anything or anyone to have his place.

The psalmist seems to catch this important aspect of our spiritual journey. "When I awake I shall be satisfied beholding thy likeness," he says. Whatever of happiness or fulfillment he knew in life, he could still look forward to greater fulfillment and greater happiness when the journey reached its goal. Part of being satisfied in heart is knowing that we are on the journey and that home awaits us at the end. And not only "home" but the Father's love, what the ancients called "the beatific vision."

> Miss Procter concludes her hymn thus:
> I thank Thee, Lord, that here our souls,
> Though amply blest,
> Can never find, although they seek
> A perfect rest;
> Nor ever shall, until they lean
> On Jesus' breast.

1. Identify three places in your life where you feel less than satisfied.

2. What steps can you take in each of these places this week to find the fulfillment you seek?

## DAY 7 • SATISFIED

Daily Reading: Jeremiah 31:7-14
*My people shall be satisfied with my goodness, says the Lord. (v. 14)*

The trouble with the people of Israel was their continual dissatisfaction which led them into all kinds of trouble. Here in this chapter the prophet Jeremiah foretells of a happier time, when God's people would be purged of their wanderings and would be returned to their homeland.

Jeremiah had warned his people over and again that their attitude toward God and their failure to repent were leading to disaster. He was arrested and put in prison because he predicted their defeat by the invading armies. But Jeremiah could not leave the people to face their situation without a word of hope. And here in this wonderful chapter he predicts a time when God would turn their mourning into joy. The Lord had not ceased to love his people, and promises that he will "gather them from the farthest parts of the earth."

What is this but a picture of God's care for us in all our stumblings and wanderings? Can we doubt that he who has done so much for us will continue to carry us in his bosom as a shepherd carries his lambs? I can see no other interpretation, and I see here the picture of a time when God's people will be restored to the life he created them to experience.

1. Jot down several times when Jesus has "carried you in his bosom like a lamb."

2. Do you have any difficulties believing that he will do that for you at the end? How can your past experience help you with any unbelief you have?